Peak Mind

12 minutes a day to
find your focus, meet
the challenge and be
fully present when
it matters most

Dr Amishi P. Jha

PIATKUS

PIATKUS

First published in the US in 2021 by HarperOne
First published in Great Britain in 2021 by Piatkus

13 5 7 9 10 8 6 4 2

Copyright © 2021 Amishi P. Jha

The moral right of the author has been asserted.

A CIP catalogue record for this book is available from the British Library.

ISBN 978-0-349-42496-5
Paperback ISBN 978-0-349-42494-1

Designed by Terry McGrath
Printed and bound in Great Britain by Clays Ltd. Elcograf S.p.A.

Papers used by Piatkus are from well-managed forests
and other responsible sources.

MIX
Paper from
responsible sources
FSC
www.fsc.org   FSC® C104740

Piatkus
An imprint of
Little, Brown Book Group
Carmelite House
50 Victoria Embankment
London EC4Y 0DZ

An Hachette UK Company
www.hachette.co.uk

www.littlebrown.co.uk

This book contains advice and information relating to health care. It should be
used to supplement rather than replace the advice of your doctor or another
trained health professional. If you know or suspect you have a health problem,
it is recommended that you seek your doctor's advice before embarking on any
medical programme or treatment. All efforts have been made to ensure the accuracy
of the information contained in this book as of the date of publication. This
publisher and the author disclaim liability for any outcomes, medical or otherwise,
that may occur as a result of applying the methods suggested in this book.

About the author

Amishi P. Jha PhD is Director of Contemplative Neuroscience and Professor of Psychology at the University of Miami. She leads research on the neural bases of attention and the effects of mindfulness-based training programs on cognition, emotion, and resilience. She has spoken at TED.com, the World Economic Forum, NATO, and has been covered by *Scientific American*, the *New York Times*, *NPR*, and *Forbes*.

www.Amishi.com

Advance praise for *Peak Mind*

'Proven practices to take control of our focus and become our best selves. A must read for our distracted times'

Daniel Goleman, author of #1 *New York Times* bestseller *Emotional Intelligence*

'Thriving starts with our attention and what we do with it. In *Peak Mind*, Amishi Jha combines the science of attention with compelling stories from those in high stakes professions to show us all how to be more present in our lives so that we can unlock our full potential'

Arianna Huffington, author of #1 *New York Times* bestseller *Thrive*

'Dr Jha brilliantly blends cutting-edge science, compelling stories and strong practical instructions – the perfect antidote for our distracted over-busy times'

Jack Kornfield, bestselling author of *The Wise Heart*

'For a while now I've thought of experiences we long for, like love and connection, as emergent properties of how we pay attention. Attention is the key factor in moving beyond just living mechanically into a life of clarity and joy. Dr Jha brilliantly shows us how that can be so, offering a clear and useful path to paying attention differently'

Sharon Salzberg, author of *New York Times* bestseller *Real Happiness*

'*Peak Mind* delivers crucial insights about the human mind along with practical, accessible tools to enhance it. With clarity and skill, Amishi Jha brings you into the lab to learn how attention works, why it's essential for well-being, and how it can be trained to reach your greatest potential. Required reading for our modern world!'

Wendy Hasenkamp, PhD, Science Director, Mind & Life Institute

'In *Peak Mind*, Amishi Jha offers a brilliant guide for training our attention with mindful awareness and maximizing our human potential. You will learn the science behind mindfulness, and well-researched strategies that promote resilience against stress, and increased mental focus, creativity, clarity and strength. The true gift is the capacity to be fully here-present and engaged in your relationships and your life'

Tara Brach, author of *Radical Acceptance*

For Michael, Leo, and Sophie

CONTENTS

INTRODUCTION **"May I Have Your Attention, Please?"** *1*

CHAPTER 1 **Attention Is Your Superpower** *19*
A user's guide to the powerful attention system
and how it defines your life

CHAPTER 2 **. . . But There's Kryptonite** *43*
The vulnerabilities of the mind and the failed
strategies that make things worse

CHAPTER 3 **Push-ups for the Mind** *63*
The new science behind the ancient solution that
works to train attention

CHAPTER 4 **Find Your Focus** *91*
Keep your "flashlight" where you need it in a
distracting world

CHAPTER 5 **Stay in *Play*** *127*
Use attention powerfully in the here and now

CHAPTER 6 **Press *Record*** *159*
What you pay attention to is what you experience . . .
and what you remember

CHAPTER 7 **Drop the Story** *187*
Stop "biased thinking" from affecting your attention and clarity

CHAPTER 8 **Go Big** *213*
Use meta-awareness to unlock your attentional powers

CHAPTER 9 **Get Connected** *237*
Revolutionize your interactions and relationships

CHAPTER 10 **Feel the Burn** *263*
Get the "minimum required dose" to transform your mind

CONCLUSION **The Peak Mind in Action** *293*

The Peak Mind Practice Guide:
Core Training for the Brain *301*
Week One *307*
Week Two *311*
Week Three *315*
Week Four *319*
Weeks Five Through Forever *323*

Acknowledgments *327*
Notes *335*

"MAY I HAVE YOUR ATTENTION, PLEASE?"

You are missing 50 percent of your life. And you're not alone: everyone is.

Take a minute to picture it—your life, I mean. Scroll through the individual events, interactions, and instances that come together over the course of a day, a week, a month, a year, a *lifetime*. Think of it like a quilt, each square a small block of time: Here, pouring yourself a cup of coffee. Over there, reading a book to your child. Celebrating a success at work. Taking a walk in your neighborhood, climbing a mountain, diving with sharks. The mundane and the extraordinary woven together and working together, forming the story of your life.

Now, take half those quilt squares and rip them out. The irregular patchwork that's left—a cold, drafty blanket full of holes—is the part of your life for which you're mentally present. The rest is gone. You didn't truly experience it. And chances are, you won't remember it.

Why? Because you weren't paying attention.

Do I have your attention right now? I hope so—the idea that we're missing so much of our own lives is pretty alarming. But now that I have it, I won't be able to keep it for very long. As you read this chapter, it's likely that you'll miss up to half of what I say. And on top of that, you'll finish reading these pages convinced that you didn't miss a thing.

I say this confidently, even without knowing who you are, or how your brain might be different from the last one we tested in my lab at the University of Miami, where I research the science of attention and teach cognitive neuroscience courses. That's because over the course of my career as a brain scientist, I've seen certain universal patterns in the way *all* of our brains function—both how powerfully they can focus, and how extraordinarily vulnerable they are to distraction—no matter who you are or what you do. I've had the opportunity to peek inside the living human brain using the most advanced brain imaging technologies available, and I know that at any given moment, there's a high probability that your mind just isn't **here**. Instead, you're planning for the next item on your to-do list. You're ruminating on something that's been bothering you, a worry or a regret. You're thinking about something that could happen tomorrow, or the next day, or never. Any way you slice it, you're not *here,* experiencing your life. You're somewhere else.

Is this just part of being alive? A side effect of the human condition, something we all just have to live with? Is it really that big of a deal?

After twenty-five years of studying the science of attention, I can answer these questions. Yes, it *is* part of being alive—in many ways, because our brain's evolution was driven by specific survival pressures, our attention waxes and wanes, making us prone to being distractible. Our distractibility served us well when predators lurked around every corner. However, in today's technologically saturated, fast-paced, and rapidly shifting world, we're feeling that distractibility more than ever, and we face new predators that rely on and exploit our distractibility. But no, it's not something we have to just live with—we can train our brains to pay attention *differently*. And finally, and most importantly: yes, it *is* that big of a deal.

The Extraordinary Impact of Attention

Tell me if this ever describes you: At times, it feels like a struggle to stay focused. Your mind toggles between boredom and overwhelm. You feel foggy—as if the crisp thinking you need to rely on is simply not there. You have a short fuse. You're irritable. Stressed. You notice mistakes you've made: typos, skipped words, or or repeated ones. (Did you catch that?) Deadlines loom but you find it difficult to pull yourself away from your news and social media feeds. You cruise through your phone, opening app after app—then you look up, some amount of time later, wondering what you were even looking for in the first place. You're spending a lot of time in your head, out of sync with the flow of all that is happening around you. You find yourself spinning on interactions—something you wish you had said, something you *shouldn't* have said, something you should have done better.

You may be surprised to know that *all* of this ultimately comes down to one thing: your attention.

- If you're feeling that you're in a cognitive fog: *depleted attention.*

- If you're feeling anxious, worried, or overwhelmed by your emotions: *hijacked attention.*

- If you can't seem to focus so you can take action or dive into urgent work: *fragmented attention.*

- If you feel out of step and detached from others: *disconnected attention.*

In my research lab at the University of Miami, my team and I study and train people in some of the most extreme, high-stress, high-demand professions. We study medical and business professionals, firefighters, soldiers, and elite athletes, among others. They need to deploy their attention—and do it well—through extraordinarily high-stakes circumstances where their decisions could affect many people. As in critical surgeries. Deadly wildfires. Rescue operations. Active war zones. A single moment when performance can make or break a career, end or save a life. For some of these folks, if and how they pay attention is literally a matter of life and death. For all of us, it's a powerful force that shapes our lives far more than we realize.

Your attention determines:

• what you perceive, learn, and remember;

• how steady or how reactive you feel;

• which decisions you make and actions you take;

• how you interact with others; and

• ultimately, your sense of fulfillment and accomplishment.

On a certain level, we all sense this already—consider the language we use when we talk about attention. *Pay attention,* we say. We ask, *May I have your attention?* We see and hear information that is *attention-grabbing.* These common phrases illuminate what we already know instinctively: that, like currency, attention can be paid, given, or stolen; that it is extremely valuable, and also finite.

Recently, the commercial value of attention has taken center stage. As the saying goes for social media apps, "If you aren't paying for the product, you *are* the product." More precisely, your attention is the product—a commodity that can be sold to the highest bidder. We now have attention merchants and attention markets. All this forecasts a brave new dystopia involving trading in human "attention futures" alongside cattle, oil, and silver. Yet attention is not something that can be banked or borrowed. It cannot be saved to use later. We can only use our attention in the here and now—in *this* moment.

What Is Attention, Exactly?

The *attention system* exists to solve one of your brain's biggest problems: there is far too much information in the environment for your brain to fully process. To avoid getting overloaded, your brain uses *attention* to filter out both the unnecessary noise and chatter around you, and the background thoughts and distractions that constantly bubble up to the surface of your mind.

All day, every day, your attention system is in action: In a crowded coffee shop, you zero in on your computer screen and your work, while the conversation at the table next to you or the hissing of the espresso machine seem muffled. At the playground, you scan all the kids in their colorful clothing on the slides and swings but can quickly pick out your own. During a conversation with your co-worker, you hold a point you want to make in your mind, even while listening and absorbing what she's saying. As you cross a busy street, you notice a car moving too fast toward you, even as a hundred other distractions exist—people flowing down the sidewalk, a blinking crosswalk sign, horns honking.

Without attention, you would be completely at sea in the world. You'd either be blank, unaware and unresponsive to events happening around you, or you'd be overwhelmed and paralyzed by the sheer, incoherent mass of information assaulting you. Add to that the relentless flow of thoughts generated by your own mind, and it would all be incapacitating.

To study *how* the human brain pays attention, my research team uses a range of techniques—functional MRI, electrophysiological recordings, behavioral tasks, and more. We bring people into the lab and follow them out into their world—what we call going "in the field." We've conducted dozens of large-scale studies and published numerous peer-reviewed articles in professional journals about our findings. We've learned three major things:

First, **attention is *powerful*.** I refer to it as the "brain's boss," because attention guides how information processing happens in the brain. Whatever we pay attention to is *amplified*. It feels brighter, louder, crisper than everything else. What you focus on becomes most prominent in your present-moment reality: you feel the corresponding emotions; you view the world through that lens.

Second, **attention is *fragile*.** It can be rapidly depleted under certain circumstances—circumstances that turn out, unfortunately, to be the ones that pervade our lives. When we experience stress, threat, or poor mood—the three main things I call "kryptonite" for attention—this valuable resource is drained.

And third, **attention is *trainable*.** It is possible to change the way our attention systems operate. This is a critical new discovery, not only because we *are* missing half our lives, but because the half we're here for can feel like a constant struggle. With training, however, we can strengthen our capacity to fully experience and enjoy the moments we are in, to embark on new adventures, and to navigate life's challenges more effectively.

We're in a Crisis of Attention . . . but It's Not What You Think

We're in a crisis of attention. We are exhausted and depleted, cognitively fuzzy, less effective, and less fulfilled in our lives. This crisis is partly systemic, driven by the *attention economy*, where inviting and highly addictive content-delivery vehicles that take the form of news, entertainment, and social media apps keep us scrolling and scrolling. Driven by predatory practices and a lack of regulation, our attention is lured and mined. And then, like mortgages and other financial products, our individual attention is pooled, repackaged, and sold for big profit.

If attention evolved because there was too much information for us to process, then right now there's *really* too much. The content stream is too loud, too fast, too intense, too interesting, too unrelenting. And we are not only recipients of this information explosion, but also willing participants in it. We're going full throttle to keep up and not miss out, because we or others expect that of us.

This doesn't feel good. So why is it so hard to fix? We're told to "unplug." To "break up" with our phones. To work in shorter, more focused bursts. But our brains don't stand a fighting chance. We can't outsmart the algorithms designed by an army of software engineers and psychologists. The power of this artificial intelligence lies in its adaptability—constantly learning from us how to best grab our attention, and keep us locked in. It uses the same type of reinforcement that keeps people sitting in front of slot machines in smoky casinos for hours on end, with a dazed look on their faces and a bucket of coins in their laps. But it's not a slot machine in front of us, it's an app. And it's not coins we're feeding, *it's our attention.*

I want to make one thing crystal clear: *there is nothing wrong with your attention.* In fact, it's working so well, and so on cue, that computer programs can predict how it will respond. We're in a crisis *because* our attention works so well. It's doing exactly what it was designed to do: respond powerfully to certain stimuli. You can't defeat algorithms on social media websites, the Pavlovian pull of your phone's dings and bings, the blaring red notification bubble of your inbox, or the desire to complete one more quest so you can up-level. Yet, we aren't helpless. We can solve this attention crisis.

The Art of War, traditionally accredited to Sun Tzu in the fifth century BCE, offers advice on what we should do when we are not in a fair fight—when we are plainly overpowered and outmaneuvered:

> To win one hundred victories in one hundred battles is not
>   the acme of skill.
> To subdue the enemy **without fighting** is the acme of skill.

In other words: Don't waste your energy trying to get better at fighting the pull on your attention. *You cannot win that fight.* Instead, cultivate the capacity and skill to position your mind so you don't *have* to fight.

That's the problem with existing solutions—they are instructing us to go to war against the forces that pull on our attention. Like swimming against a riptide, it's exhausting and ineffective. Instead, we need to move away from that mode of struggling with our attention. Like a skilled swimmer who recognizes the ocean's pull and swims sideways to safety, we need to be able to spot the cues.

Pay Attention to Your Attention

Think about the things that suddenly clue you in that your attention is off-track. You might get to the bottom of a page you're reading and realize you've absorbed none of it—it's the physical turning of the page (or scrolling to the next screen) that cues you. You're deep in thought when you hear the sound of your name and an irritated "Hello? Are you listening?" and you realize that you departed from the conversation quite a while ago—it's the person's voice that cues you. You block websites or limit your access by loading an app that times you out; it's the "Time's up!" notification that cues you. But by the time these external cues catch you, over and over again all day, you've already spent far too much time in a brain state that has depleted and degraded your attention, leaving you with declining cognitive resources and increasingly less capable of catching yourself—it's an exponential downward spiral.

We think of this as an exclusively contemporary problem—a crisis born out of our high-tech era. Yes, it's true that we are living in a period of unprecedented targeting of our attention. But we don't need external stimuli to have a crisis of attention—this has *always* been a challenge for humans. We have records of medieval monks in the year 420 fretting that they could not keep their thoughts on God as they were supposed to—they complained they were constantly thinking about lunch, or sex. They felt overwhelmed with information, frustrated that the minute they sat down to read something, their restless minds wanted to read something else instead. *Why could they not just focus? Why did the mind disobey?* They went so far as to cut off relationships with family and give up all their possessions—the idea being that if they had fewer earthly entanglements to think about, they'd be less distracted. Did it work? No.

Over a thousand years later, in 1890, the psychologist and philosopher William James expressed the attention struggle, and the persistent lack of a solution:

> The faculty of voluntarily bringing back a wandering attention, over and over again, is the very root of judgment, character, and will. No one is [master of himself] if he have it not. An education which should improve this faculty would be *the* education par excellence. But it is easier to define this ideal than to give practical directions for bringing it about.

Even if we could—with the swish of a magic wand—wipe away all our technology, our glowing late-night laptops and buzzing phones, it wouldn't work. The mind's nature is to forage for information and engage with it—whether it's the phone in your pocket or the bubbling thoughts in your mind. You don't need to be immersed in this digital ocean we all live in today to feel the pain of restless, depleted attention, and to suffer from it. We can look back a thousand years and see that our fellow humans were experiencing the same.

Our problem is not the phone, nor is it our rapidly filling inbox. It's not that we are surrounded by attention-grabbing news and information at all times. It's not the team of software engineers working on new and better ways to trap your attention with that buzzing and beeping rectangle tethered to you day and night. The problem is that we often don't know what's happening in our own minds. We lack **internal cues** about where our attention is moment to moment. And for this, there is a solution: *pay attention to your attention.*

You Can't Just *Decide* to Do This— the Brain Doesn't Work That Way

If you were to participate in one of our lab's studies, here's what would happen: We'd fit you with a funny little hat that looks like a swim cap, elastic and snug, covered in electrodes designed to pick up your brain's electrical activity. When enough of your neurons fire together in response to something we show you on a computer monitor, the electrodes detect tiny voltage jolts, which are transmitted to an amplifier, and passed forward to another computer to record and process. While all this is transpiring, there we sit, the research team, monitoring a screen full of jagged squiggles that shows us, in real time, millisecond by millisecond, what's happening inside your skull. At the same time, we give you computer-based tests to probe attention-related behavior.

In study after study, we looked for circumstances in which people could pay attention without getting distracted. And here's what we found: there are none. Across our increasingly targeted experiments, there were *zero* circumstances in which participants maintained their focus 100 percent of the time. And a growing body of research now finds that this isn't unique to our research participants—studies from all over the globe find the same pattern. Research participants couldn't continuously pay attention when they were instructed to. They couldn't do it when the stakes were high or when they were motivated to. They couldn't do it even when they were paid to!

Let's pause and take a quick pulse. In the very first sentence of this book, I told you that you might miss up to 50 percent of what I was about to say. You may have taken that as a challenge to pay extra-close attention. So how'd you do? Think back and see if you can take a mental inventory of all the *other* things you thought about (or even stopped reading to do) since you started reading these pages. You might even want to jot them down so you can see how many tasks and thoughts and to-do's your highly active mind is trying to hold all at once. Did you pause to send emails or texts? Did your attention turn to concerns about looming deadlines, worries about your kids or parents, plans to see friends, or thoughts about your finances? Did you give your dog a quick pat on the head or realize she needs a walk, or food, or a bath? Did you stop reading completely to check your news feed?

We all do it. You cannot simply decide to pay attention "better." No matter how much I tell you about how attention works and why, and no matter how motivated you are, the way your brain pays attention cannot be fundamentally altered by sheer force of will. I don't care if you're the most disciplined person alive: *it will not work.* Instead, we need to train our brains to work *differently.* And the exciting news is: at long last, we've actually figured out how.

The New Science of Attention

Scientists, scholars, and philosophers have long been focused on some key questions: *What is attention? How does it work? Why does it work that way?* I spent a long time early in my career exploring those questions. But I knew we needed to ask the next question: *How can we make it work better?*

I started searching for ways that attention could be strengthened. We'd tried all kinds of techniques in the lab, from apps offering brain exercises to mood-boosting music and even high-tech light-and-sound headsets. Yet, nothing had been consistently successful. To make matters worse, we started noticing a troubling pattern in our research with high-demand individuals in the field: soldiers, firefighters, and others who operate in high-stakes emergency situations. People in these professions often go through intense periods of preparation for what they are about to do: Soldiers go through months of intense training before they deploy to war zones; firefighters endure rigorous training before facing unpredictable and life-threatening situations. Think of anyone preparing for something important. A student studying for her exams. A lawyer preparing for trial. A football player in preseason, twice-a-day practices. We found that these individuals became attentionally depleted during that preparation period. Their attentional capacity took a nose dive. And this was happening right before they had to go out and perform at their peak.

These folks are not unique—a period of protracted stress or continuous demand is going to deplete you, leaving you with fewer resources when you actually need them most. But before we could devise a *fix*, we needed to figure out what, exactly, was degrading attention.

One of the biggest culprits? *Mental time travel.*

We do it all the time. We do it seamlessly. And we do it even more under stress. Under stress, our attention gets yanked into the past by a memory, where we get stuck in a ruminative loop. Or we may get launched into the future by a worry, leading us to catastrophize on an endless number of doomsday scenarios. The common denominator is that stressful intervals hijack attention *away from the present moment.*

This is how mindfulness first entered my lab as a possible "brain-training tool." I wanted to know whether training our participants in mindfulness exercises could help them be more effective in high-pressure situations. Our basic definition of mindfulness was this: ***paying attention to present-moment experience without conceptual elaboration or emotional reactivity.*** I wondered if training people to keep attention in the here and now without editorializing or reacting, could serve as a kind of "mental armor." Could it protect and strengthen their attention for when they most needed it?

We worked with mindfulness teachers and Buddhist scholars to identify the core mind-training practices that had persevered through the centuries. We offered these practices to hundreds of participants, exploring their effects in the lab, in the classroom, on the sports field, and on the battlefield. This work led to some exciting moments of discovery, and I'll highlight several of these studies and stories throughout this book. But for now, I'll skip to the end, to the zillion-dollar question: Did it work? Could mindfulness training protect and strengthen attention?

The answer was a resounding *yes.* In fact, mindfulness training was the *only* brain-training tool that consistently worked to strengthen attention across our studies.

Our crisis of attention is fundamentally an ancient problem, not a modern one. And an ancient solution—with some very modern updates—is *the* promising, science-based way out of it.

New Science, Ancient Solutions

As a researcher, my mission has been to bring the lens of brain science to the millennia-old practice of mindfulness meditation to explore *if* and *how* it can train the brain. What we've uncovered is new evidence that, with training, mindfulness *can change the way the brain works by default* so that our attention—that precious resource—is protected and readily available, even in the face of high stress and high demand.

We are living in a time of uncertainty and change. Many of us are experiencing an atmosphere of stress and threat that constantly activates our minds' tendency to mentally travel to an alternate reality. The more stress and uncertainty we face, the more our minds journey to a desired or dystopic mental destination. Often we are in fast-forward mode. We're trying to puzzle through all the uncertainty. We're mentally planning for events that aren't plannable. We're gaming out scenarios that may never come to pass.

Sometimes we mentally travel out of the present moment because it's tough to be in it. Military service members tell me, "I don't want to be in this situation. Why should I stay in the present?" We all want to escape sometimes. But as we'll see in the coming chapters, escapism and other mental coping tactics, like positive thinking and suppression (*Just don't think about it!*), don't help us under high-stress circumstances. In fact, they make things worse.

We're missing out on what's happening right here, right now, right in front of us. And not only do we want to experience the moments of our lives, we need to be able to *gather information from the present moment,* to observe and absorb what's happening in the here and now, so that we can navigate the actual future that unfolds, meet challenges as they arise, and be fully present when it matters most.

A Mental Workout That Works

At the beginning of this chapter, I told you that your mind would wander, that you wouldn't be able to keep your attention steady all the way through—that you'd miss half of what I said. It was, admittedly, meant as a bit of a challenge for you to try. But it wasn't really fair. Imagine that, instead, I'd asked you to pick up the heaviest ball you can lift and then hold it in your hands the entire time you were reading, with no warning or preparation. Of course, you couldn't do it for very long without training for this task first—by practicing holding up that weight for longer and longer stretches of time.

We tend to accept that, to improve our physical health, we need to engage in physical exercise. Somehow, we just don't think the same way about psychological health or cognitive capacity. But we should! Just as specific types of physical training can strengthen certain muscle groups, this type of mental training can strengthen attention—*if you do it*. Lieutenant General Walter (Walt) Piatt—one of the many people you'll meet in these pages who has transformed his life and leadership style through mindfulness practice—immediately saw the parallel between physical training and mental training when I started working with his troops. He said, "Mindfulness training gave our soldiers push-ups for the mind."

I wish I could just tell you how to reclaim your attention, and you could go off and do it. I wish that reading this introduction was all you needed to do. But as we've seen over and over again, knowledge isn't enough. Wanting it to be different isn't enough. *Trying* isn't enough. You actually have to train in a particular way. Our evolutionary history has primed our minds to work a certain way *by default*—we can't simply stop it. Instead, we can train the brain to shift away from specific default tendencies that aren't serving us. We can train our attention to better serve us when we need it most.

And here's the good news you may have been waiting for: you can do this in as little as twelve minutes a day.

The precise science of how much and what kind of mindfulness practice is most beneficial is a rapidly developing field. But as of this moment, our research and best understanding of how to train the brain indicates that if you engage in regular mindfulness practice, for as little as twelve minutes per day, you can protect against that stress- and overwhelm-related decline in attention. If you can do more than twelve minutes? Great! The more you do, the more you benefit.

This book will take you deep into your brain's attention system: how it works, why it's so critical for everything you do, how and why it gets depleted, and what kind of consequences you suffer when it does. Then—like the finely tuned exercises that a personal trainer gives you—I'll take you through specific exercises that target, train, and optimize the brain networks of your attention system. By the end, you'll understand the vulnerabilities of attention, and know how to overcome them by training the brain. We'll start with a "push-up," and build up to a full workout.

Mindfulness training is a form of *brain training*. This ancient but enduring mental practice isn't an abstract or exclusively philosophical endeavor. It's a battle for the resources to live your life.

You Can Start Now— You Have Everything You Need

When I started this research, I was on a mission to recruit people who had highly demanding, time-pressured, and stressful professional lives. One group we partnered with consisted of active-duty military service members, deploying to war zones. During active combat, they experienced circumstances that were *volatile, uncertain, complex,* and *ambiguous*—VUCA for short. They helped us put mindfulness training to the test. We wanted to know if it could help them under the *most* challenging circumstances—and it did. But when I began this work back in 2007, I never expected that a dozen years later, the whole world would become a VUCA laboratory.

We are all in a period of high demand. It can be intense, unpredictable, even scary. And we still need to get through it. Right now, this is what the future looks like: it's going to get more information-dense, more interconnected, more technology-reliant. It may even become more divisive and disorienting as we rise to meet the challenges of the twenty-first century. If that's what we're up against, we need to train as if our lives depend on it—because they do. Our goal: not only to survive, but also to thrive. We need to continue to navigate toward *what* we most want to do, *whom* we most want to be, and *how* we want to lead both others and ourselves through the inevitable stresses of life, through times of uncertainty.

People talk a lot about resilience. What you'll learn in this book is really about what I call "pre-silience." Resilience means bouncing back from adversity. But what we want is to train our minds so that we maintain our capacities *even as we are experiencing challenge.* This means we need something that we can start doing right now. And that's what we have at our fingertips with mindfulness training. You don't need any special equipment. All you need is your mind, your body, and your breath. You can start immediately.

With mindfulness training we can learn to protect and strengthen our most precious resource: *our attention.* You can train yourself to pay attention to *your* attention, to know—moment to moment—what your mind is up to, if it's serving you well, and how to intervene if it's not. As you do, you will build the capacity not only to greet moments of joy and awe more fully, but also to rise to the moments of challenge with skill and even ease. A riptide can carry you farther out to sea if you fight against it. But if you know how to navigate those waters, you can even use that strong current more effectively to get to where you want to go.

1

ATTENTION IS YOUR SUPERPOWER

I threw open the bedroom door.

"I can't feel my teeth," I said, an edge of panic in my voice. My husband looked up, startled. He was sitting up in bed, tapping away at a homework assignment on his laptop.

"What?" Michael asked.

"I said *I can't feel my teeth!*"

It was the strangest feeling, a numbness as if from novocaine. I was struggling to talk, and I felt a little shaky. How would I eat? How would I *teach?* I was supposed to be giving a major talk later that week on my latest research. What was I going to do—get up on stage in front of hundreds of people and mumble as if I'd just had a cavity filled?

Michael asked me to sit down. He tried to talk me through it. He suggested that perhaps I needed more rest, and the problem would go away. Had I crunched down on something too hard while eating? Did I feel sick in any way?

He picked up my hand and held it. "What's going on?" he asked gently.

What *was* going on? Well, a lot. Our son, Leo, was almost three. As it is for many, the first few years of integrating new parenthood into an already busy life had been . . . well, challenging. I'd finished up a postdoctoral fellowship at Duke University and then landed my very first faculty position at the University of Pennsylvania. We relocated, purchasing a hundred-year-old fixer-upper in West Philly, which Michael immediately got to work renovating. Now, as an assistant professor, I had set up my own lab and was on the tenure track—an arduous process during which you are constantly asked to prove your worth and defend your work. I was engaged in the constant, all-consuming work of running the lab: writing grants, conducting studies, teaching courses, mentoring students, publishing. And Michael, who was working full-time as a computer programmer, had also started a demanding graduate program in computer science at Penn. I felt extraordinarily scattered, as if I was being pulled in all directions. At the same time, I felt I should be able to just handle it. Our lives were demanding, sure, but these were all things we *wanted* to be doing.

When I went to the dentist, he said I must be grinding my teeth in my sleep.

"It's probably just stress," he said. "Have a glass of wine to take the edge off."

One night at bedtime, I began reading Leo his favorite book, *One Fish, Two Fish, Red Fish, Blue Fish*. A short section of this classic Dr. Seuss book was about wumps—the wumps went here, the wumps went there, the wumps did this or that. Halfway through the book, my son put his little hand on the page to stop me from turning to the next and asked, "What is a wump?"

I opened my mouth to answer him and then stopped. I had no idea what a wump was. I was in the middle of reading a book—one I'd read aloud probably *a hundred times,* and I could not answer the simplest question about it. Like one of my undergrad students caught off guard by a pop quiz, I tried to salvage the situation, focusing on the page in front of me—what the heck *was* a wump? It looked like some kind of fuzzy brown lumpy thing, maybe an oversize guinea pig? Whatever it was, I had somehow completely missed it, even with my little boy nestled in my lap, turning the pages, saying the words.

Oh no, I thought. *What* else *am I missing? Am I missing my whole life?*

And if I was this way with my son when he was not even three, when he was safe and small and the parenting challenges were also relatively minor—getting him to take a nap, coaxing him to eat his vegetables, helping him find his favorite toy—then what was going to happen when things got really challenging someday? Was I going to be able to be there for him?

It was ironic. I'd spent years as a devoted student of the human brain's attention system. And now, the lab I ran at a top-notch university was entirely dedicated to the study of attention. Our mission was to investigate how attention worked, what made it worse, and what made it better. When the university's media team got requests to interview a subject matter expert on the science of attention, they called me. Yet, now, I had no obvious answers for myself. I was distracted and unable to grab hold of my own attention. Nothing I'd learned in my professional life was helping me with this situation. I was used to being able to "study my way" to success, reading everything I could get my hands on to track down an answer, conducting research studies to glean scientific insights. This approach had gotten me far in life, my education, and my work—but it wasn't working now.

For the first time, I couldn't "logic" my way out of a problem. I couldn't analyze or *think* my way back from feeling out of step with my life, as hard as I tried. I thought about what I could change to make things easier. I thought about my career—the thrill of being on the frontiers of brain science, collaborating with smart colleagues, using cutting-edge neuroscience tools, and guiding the next generation of scientific minds on their journeys. I thought about my family—the all-encompassing love of being a parent and coparenting with the spouse I adore. When I reviewed this life of mine—which was, in so many ways, exactly what I wanted—I felt uneasy instead of happy, just as I had when reading my son his book. A troubling thought bubbled up: *I'm not here for this story, either.*

I was perpetually preoccupied by a blaring, unrelenting onslaught of mental chatter, ranging from what I should have done differently on the last experiment we ran in the lab, to the most recent lecture I gave, to chasing the next work, parenting, or home-renovation demand. It felt like a perfect storm of overwhelm. Yet, I wanted this life. None of these very real demands were going to magically vanish anytime soon—nor did I want them to. In that moment, I realized something: if I was unwilling to change my life, I was going to have to change my brain.

Can the Brain Really Change?

I was born in the city of Ahmedabad, in Gujarat, a state on the western border of India. It's notable for being the location of Mahatma Gandhi's ashram—his legacy looms large there. But when I was a baby, my parents moved to the United States so that my dad could complete his graduate work in engineering. We lived in the suburbs of Chicago, where the neat, straight road grids of the city dissolved into curvy, subdivision cul-de-sacs. In many ways my sister and I were like typical American kids growing up in the 1980s—we listened to Wham and Depeche Mode, and did our best to look like characters from *Ferris Bueller's Day Off*. But inside our house, we were on our own little island, surrounded by the ocean of America. Our parents had carried 1970s Indian culture and traditions here with them, and when we were at home, that was the world we lived in. Walking out the door to go to school each morning was a little bit like crossing a bridge to another world, one with rules and rhythms very different from those within the walls of my home.

As Indian kids, the children of hard-working and educated immigrants, my sister and I knew there were but three choices for our eventual professions that would be acceptable to our parents: doctor, engineer, or accountant. This was, of course, an almost comically restrictive stereotype, but I also knew that their expectations for us to pursue and achieve professional success were real. I figured *doctor* would be the most thrilling, so as a teenager, I declared my intention to get my MD. First step: volunteer in a hospital.

On my first day as a candy striper, I had the realization that I absolutely could *not* become a doctor. I felt uncomfortable, and thoughts of being surrounded by sickness and death were troubling to me. Unlike my friends who felt purposeful in that environment, I had to accept that it was not for me—all the bad news and uncertainty, the long waits, the fluorescent lights and institutional hallways. But I had signed up, so I stuck to my volunteer hours, disliking nearly every single shift—until they sent me down to the brain injury unit.

My job there was to take people who were recovering from traumatic brain injuries outside for some fresh air. One of the orderlies would get them into a wheelchair (most had varying levels of paralysis), and I would wheel them down the long, windowless hallways with their smells of bleach and cafeteria food and through the double doors into the fresh air. I got to know one of the patients particularly well. His name was Gordon, and he'd been in a motorcycle accident. At first, I thought he was a quadriplegic, paralyzed from the neck down, but as time went on, he started to regain the use of one of his arms. Initially, I had to push his wheelchair when we went outside. Then, gradually, he started to be able to move his hand *just* enough to press a little lever on the armrest of an electric wheelchair so he could move it forward without my help. I'd walk next to him, in case he had any trouble, but he did better and better. He was getting physical therapy to help with the recovery, but he told me something else— that at night, when he was lying in bed in the dark, trying to fall asleep, he'd vividly imagine the hand motion of pressing that lever in his mind. Even after the hours of physical therapy he was receiving, he'd still spend even *more* time every night going over the motion in his mind, memorizing that muscle movement, repeating it to himself like the lyrics to a favorite song he never wanted to forget.

"It exercises my brain!" he would say to me as we stuttered along the sidewalk, his hand pressing the lever and then pressing it again and again as he rolled along.

That was it—the moment that it dawned on me. I thought, *Wow, he's training his brain to be different. He's actually changing his own brain!*

Later, in the midst of my undergraduate neuroscience studies, I discovered that professional athletes use this tactic—it's a known strategy of "mental practice" in sports psychology. Even when athletes aren't physically training, they'll go over a move or motion in their minds as a form of practice. Golfers talk about visualizing their swing, while pitchers imagine the pitch, from the first muscle twitch to the last. After the superstar swimmer Michael Phelps won one of his gold medals at the Olympics, he described the way he "lives the strokes" in his head all the time, even when he's not in the water. And brain imaging research shows that this mental rehearsal activates the motor cortex similar to the way actual physical movement does, exercising and strengthening neural networks that control movement, similar to the way physical exercise does for muscles.

After my stint volunteering in the brain injury unit, my fascination with the brain only grew. I became captivated by its fragility, its resilience, its capacity for change. I wondered: How does the brain work? How can it control all these different functions? How can it adapt and change so radically? How does it manage to be this shifting map that can rewrite itself, altering and updating its roads and boundaries—all those things that seemed so permanent, as if carved in stone?

Eventually, my pursuit of these questions led me to the brain system that has been the passion and focus of my career: *attention*.

Super-powerful

The attention system performs some of the brain's most powerful functions. It reconfigures the brain's information processing in important ways that allow us to survive and thrive in an ever-complicated, information-dense, and rapidly changing world. Like X-ray vision, your attention zooms through a crowded sea of thousands of people, a cacophony of sounds and flashing lights, to find your friends and your seat at a concert. Attention gives you the ability to *slow down time*: you can do everything from watching the sun slowly sink over the horizon to meticulously checking your gear before a rock-climbing trip or following a checklist or instruction sheet for an intricate job you're about to perform—as medical teams do before surgery—and not miss a thing. (As my military friends put it: "Slow is smooth and smooth is fast.")

Attention allows you to *time travel*—you can browse through your happy memories and select one to unpack, relive, and savor. You can use it to peer into the future as if clairvoyant, planning and dreaming and imagining what fun or exciting things might happen next. Of course, we can't use our attention to move mountains, fly, or walk through walls, but it *does* allow us to get transported into these thrilling alternate realities, either while watching a movie, reading a book, or letting our imaginations run wild. If I haven't convinced you yet that your attention is a superpower, consider what life would be like if your mind couldn't do any of these things: *superdull.*

Attention simultaneously highlights what's important and dims distractions so we can think deeply, problem-solve, plan, prioritize, and innovate. It's the portal to learning, taking in new information so we can remember and use it. It's a key player in how we regulate our emotions—and by that I don't mean suppressing or denying; I mean having awareness of our emotions and generating proportionate responses based on our feelings. And attention is the entry point to another important system: *working memory*, a dynamic cognitive workspace that you use for nearly everything you do. (We'll get into this more deeply in the chapters that follow.) Yet perhaps the greatest power attention holds is that it threads together the moment-by-moment colors, flavors, textures, insights, memories, emotions, decisions, and actions that create the fabric of our lives.

What you pay attention to *is* your life.

There's a famous study on attention that goes like this: A group of research participants is shown a video of two teams on a basketball court, practicing passing and intercepting the ball. One team wears white shirts, the other wears black shirts. Participants are told that their job is to count the number of passes between the white-shirted players over the course of a few minutes. There are two balls in play, one for each team. While moving around, behind, and in front of each other, the black-shirted players pass a ball from player to player and the white-shirted players do the same. It's a little bit hard to track the movement of the ball between the white-shirted players, but if you really focus you can do it. At the end of the video, the researcher asks the study group: "How many passes did you count?"

Anybody who answers "Fifteen" is correct. But there's another question.

"Did you see the gorilla?"

The response to that is usually total confusion. *What gorilla?!*

When the video is rewound, it's obvious: halfway through, a person in a gorilla suit strolls into the middle of the basketball game, stops and waves (or even does a little dance, in some variations—this study has been run many times), and then meanders offscreen. *And nobody sees it.* If you're thinking to yourself, "Well, *I'd* see it—there's no way I'd miss a gorilla!" then consider this: This demo was run with a group of astronauts at NASA, arguably some of the most intelligent, highly focused people on the planet. Did any of them see the gorilla? Nope.

When scientists talk about this study, they usually discuss it as a *failure* of attention. It's a "gotcha" moment at the end of the activity—you missed something you should have noticed: *fail*! However, I see it as an example of how incredibly powerful your attention can be. It shows that your attention system can be highly effective at shutting out distractions. In this instance, you were given a mission—count the passes—so you focused on those white shirts and filtered out anything dark, including that gorilla. To me, that sounds like an incredible *strength* of attention. It's so effective at illuminating the relevant and blocking out the irrelevant that it made a dancing gorilla invisible.

But this next point is important: your attention system is doing this constantly—highlighting certain things and shutting out others. It was my attention system's capacity to do this that was messing with me during those overwhelming teeth-numbing months. I had "selected" certain things to focus on—worries about work, the house, the future—and everything else was dimmed: my husband, my son, the rest of my life.

We all need to be asking ourselves:

What is my attention highlighting right now?
What is it shutting out?
And how does this factor into the experience I have of my life?

This Is Your Brain on Attention

Your brain is built for bias. That might sound like a bad thing—immediately we think of biases based on race, gender, sexual orientation, age, or any number of other aspects of someone's core personhood that lead to unjust mistreatment or privilege—but this isn't the bias I'm talking about right now. By *built for bias*, I mean that the brain does not treat all information it encounters equally. And as a matter of fact, neither do you. Maybe you like the color green more than the color blue, or dark chocolate more than milk chocolate, deep house or country music more than classical. You can probably think up all kinds of explanations (from your past, your relationships, your experiences, and so on) for why you have these particular preferences, but when it comes to how the brain functions, *evolutionary pressures* are actually what have led to many of its biases.

Here's an example: We humans can see better than we can smell. Meanwhile, our dogs can smell better than they can see. Why? Our ancestors thousands of years ago almost certainly relied on sight more than smell to survive—and vice versa with our furry friends. How much of your brain do you think is devoted to vision? Take a guess. And keep in mind that the brain has many functions outside of vision. Five percent? Ten percent? Twenty-five percent?

The answer is *50 percent.*

A full half of your brain is devoted to one job: visual perception. So, right off the bat, your brain is *biased* toward visual cues over other sensory inputs. Then it gets even more intense.

Look up from this page for a minute and keep your head and eyes facing straight ahead. You just experienced your "field of view": the extent of the observable world that is possible for you to see at any moment in time. For humans who have two functioning eyes, that field of view is about 200 degrees. So if you were to draw a big 360-degree circle around yourself, you can perceive a little more than half of that range. And the place where you have the best acuity is right smack at the center of your field of view. This little wedge is the only region where we have 20/20 vision. And when I say "little," I mean *little*. Out of those 200 degrees that you can perceive, you have high visual acuity in just *two* of them.

Try this: Take both of your arms and extend them out in front of you. Now hold up both thumbs so they are side by side, touching. The width of your two thumbnails next to each other is roughly two degrees. That's it—that's the narrow little slice of your visual field that has high acuity. If you don't believe me, try gradually moving your thumbs apart, while keeping your eyes steady. Very quickly you'll notice that things get fuzzy. To keep both thumbs crisp and clear, you have to dart your eyes back and forth, which is basically rapidly shifting your field of view, again and again, so that each thumb is briefly in the center again.

Those two degrees of high visual acuity you have? They rely on 50 percent of the cells in your brain's visual cortex. The reason I'm mentioning this is to illustrate exactly how much bias there really *is* in your brain, all the time, no matter what you're doing: your brain is *biased* toward visual information. And it's even more biased toward that tiny slice of your visual field. Whatever's in those precious two degrees is going to have a massive overrepresentation in your brain.

Representation of your body in your brain is also highly biased. You won't be all that surprised to learn that we have many more neurons devoted to tactile sensation on our fingertips compared to the forearm. Which would you rather use to feel the soft fur of a cute bunny, your fingertips or your arm? Reach out right now and touch something textured—a blanket, your sweater, anything. Stroke it with the back of your hand; then stroke it with your fingertips. Notice the difference. This is you having *direct contact* with one of your brain's "biases." Many more neurons are involved and firing as your fingertips touch your sweater compared to other parts of your hands or arms.

These built-in structural biases we have in the brain are essential. They were born out of the evolutionary pressures endured by our ancestors to advantage their survival. We rely on them all the time: think of moving your eyes to the doorway to check who's coming in. Our gaze and our attention are tightly yoked, like dancing partners always in step. Moving our gaze is often how we direct attention and how we show others (including your dog) where our attention is. Eye gaze is an incredibly powerful social cue.

However, having your eyes somewhere doesn't guarantee that your attention is there too or that information processing will be successful—think about the last time you zoned out in the middle

Read the text on the bottom right of this box

This is the bottom left   That's much better

of a conversation. In other words: you could be petting that bunny without really feeling the soft fur; you could be looking at your child's face without hearing what he's saying. Why? Because inside your own brain, there is a continuous battle unfolding over which information gets processed versus which gets suppressed. And *attention* is the powerful force that can tip the scale.

Your Brain Is a War Zone and Attention Rigs the Fight

The brain is a war zone where neurons, nodes (clusters of neurons), and networks (interconnected nodes, like a subway map with hubs) compete for prominence, fighting to suppress each other's activity. Sometimes they form alliances, enhancing each other's activity; other times they go to war with each other. Nodes can exert more influence than individual neurons, and even more so when they link up into networks, like a national political party opening offices across the country, solidifying its influence into a coherent message and strong collective action. There are multiple networks warring for prominence in your brain at any moment in time.

Forget the myth that you only use 10 percent of your brain. One hundred percent of your brain is active right now, with all of its 86 billion neurons—organized into nodes and networks—coordinating, enhancing, and suppressing each other. As the activity of one network goes up, another's is tamped down. This is mostly a very good thing! If the network activity tied to moving your hand in an *upward* direction didn't suppress network activity for *downward* movement, you would not be able to move your hand. In fact, this is the kind of thing that can happen with certain neurodegenerative diseases that impair cognition, movement, vision, and more—neurons lose their clear marching orders and stop coordinating the way they're supposed to.

In the brain wars, we *want* to have definitive winners and losers in the moment-to-moment dynamics of brain function. This allows us to do everything from moving our bodies to pursuing certain lines of thought and not others.

In my lab, we use complex visual items like *faces* and *scenes* to explore perception and attention. Faces are special. There is a unique electrical brain signature that we can index by putting electrodes on your scalp. Our recording equipment reliably picks it up 170 milliseconds after you are shown an image of a human face. And the amplitude of the signal—in other words, the voltage that is produced by the sheer number of neurons that fire together in response to the face—is high. It's a strong, reliable brain signature. We call it the N170.

If I were to show you the image of a face while recording the ongoing electrical activity in your brain, I'd see a strong N170 from you. If I showed you a second face half a second later, I'd see another strong N170. But if I showed you two faces at the same time, the N170 would suddenly drop to being smaller in amplitude. It immediately shrinks and weakens.

That seems very strange—why would *more* visual information lead to a *smaller* brain response? Answer: *the brain wars!* The groups of neurons processing each face *suppress each other.* We get a weaker signal because the faces are in competition for our neural activity. As a result, neither face gets processed well.

So what? Well, consider the consequences for our experience of the world: the amount of neural activity determines the richness of the perceptual experience we have. Our ability to perceive details, or act based on what we perceive, is tied to the activity of our perceptual neurons. Think of the last Zoom call you were on. If it was a call with one other person, you probably had a sharp read on their expressions, their appearance. But if you had a fifteen-person meeting, it might have felt both fuzzy and overwhelming. With more faces, there will be even more inhibition driving down and compromising the richness of your perception. And this is true for anything—not just faces. Everything around us is competing for brain activity at all times.

This is where *attention* becomes the superhero.

Let's come back to those two faces. This time, I tell you to *pay attention* to the face on the left. You aren't allowed to move your eyes—keep them perfectly still while shifting your attention to the left face. What we'd see in the lab is that even though there are still two faces on the screen, and nothing has changed, you will be much better at perceiving and reporting back information regarding the left face. *Paying attention* to the face boosts the activity of the corresponding neurons, and more activity means more richness of perception. It won the fight! And attention is what determined the winner.

Here's the recap: *attention biases brain activity.* It gives a competitive advantage to the information it selects. Whatever it is you pay attention to will have more neural activity associated with it. Your attention, quite literally, *alters the functioning of your brain at the cellular level.* It truly is a superpower.

Attention Is Not Just One Thing

So far I've been talking about *attention* as if it were a single brain system—one that you can direct somewhere to selectively enhance information processing. But this is only one form of attention. There are actually three subsystems that work together to allow us to fluidly and successfully function in our complex world.

The Flashlight

Your attention can be like a flashlight. Where you point it becomes brighter, highlighted, more salient. Whatever's not in the flashlight's beam? That information remains suppressed—it stays dampened, dimmed, and blocked out. Attention researchers call this your *orienting system,* and it's what you use to select information. You can point that flashlight beam anywhere: outward at your external environment, or inward, to your own thoughts, memories, emotions, body sensations, and the like. We have this fantastic capacity to willfully direct and select with this flashlight of ours. We can shine it at a person we're with, into the past or into the future—anywhere we want, we can point it.

The Floodlight

This is, in some ways, the opposite of the flashlight. Where the flashlight is narrow and focused, this subsystem, called the *alerting system*, is broad and open. I have a giant floodlight above my garage door. It's not always on, but when the motion detector gets triggered, on it goes. When I look out my window, I can scan to see what's happening. Is there a package? A racoon? A visitor? My attention is ready for whatever or whomever it is. Think of what happens when you see a flashing yellow light as you're driving—you immediately go "on alert" as your attention system shines its floodlight. Diffuse and ready, just like me looking out my window at home, it has a broad, receptive stance. You are now in a state of vigilance. You're not sure what you're looking for, but you know you're looking for *something,* and you're ready to rapidly deploy your attention in any direction as you respond. What you're alerted to could be something in your environment, or it could be a thought or emotion generated from within.

The Juggler

To direct, oversee, and manage what we're doing, moment to moment, as well as ensure that our *actions* are aligned with *what we're aiming to do*: this is the job of the juggler. This subsystem is what people are referring to when they talk about "executive function," and the formal name for it is actually the "central executive." This is the overseer that makes sure we stay on track. We may be aiming to accomplish microgoals that are near-term, such as finish reading this chapter, draft an email, clean up the kitchen. Or we may have big long-term goals, like train for a marathon, raise happy children, earn a promotion. No matter how big the goal or how far away it is on the horizon, there will always be challenges along the way, distractions to overcome, competing forces to contend with. So we will need to navigate multiple demands at once.

The central executive functions like a juggler, keeping all the balls in the air. The juggler's job isn't to do everything itself. It's to make sure that the whole operation is fluidly ongoing. It's to match up *goals* with *behaviors* to make sure those goals get accomplished. Example: Your goal is to finish a time-sensitive project by 6:00 p.m. But instead, you're on a group chat until 5:00 p.m., planning an event six months away. That's a failure of the central executive: your juggler has lost track of your current goal. It failed to override the pull of your phone as the pinging messages came in one after another in rapid fire. Soon your behavior no longer aligns with what you wanted to accomplish. Now multiply that by all the things you need to accomplish in a day, a week, a month . . .

Importantly, you use your juggler to *override automatic tendencies* (like picking up that phone at every ping), as well as to update and revise a goal based on new information that's come in, and to refresh the goal to remind you of what you are aiming to do. Override. Update. Refresh. Every time we do any of these things, we're engaging our *central executive*. The more tasks you're planning and managing, the more you rely on this form of attention. Sometimes, you're juggling and somebody throws another ball (task) at you—you have no choice but to deal with it. It might bump another ball out of orbit. Or maybe you chose to keep picking up more and more balls, thinking you can handle them all—and maybe you can, depending on how well your juggler is able to align your behaviors and goals.

As effective as your attention can be when it's in any of these three modes, it won't typically operate in multiple modes at once. For instance, it can't really be the flashlight *and* the floodlight in the same moment. Think of a time when you've been deeply focused and engaged in an activity. If someone were to walk up and speak to you right then, it might take you a few extra seconds just to realize that something had been said, much less be able to start the process of deciphering what was actually said! (How many times have you looked up from a book, your phone, video game screen, or laptop, and said, "What?") That's *high-orienting, low-alerting functioning*: your flashlight was so fixed on its target that everything else—from sights and sounds in your environment to random thoughts generated in your mind—went dark.

Now imagine walking home and taking a shortcut down a dark and deserted alley. Before, you were deep in thought planning out your day tomorrow, but now you drop that mental activity and shift into high alert, scanning for possible threats. That's *high-alerting, low-executive functioning*—the floodlight is on, and the juggler's got only one job: to manage your safety.

If you're "on alert" for whatever reason (you don't have to *be* threatened, you just have to *feel* threatened), you won't be able to focus or plan. And while it might seem like it, this is not actually a failing of attention. This is exactly how attention is supposed to work, so that we can:

- *focus* when we need to,

- *notice* when we need to, and

- *plan and manage our behavior* when we need to.

When we tell someone to "pay attention," what we often mean is *focus*. But attention is about so much more than that. Attention is a currency, a multipurpose resource. We need it for nearly every aspect of our lives, and each form that it takes (the flashlight, the floodlight, the juggler) is relevant for everything we do. We've talked about how attention enables you to perceive the environment around you. In addition to perception, the three forms of attention operate across **three types of information-processing domains:** *cognitive, social,* and *emotional.* Take a look at the three simple charts below to get a sense of how attention is used in each of these domains—this pretty much encompasses all the "information processing" you're going to do over the course of a day, and over the course of your life.

Cognitive (thinking, planning, decision making)

Flashlight	You can follow and sustain a train of thought.
Floodlight	You have situational awareness—you can notice thoughts, concepts, and perspectives that relate to your task.
Juggler	You have a goal and can hold it in mind, knowing what you need to do next to move toward accomplishing it. You overcome distractions and "autopilot" behaviors (like picking up your phone) that could derail you.

Social (connecting, interacting)

Flashlight	You can direct the beam of your flashlight toward other people to listen and connect.
Floodlight	You can gain awareness of the tone of someone's voice, and of other people's emotional states.
Juggler	You can negotiate a conversation with multiple people, select relevant points of view to hold in mind, then filter and evaluate them when conflicting opinions are expressed.

Emotional (feeling)

Flashlight	You can turn your flashlight toward your own emotional state, first to know what it is, and then to recognize when it's interfering with your ability to do other things.
Floodlight	Your emotional reactions alert you to how you are feeling. You can see if they're "proportionate" (appropriate to the situation) or not.
Juggler	You can execute an emotional course-correction when required.

There is another, critical brain system that you use for all of this. It's not a part of your attention system, yet is a close cousin to it: *working memory*. Your working memory is a kind of temporary "workspace" in the brain where you can manipulate information over very short periods of time, from a few seconds to a minute, max.

Attention and working memory work together: anytime we pay attention, in any way (whether it's narrow, broad, or juggled), the information that's processed has to be temporarily stored somewhere long enough for us to work with it. Attention and working memory form not only the current contents of our conscious experience, but also our ability to *use* that information as we maneuver through life.

Do I Need a Better "Boss"?

We've spent a fair amount of time thus far talking about how powerful attention is, so you might be wondering—*if my attention is already a superpower, why do I need to improve it?*

Attention *is* powerful. I do want you to come away from this book really understanding, and fully appreciating, the innate power of your attention system. I want you to gain an awareness of everything your attention is doing for you that you might not have had before. We often take for granted the superpowers of attention, the same way we might take for granted the other amazing things our bodies and minds do for us moment to moment. You might not sit around thinking about the fact that your heart pumps *two thousand* gallons of blood per day, but it does. It's constantly working for you, circulating oxygen and nutrients through your body. Your attention may be similarly underappreciated. Often, we don't clue into the powers of our minds or bodies until, for whatever reason, something goes awry.

And that's where getting a better boss comes in.

When my own attention crisis struck, it was a really unusual symptom (I'd never heard of anyone losing the ability to feel their teeth before!). But having an attentional crisis is hardly rare. Look around, and it might seem that everyone you know is in a crisis of attention. It may feel as if your focus is constantly flicking from one thing to the next, that you're scattered and ineffective. You may have realized this even as you have been reading this book, putting it down to check your phone. If attention is supposed to be so powerful, then why all the struggle?

Some of the very things that make attention so powerful—like its ability to constrain and limit what you perceive, to zoom through time and space, and to simulate imagined futures and other realities—can all be turned against you. They turn on you for a few key reasons. One is the human brain's natural, millennia-old tendencies—some of which we may find frustrating, though they have very good reasons for existing that relate to our survival. Yet another reason has to do with the world we live in.

Attention Disruption

Imagine your ancestors, picking berries or hunting. All of a sudden they spot a face through a thicket of branches. Is it a predator (run!) or a possible meal (charge!)? They needed to be able to decide—*fast.*

In the lab, we showed people the image on page 40. Watching their brains' electrical activity, we asked them questions about the scene (*Is it inside or outside? Urban or rural?*) or about the face (*Is this person male or female? Are they happy or sad?*). When people paid attention to the face, the N170 was much stronger compared to when we asked them to pay attention to the scene. *Attention enhanced face perception.* This helped our participants perform well on the task, just as it helped our ancestors survive to eat another day, and not be eaten themselves! But sometimes, our ancestors *did* get eaten. So why does attention sometimes fail us?

In a variant of the experiment, we showed the same face/scene images. But every now and then, we'd flicker a different image on the screen: a negative image, something violent or upsetting. These were pulled from the media—the kind of stuff you might see on a twenty-four-hour news network, in your Facebook feed, or on whatever method of *doom scrolling* you prefer. Even though our participants were doing the same "pay attention" task, their ability to distinguish between "relevant" and "irrelevant" nearly vanished. The mere presentation of stressful images, like those we are surrounded by all the time, was enough to diminish the power of attention.

Every superpower has its corresponding kryptonite—that thing that breaks it down *fast*. As attention breaks down, those amazing strengths can quickly turn against you. Your attention morphs into a glitchy DeLorean, hopping through time without intention or control, ruminating on regrets and predicting catastrophes that may never come to pass; it fixates on things that are not productive; it fills up working memory with irrelevant clutter.

Attention is powerful, but it's not invincible. Certain circumstances are potent kryptonite for attention. And unfortunately, they just so happen to be the circumstances of our lives.

2

. . . BUT THERE'S KRYPTONITE

It's 2007, on Florida's Gulf Coast. Jeff Davis, then a captain in the US Marines who recently returned from Iraq, is driving across a long bridge. The view from the bridge is gorgeous. The sun is bright on the water, the sky cloudless and perfect—that color of blue that always seems impossible. But Davis isn't seeing any of it. Instead, his mind is occupied with scenes of dusty roads and fields of dirt: deep shadows that seem to move. His body is flooded with stress hormones as he feels the same anxiety he used to feel as he drove those roads. His body is on that bridge in Florida, his foot pressing harder and harder on the gas pedal, the car dangerously picking up speed. But his mind—his attention—is halfway around the globe, in Iraq, and he can't pull it back. What he wants more than anything is to turn the wheel just slightly and drive right off that bridge. It takes everything he has not to do it.

What we see Captain Davis experiencing in this moment is called *attentional hijacking*. While this example is certainly more extreme and consequential than what most of us may experience, attentional hijacking is quite common. Your attention, that spotlight created by your mind, is constantly being yanked away from where you want it to be and onto something else, something that your mind, in all its complexity, has decided is more "relevant" and "urgent"—even if that's the furthest thing from true.

In the previous chapter, we talked about how attention is a powerful system that determines the victor in the war inside your brain. Well, there's a war for your attention *outside* your brain, too.

Your Attention Is a Hot Commodity

In the lab, attention research is a tightly controlled operation. We keep the environment dim, specifying the exact lumens of light. We seat you, our participant, exactly fifty-six inches from the screen. We check your eye movements to make sure you're keeping them fixed straight ahead as we've instructed. And most important, to make sure all the parameters we are testing are known to us, we direct you precisely where to pay attention, which is a highly contrived and unnatural situation—the real world is so much more complex, unknown, and dynamic. And the real world is where our attention really matters.

Inside your brain, attention *biases* brain activity. Whatever it advantages "wins the prize" of gaining more influence over your ongoing brain activity. Outside the brain, in the "attention marketplace," the grand prize is access to your wallet. And attention merchants are doing their best, with teams of designers and programmers all training their algorithms to win your attention, and therefore your money. And it *works*.

I recently went hunting for a set of magnetic-bottomed pans for my family's new induction cooktop. I waded through the pages of hits after I Googled "induction pans." I watched a video from a food blogger I like, cruised through a few pages that looked promising, but nothing was exactly what I wanted. The next day, when I opened Gmail, an ad banner said, *"Hello cookware enthusiast!"* When I checked my social media apps, there were pans all over my feed. I'm sure it's not news to you that advertisers pursue you this way, tracking your digital footprint like bloodhounds and throwing their products in your path, hoping you'll click. And I *did.* I clicked on one of the ads when I recognized the name of the company; I clicked another that had red flashing text: *AMISHI, WE'VE GOT A DEAL FOR YOU! BUT ACT FAST—ONLY LASTS 7 MORE MINUTES!*

Our attention is always being hunted. Advertisers know better than anyone how precious it is, and they know exactly how to capture yours. The neuroscience literature points to three main factors that determine when our attention is deployed:

1. *Familiarity.* The first time I clicked, it was because I'd heard the company name before. My attention was immediately and powerfully biased by prior history. That familiar name leapt out and pulled my flashlight like a magnet.

2. *Salience.* The second time I clicked, I was sucked in by the physical features of the ad. The color, the flashing, the size of the text—all of these physical features of the ad were screaming *LOOK AT ME!* Salience (novelty, loud noises, bright lights and colors, motion) yanks us toward that stimulus—we can't resist. *Salience* is tailor-made for each of us—seeing my name, "AMISHI," got me—which is precisely why so many apps ask us to customize our profiles. We are gripped by personally relevant stuff. Our attention moves—fast and ballistic. It is easily captured.

3. *Our own goal.* Finally, our attention can be "goal-driven," biased by our own chosen goal. Mine was to find high-quality, affordable pans, so I finally restricted my online search terms to show only

those options. This is *exactly* how attention works when we have a goal in mind: *it restricts our perception based on that goal.* But my pan-hunting example also highlights a weakness: our goals are the most vulnerable of all these "attentional pulls." Familiarity and salience were easily able to pull me away.

This was a battle for my *orienting system*—my flashlight. It was pulled by familiarity, like a magnet drawing it; it was yanked by salience. Ultimately, my goal won the battle—but it took a lot of time and a few detours before I ended up with what I wanted and needed. This isn't just about buying pans, of course: it can happen with anything we set out to do. Attention is a superpower, but we often have very little awareness of where it is and who or what is in control, not to mention how or when it gets deployed. And on top of that, we spend much of our lives—as we navigate not just the internet but also our careers, our relationships, and all the curveballs life has to offer—under conditions that are like *kryptonite* for our attentional superpower.

What Is "Kryptonite"?

Three major forces degrade our attention: *stress, poor mood,* and *threat.* It's not always possible to pick them apart—they often function in unison, working together to thwack at the attention system. But I'll take you through them one by one so we can look at how, and why, these forces can disrupt your attention catastrophically.

Stress

That perceived feeling of being overwhelmed that we call *stress* fuels mental time travel. We experience a skyrocketing of attentional hijacking, like Captain Davis did on that bridge. The tendency of our minds to get pulled by a memory or worry, and to incessantly create stories, takes us away from the here and now as our stress increases. You're ruminating on something that occurred in the past, long after the time when reliving it is helpful or instructive. Or you're worrying about things that not only haven't happened yet, but may never happen. And this only serves to aggravate and accelerate the amount of stress you're under. When you experience too much stress for too long, you get caught in the downward spiral of attention degradation: the worse attention gets, the less you're able to control it; the less you're able to control it, the worse stress gets.

How much stress is "too much" can be pretty individual and subjective. For a lot of the people I work with—and this might be true for you, too—the idea of stress as a problem doesn't immediately resonate. They see stress as a powerful motivator, something that challenges and inspires them to overcome, push harder, strive for excellence. I get that. Take a look at the graph on page 48, which shows how stress intersects with performance. What it suggests is that, indeed, when our stress is low—when we have nothing driving us, no immediate deadlines for example—our performance isn't that great, but as our stress increases, we rise to the challenge. This type of "good" stress, called *eustress* (pronounced "you-stress"), is a powerful engine for performance, all the way up to the very top of that chart, where we reach the optimum level (what I affectionately call the "sweet spot") where stress is a positive motivator, something that drives and focuses us.

If we could stay here forever, we'd be all set. But the reality is that even this optimum amount of stress, if experienced over a long enough period, starts to push us over that hill and into the long slope down, where *eustress* becomes *distress*.

Even if stress begins as motivating or productive, the longer we're under high-demand conditions, the more that ongoing stress is going

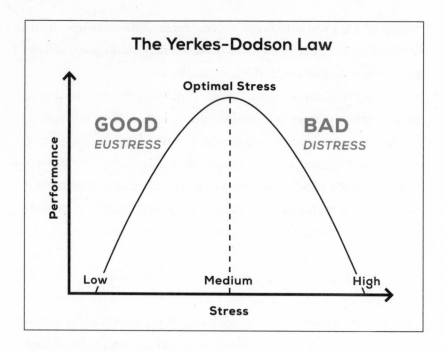

The Yerkes-Dodson Law

to affect us. We'll start to tip over the optimum stress point and drop down the far side of the stress curve. We rapidly lose any benefits from the stress we're experiencing, and it becomes a corrosive, degrading force on our attention. More and more, your flashlight gets stuck on negative thoughts. Your alerting system amps up so that *everything* you encounter feels like a flashing caution sign, pulling you into a hypervigilant mode, making it impossible to focus deeply on anything. And your central executive, the juggler, drops balls so what you *want* to do and what you *actually* do no longer match; your actions and goals fall out of alignment. And as all this happens, there's a natural consequence: mood plummets.

Poor Mood

Everything from chronic depression to how you feel after receiving bad news can constitute *poor mood*. Whatever the source, the effect can be to send you into loops of repetitive negative thought. In the lab, when we induce a negative mood in study participants, performance on attention tests declines.

How do we "induce a negative mood"? Sometimes we show participants upsetting images, similar to those in the study I mentioned earlier. Or we may ask people to conjure up a negative memory. Then we give them cognitive tasks that tax attention and working memory—such as remembering a few letters and then doing a math problem in their head. Performance is always worse—lower accuracy, slower and more variable responses—after the negative mood induction.

Threat

When you're under threat—or feel that you are—it can be impossible to focus on the task-at-hand or pursue any goal or plan. That flashlight I described to you in chapter 1? Your powerful ability to direct your attention at will? Poof. Gone. Imagine that steady, brilliant beam of light now haphazardly shaking about, and all of that focus scattering to the shadows. Whatever you were trying to do? It's not going to happen.

Under threat, attention is reconfigured in two ways: (1) threat vigilance increases, and (2) attention becomes *stimulus-driven*, so that anything that is threat-related captures and holds attention. There's an obvious survival reason for this: at pivotal points in human evolution, high vigilance was a requirement, otherwise you wouldn't survive to pass on your genes. If you were too absorbed in a task to notice a predator stalking you, that was pretty much it. A sense of being threatened had to trigger a rapid switch to being on "high alert." And, as extra life insurance, evolution doubled down so that the threatening stimulus would capture and hold your focus, ensuring that your attention remained steadfastly and compulsively fixated on it—which allowed you to stay on the watch for a predator and, if you saw one, to know where it was at all times. This probably saved our ancestors' lives many times over. But it had other consequences that explain why they never wrote brilliant tomes or designed complex machines. If you feel threatened all the time, you aren't going to be able to engage deeply in any other task or experience. And it doesn't matter whether the "threat" in question is a literal one or a metaphorical one.

When we study threat in the lab, we don't put people in situations where they truly feel their physical safety is at risk—that wouldn't be ethical. However, plenty of people that I work with do face true threats to their physical safety: a soldier going into combat or a live-fire training exercise, or a fire jumper confronting a dangerous blaze in high winds. For most of us, threat will be less literal—but that doesn't mean its impact on our attention will be less. A meeting with a supervisor regarding a performance review, a dispute with your insurance company, testifying at a public hearing with city officials regarding a new ordinance that affects your neighborhood—these types of circumstances, while not representing threats to our physical safety, can still be threatening. Our reputation, financial well-being, or sense of justice can all be under threat.

Even if you have the highest IQ on the block, here's a truth about human brains: in some ways, they haven't changed in thirty-five thousand years. If the brain believes it's under threat, it's going to re-configure attention accordingly, regardless of whether what's actually in front of you *is* a threat.

Kryptonite Is Sneaky

Even if you haven't visited a neuroscience lab or seen the scientific evidence from study after study, it probably makes sense to you that stress, poor mood, and threat are tough on your attention. *Okay, we think, then I'll just reduce stress, keep an eye on my mood, and make sure I'm not feeling threatened by stuff that isn't really a threat.*

The fact is, we're really bad at identifying forces that degrade attention, even when we're immersed in them. We often aren't able to recognize them for what they are. And further, without training to gain a stronger awareness of our own minds, we simply aren't very cognizant of the effects.

Here's a good example: *stereotype threat.* It happens when societal preconceptions about some aspect of one's identity—often related to gender, ethnicity, or age—function as an obstacle to our performance or well-being. A study on Asian undergraduate women played two common stereotypes against each other: one, that females are inherently bad at math; the other, that Asians are naturally skilled at math. One group of students was asked to record their gender before taking a mathematics test: they simply had to write down "female." The other group was asked instead to indicate only their ethnicity. The group that was "primed" to hold their ethnicity in mind performed well on the test, while the group set up to identify with their gender performed more poorly.

And there's a twist: it's not just when the stereotype is "bad" that performance suffers. In a related study, researchers emphasized an expectation that the participants would do well on a test ("Asians are good at math")—and yet they ended up doing poorly! In that instance, the *high* expectation based on the stereotype also functioned as a threat—the "threat" being that they might not live up to those expectations and would fail to confirm that positive stereotype. Stereotype threat can swing both ways: you might promote the *low*-opinion stereotype ("women can't do math"), or you might (or might not) promote the high expectation ("Asians are great at math"). Either case threatens some core part of your identity, and that threat shatters your focus. And finally, across all studies, the pattern was only observed in participants who knew of the stereotype—if you feel you are a member of that group, it will hurt you.

Why is this important? Because it highlights why stereotypes become a threat to attention: it's *preoccupying*. "I'm getting older, so I'll be slow and forgetful," or "I'm too young to be respected as a leader"—these are distractions because they function, in our brain's attention system, as threats. We take on a major cognitive burden when worrying about confirming the low expectations of others—or failing to confirm the high ones.

Stereotype threat played a role in a pivotal moment in my own life. As an undergrad student in neuroscience, I once worked in a lab that focused on *theory of mind*—the ability to attribute mental states to oneself and others, and to understand that others have perceptions different from one's own. I found it fascinating and considered pursuing this research topic in grad school. The professor who ran the lab was a senior faculty member in the department, well-respected. At the end of my junior year, after a year in his lab, I went to him for advice on which graduate programs I might apply to. I remember the look on his face: he was surprised, and then dubious.

"You're going to grad school?" he asked. "Women from your culture don't typically go on to have professional lives."

I remember how hard it hit me—that when he looked at me, he saw my gender and some antiquated version of my culture. Not a talented young student with a lot of potential.

When I left his lab that semester, I never went back. There was a fantastic class I had just finished, one of my favorites in my major, with a professor named Dr. Patti Reuter-Lorenz, who I thought was articulate, brilliant, clear, funny, and, frankly, a real rock star. She'd taught through her third trimester of pregnancy. She was strong, energetic, and undaunted. At the beginning of my senior year, I con-

tacted her and asked if she had any space in her lab, which studied . . .
attention.

That incident set me on my life course. I felt the gut punch of
stereotype threat, and I wasn't willing to operate under those kinds
of contrary conditions—ones that I knew wouldn't be conducive to
learning and success. If I could speak to that first professor now, I'd
thank him—for alerting me to his true colors, just in time for me to
change course and find this work, which has changed my life in so
many ways.

Think of all the ways you might categorize yourself—by gender,
race, sexual identity, ability or disability, weight, appearance, socioeconomic background, educational background, nationality, reli-
gion, work experience or inexperience. No matter the historical or
prejudicial forces driving our experience of stereotype threat, when
we feel it, it undermines our performance, our goal achievement, and
even our overall psychological well-being. This is the cultural soup we
live in. As great as it would be if we could just drain it away, we can't.
Stereotype threat can put us constantly "on alert" in ways that keep
our attention diffused, shallow, and unable to focus.

Stress can also be sneaky.

When Stress Doesn't Feel Like Stress

Recently, I gave a presentation on my work to the president of my
university, the University of Miami, Dr. Julio Frenk. He had heard
about my team's research and was interested in the possibility of having us offer a mindfulness training program for his leadership cabinet. But if his team members were going to spend time on something
like this, he needed more information about what they stood to gain.

So I delivered a one-on-one briefing, and began by describing the cognitive costs of high-stress intervals. He listened attentively, but when I was done talking about the damage that these attention-degrading factors can do, he had a question.

"But what if I'm *not* stressed?"

He acknowledged that he had a lot going on. But it didn't feel like *stress*. He wasn't feeling that sense of overwhelm, urgency, panic, or any of the typical emotions associated with stress. He described it instead as "a lot of things happening in the background that pull me away."

I nodded. It made sense that someone at his level wouldn't experience "stress" in the usual way. Often, high-achieving, high-performing leaders don't identify their experience as stressful. While he understood the concept of one's attention getting hijacked by preoccupations, the notion of "stress" simply didn't resonate with him.

As I knew from work in the lab, you don't have to be *feeling* stressed for attention to be compromised. Many things leaders deal with—high-cognitive demands, evaluative pressure, tense social interactions, uncertainty—are known to degrade attention, as well. In a recent study, participants were told that they *might* have to give a speech after completing an attentionally demanding task that would take several minutes. These participants had poorer task performance than those who were told that they would *not* have to give a speech. That might not be surprising. But here is what was: the "uncertain" group's task performance was worse than a third group that was told they would definitely be giving a speech—suggesting that the uncertainty itself adds a preoccupying cognitive load that further depletes attention.

This research tells us that it doesn't have to feel like stress for it to degrade our attention. I knew it from my own personal experience, as well. I hadn't identified what I was going through during my teeth-numbing episode as "stress"—I never would have labeled it that way.

You might just be feeling like your plate is extremely full, so much so that you start to notice some challenges in isolating and homing in on the most important priorities, or in maintaining that mental clarity you need to function at the top of your game.

We're all going to have varying levels of stress tolerance (also called "distress tolerance"). You might not experience your life as stressful. But know that when the demands on you are intensive and protracted (from a few weeks to months), in all likelihood they're having an impact on your attention. Call it "high demand" if that feels right for you. What we're talking about here is "demand" as a tipping point, when you go past what is comfortable or productive. When there is more going on than your attention system (in its current state) is able to handle, you're far more prone to discomfort and dysfunction.

Regardless of how you label it, periods of high demand can have a corrosive effect on your attention. Is the obvious solution, then, to avoid the offending circumstances? To set lower expectations? To achieve less? To scale down demands?

My answer is a resounding *no*. Many stressors are unavoidable, while others are part of our journey to fulfillment and success—if we removed them, we would be limiting ourselves. I'm not here to tell you to change your life, switch careers, or lower your expectations for yourself as a professional, a parent, a community organizer, an athlete—whatever it is that you've set out to become. I wasn't willing to do that, and I'm betting you aren't, either. This book is not about reducing your demands to optimize attention, or learning how to say no. It's about optimizing *in the face of* stress, challenge, and high demand. Things worth doing are demanding. Our jobs are demanding. Parenting is demanding. Achieving success is demanding.

Having big life goals that you're aiming to reach can be stressful. Our lives are far from perfect—maybe if I hadn't had my first baby while starting my first tenure-track job and opening my first research lab, my teeth wouldn't have gone numb! But I wanted to be a mother, *and* a professor, *and* a scientist. They all needed to happen on a certain nonnegotiable schedule (according to the laws of biology and the challenging academic career path), and I wasn't willing to give any of them up.

It's a classic Catch-22: You're in a long-term period of high demand, which means you need to be functioning at a high level. And the *exact* cognitive resources you need in order to function at that high level are being rapidly depleted by that very period of high demand you're in.

The Attention Continuum

Remember that attention doesn't *only* impact job performance. Attention is a multipurpose resource that you use for *everything you do*. This means that when it starts to break down, we're not simply talking about your ability to write an email or finish a report. We're talking about your relationships with the people who are important to you. We're talking about being able to navigate toward your big life goals, whatever they are—they might be pretty far off, but you need to start closing the gap if you're going to get there, and attention issues are going to either send you in the wrong direction or leave you drifting. And we're talking about your ability to respond well during a critical moment, whether in a life-threatening emergency or in an emotional or interpersonal crisis that could determine how a key event or relationship plays out moving forward.

All three modes of attention across all information-processing domains are highly sensitive to the depleting influences of stress, poor mood, and threat, as well as to other adverse conditions—attentional

The Attention Continuum

MAXIMIZED ⟷ COMPROMISED

MAXIMIZED		COMPROMISED
You can follow a train of thought, strategize, plan, and make decisions. You have situational awareness and can triage and prioritize tasks.	**Cognitive**	Your thought train can be derailed; you switch tracks frequently. You get bogged down in details or scattered by what seem like insurmountable problems.
You can connect with and engage directly and meaningfully with others.	**Social**	You're not perceptive or attuned to others; you miss important cues and opportunities to connect.
You notice your own reactions; your responses are genuine but proportionate to events.	**Emotional**	You have out-of-proportion emotional responses and lack awareness of your own emotional state.

drains can take the shape of anything from an uncomfortably low temperature to *mortality salience* (thinking about your own death).

The table above provides a visual overview of what it looks like when attention is *maximized,* and what it looks like when attention is *compromised.*

Glance down the left-hand column of the table and what you'll see is, in essence, the profile of a person successfully using attention. This is what it looks like when attention is strong, flexible, and well-trained. But the truth (supported by mounting evidence from my own lab as well as the broader research field) is that none of us fall reliably or exclusively into that column.

Not students.

Not lawyers.

Not CEOs.

Not generals.

Not top scientists at NASA, Boeing, or SpaceX.

Nobody.

What Makes Kryptonite So Powerful?

There's a famous test of attention given to people of all ages: You sit at a computer, and a series of letters appears on the screen before you, one after the other. Your job is to say the color of the ink for each cluster of letters, as quickly as you can. Sounds simple, right?

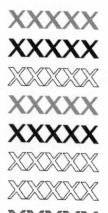

Try it with the graphic shown on this page. Skim down and say out loud the color of the ink, as quickly and accurately as you can.

Easy, right? No problem. But now I want you to do this again with the list on the opposite page. Your task is the same: go down the list and say the ink color one by one. To be clear: say the *color of the ink*—not the word itself. Ready, set, go!

Easy again? Probably not.

There's no computer measuring your response times right now, as there would be if you were taking this test in my lab. But you might have noticed that you were slower than you were with the first list. And you likely hesitated, taking just a beat longer when you came across the fourth one down. Your urge to say "black" was probably very strong. You might have

GRAY
BLACK
WHITE
BLACK
WHITE
BLACK
GRAY
WHITE

even blurted it out and then corrected yourself, to say "gray."

The instructions were so simple. So why did this happen? *Because I set your brain up to battle with itself.* The battle was between what happened automatically (you read the word) and what the instructions asked you to do (report the color of the ink). This mismatch produced what we call a "high-conflict" moment.

And in the brain, such moments signal that there is a problem. In response, executive attention is summoned to provide a "power boost." With attention on hand, you can more easily override automatically reading and saying the word. Your behavior becomes more aligned with your goals. We can track this in the lab. Responses are faster and more accurate for high-conflict trials that follow other high-conflict trials versus those that follow low-conflict trials—which sounds like a good thing. And sometimes it is. But it can also become a root cause of depleting our attention.

In our lives, what we consider *challenging situations* are often "conflict states." There is a mismatch between what we perceive *is happening* and what *should be* happening. Our minds experience these conflicts in different ways:

- *Resisting Mind:* We may want whatever is happening to stop—filling us with fear, sadness, worry, resentment, or even hatred.

- *Doubting Mind:* We may have a distrust in our assessment of what is or should be happening, increasing our sense of doubt.

- *Restless Mind:* We are restless and agitated, uncertain about what is occurring but dissatisfied nonetheless.

- *Craving Mind:* We may want more of what is happening, leaving us desiring and craving for it.

These conflict states signal that there is a problem. Attention is summoned to solve it. Yet the problems in our lives aren't like math problems that can be solved and then checked off our to-do list. These are, more often than not, long-term, complex problems—or simply threads in the texture of being human—and can't be efficiently "figured out" in that way.

The reason that conflict states are attention-draining: *they keep summoning attention over and over again.* This *continuous engagement* of attention depletes it. And as your attention becomes depleted, you go on autopilot. Your mind gets easily "captured" and carried away by whatever is most salient.

When you carry conflict states around with you they can occupy and compete for your mental workspace and attentional resources. You're so busy carrying that load that very few attentional resources remain to overcome automatic tendencies. Any *salient* thing will grab you—and keep you longer. So, if you've had a long and demanding day—say, you're stressed, anxious, or preoccupied—you're more likely to go for the bright shiny thing. You'll grab the cookies instead of the carrots. You'll click the flashing ad. You'll spend the money you meant to save. You'll spend something even more precious—*your attention*—in places you never intended to.

And in these situations, we tend to turn to a handful of common strategies to cope. They're common and natural, thus we default to them often. The problem is, they don't work.

We're Using Failed Strategies

Think positive. Focus on the good. Do something relaxing. Set goals and visualize them. Suppress upsetting thoughts. Concentrate on something else. We've all heard these types of advice for coping and focusing under stress. Some of them make up a big part of performance psychology and professional leadership training. We often default to these tactics when we find ourselves mind-wandering or caught in a loop of negative thinking. The problem? All these strategies actually require attentional resources to implement. They use up attention instead of strengthening it. As much as we're told that we can and should "change our experience by changing our thoughts"—by putting on rosier glasses—this strategy, like others, exacts a very high toll. And worse: under high stress, it usually doesn't work.

Try this: don't think about a polar bear. I mean it! Don't. It's your one job right now. Stop thinking about a polar bear!

What are you thinking about?

I have one guess.

We did a study with active-duty soldiers whom we tested to see if positivity training could help them over a high-demand period of military training. It didn't. And not only did it not work to improve or protect attention, attention actually got worse over time.

Why? Part of the reason is that it takes a lot of attention to positively reframe an experience when undergoing distressing or demanding circumstances. When attention is already beginning to degrade, it's hard to build this mental model, and the whole thing crumbles like a sandcastle at high tide. You then pour a lot of your cognitive resources into rebuilding and repairing it—which is like trying to keep your sandcastle from being washed away. You can't. You end up mentally (and attentionally) exhausted, without anything to show for it.

While there is substantial research that positivity is beneficial under many circumstances, tactics like positivity or suppression are not merely ineffective during periods of high stress and high demand—they can be actively damaging. I call these "failed strategies" because while we try to use them to solve our attention problems, what they do is degrade attention even further. (Imagine having a sprained ankle and trying to run on it.) It's cyclical and exponential: as our focus fades and distractions intrude, we try to look on the bright side, suppress, escape, push away, barrel through. This effort sucks up cognitive resources. Stress goes up, mood worsens. The attention-degrading forces intensify. As attention degrades further and faster, you lean into these ineffective strategies harder, burning even more cognitive fuel. You're in a downward spiral, cognitively depleted and less able to cope and function.

You simply can't *not* think about that polar bear, and trying not to drains you—*fast*. These strategies drive up attentional engagement. Using them is like trying to put out a fire with gasoline—it just makes things worse. In our struggle to control our attention, we're pouring all our cognitive efforts into methods that simply do not work.

The obvious question then becomes: What *does*?

3

PUSH-UPS FOR THE MIND

When my son was little—when I was at the peak of struggling with my own attention—he had this toy he loved. Called "the water wiggler," it was basically a clear plastic, slippery tube filled with water and sealed at both ends. When you tried to pick it up and grasp it, it doubled in on itself and shot out of your grip. It was impossible to hang onto. Leo would wrap his tiny hands around it, and it would pop into the air and go bouncing across the floor—endless entertainment.

Meanwhile, I was having no fun at all. I was locked into the same kind of cycle, but instead of a water wiggler, it was my attention I was trying to hang onto. Yet the tighter I grabbed, the more it shot away.

I remember *commanding* my mind to calm down and be still. I remember trying harder and harder to control it. It royally backfired. The distressing and distracting inner monologue just got louder. I felt hopeless—it seemed like the harder I tried, the worse it got. And the hopelessness was compounded by a growing sense of longing. I longed to really experience my life—not live in fast-forward or reverse.

Many of us experience this existential longing. Some event—a health scare, a divorce, a tragedy or loss, a global pandemic—prompts us to take stock of how present (or not) we are to the unfolding of our lives. The trigger might even be a good thing: a success, a promotion, a sweet moment with a loved one. Or it might be a gradual realization—a hunch you have that there *must* be some way to "up-level" your performance and well-being. Whatever it is, something clues you in that you are more distracted, dysregulated, and disconnected than you'd like to be—than you *need* to be to live your life to its peak. We've tried all the available tricks and tactics, from digital detox weekends to hack-your-life apps. We need a real solution to this predicament—something we can do to become more focused, less reactive, and more connected.

We understand now that our attention is powerful but vulnerable—that we are built for distraction, and that the world around us will relentlessly exploit that. I've also told you that there's something you can do about this. But one challenge is that there's a widespread belief that the brain doesn't change that much. People often believe that they are "wired" one way or another, and that this wiring is relatively permanent, part of their genetic makeup or personality.

Neuroplasticity: Train Your Brain to Change Your Brain

Neuroscientists used to think the brain's wiring was relatively permanent. We thought that by the time you reached adulthood—after you passed out of those malleable, formative teenage years—"the brain you had was the brain you had." Sure, new connections could be made when you learned something or had a new experience, but that was simply making connections between existing landmarks—like putting a bridge up to connect two landmasses or adding an access road to connect two highways. You were still working with the same basic terrain. By adulthood, the map was already drawn in semipermanent ink.

Until we realized, as often happens in science, that we were wrong. The human brain—the fully developed brain, the adult brain, even the *injured* brain—has incredible *neuroplasticity*, meaning that it can reform or reorganize itself, depending on the input it receives and the processes it engages in with regularity. Here's a quick example: In London, an old city with a complex, mind-boggling urban map, researchers ran a study comparing the brains of bus drivers with those of cab drivers. They found that the hippocampus, a key part of the brain for memory and spatial navigation, was significantly bigger in the cab drivers than in the bus drivers. They mostly had the same job—driving through the city—so why? Because while the bus drivers only had to memorize and use one specific route, the cab drivers had to hold the entirety of the cityscape in their minds, flexibly scrolling through the mental map to find each new route. These people, obviously, hadn't been driving buses and cabs since they were little kids—these changes to their brains had happened relatively recently.

This research on neuroplasticity has been out there for years. But it hasn't quite trickled out into the general consciousness. We still think of our brains as "hardwired"; we still believe that how we respond to situations—whether cognitively or emotionally—is an immutable fact, a facet of our personality or identity, something we have to deal with or work around but can't actually change. That it even occurred to me during my "attentional" crisis that I could change my brain instead of my entire life is a consequence of my particular choice of career. When you're faced with a crisis like the one I was in, the natural approach might be to figure out how to change your life so you can cope better—switch jobs, drop responsibilities, and so on. Yet to me, nothing was particularly negotiable. I was already on the right path, doing what I loved. There wasn't anything I was wanting to change—except for the way I was feeling in the midst of it all. And as a neuroscientist, I already had an intimate knowledge of the brain's incredible neuroplasticity. Brain injuries like those suffered by Gordon, the paraplegic I met all those years ago as a hospital volunteer, gave me my first inkling of what might be possible when it comes to neuroplasticity. After damage, the brain could dramatically recover some of the functions that it had seemingly lost. It would take time, practice, and persistence, but it was possible. This told me that the brain *could* change. So the next step, after going from injury to recovery, was to take people who are already healthy and provide them with opportunities for repeated practice. The hope was that with repetition they could *optimize* some of their functions. Could we use the brain's capacity for neuroplasticity to make the mind healthier, *more* tailored to the challenges of our times?

I *could* change my brain—that much I was certain of. What I didn't know, exactly, was *how*.

That same spring when my teeth went numb, the eminent neuroscientist Richard (Richie) Davidson happened to come to campus to give a lecture in my department. Today, Richie heads up a thriving center focused on meditation research at the University of Wisconsin–Madison, the Center for Healthy Minds, but when he came to Penn in the early 2000s he hadn't started speaking at length about his recent research into meditation. Toward the end of his lecture, he put up two separate fMRI brain images on the screen side by side: one of a person induced to be in a positive mood, and one of a person induced to be in a negative mood. To get these images, researchers triggered emotional responses in participants by having them vividly recall happy or sad memories, playing upbeat or mournful music, or having them watch movie clips of contrasting mood. Meanwhile, the giant MRI magnet, buzzing and beeping with its radio frequency pulses, captured the brain activation data.

MRI (magnetic resonance imaging), like the kind you might get for a knee or ankle injury, offers a *static* look at anatomy—a snapshot of what's inside. An fMRI, or *functional* MRI, is different. It capitalizes on handy properties of the brain and of blood in a magnetic environment. When neurons fire, they require more oxygenated blood—and blood has a different magnetic signature when it's rich with oxygen versus when it is not. fMRI illuminates the ongoing levels of oxygenated blood in different parts of the brain over time, which means it can indirectly track, moment by moment, where in the brain neurons are most active. The images in the two slides that Richie showed us had strikingly different activity patterns, like Rorschach tests with opposite inkblots. The negative brain functioned differently from the positive one.

During the Q&A, I raised my hand. "How do you get the negative brain to look like the positive one?"

He answered without hesitation. "Meditation."

I couldn't believe he'd used that word. This was a brain science lecture—how could he bring up *meditation?* It seemed as outlandish as mentioning *astrology* to an audience of astrophysicists. Meditation was not a topic worthy of scientific pursuit! Nobody would take you seriously. Plus, I had my own personal reasons for being skeptical.

Growing up, my dad was committed to meditation practice. I remember stumbling into my parents' bedroom early in the morning, bleary-eyed, to see my dad showered and dressed—*mala* (prayer beads) in hand, eyes closed, still as a statue. Although I didn't often travel back to the Indian city where I'd been born, when I was about ten, we traveled to India for the summer. One of the big events for my family that year was a Hindu rite-of-passage ceremony for a cousin, a boy who was the same age as me. During the ceremony, the priest whispered something in his ear. I later discovered that what he'd whispered was a special *mantra*, a short passage in the ancient language of Sanskrit. He was to use prayer beads with 108 beads and silently, deliberately repeat the mantra 108 times as a daily practice.

I was intrigued—it seemed like being invited into a secret club, very important and adult. I asked my mom what the mantra was, and when I might receive mine. That's when she broke the news to me: I wouldn't receive the mantra given to all boys . . . because I was a girl. In the Hindu tradition, only boys got to have this ceremony, and only boys received the mantra. This gave my mom no pleasure, since she always wanted her daughters to be treated equally, but this was the cultural reality.

That was it for me. I was done with meditation. If meditation wouldn't accept me, I wouldn't accept it. I lumped it all together and packed it away, boxing it up in my mind in the same container as the other outdated attitudes about gender roles, as well as all the other old traditions I chafed against. I was not going to learn to cook Indian food to be the perfect Indian wife, and I was certainly not going to meditate. So, when Richie Davidson said the word *meditation* in that seminar, every part of me—the scientist, the professor, the outraged young girl getting shut out of a family tradition—pushed back in opposition. I brushed his comment away, but it nagged at me.

Meanwhile, in the lab, we were looking for new routes for improving attention, mood, and performance. We tried many things—devices, brain-training games, and other strategies like mood inductions. In one study, we investigated a new device that many students called their "secret to academic success" because it made them feel more attentive. It was a small, handheld gadget that connected to earbuds and goggles. Users turned it on to experience blinking lights and soothing sounds. You didn't have to *do* anything—you passively listened to the sounds and watched the lights. It was wildly popular—in one tech-happy Asian country, people were buying it for their children, and college students said it was single-handedly responsible for helping them pass the national exams. The manufacturer claimed that it would increase focus, improve memory, and reduce stress. So, did it, really?

People who tried it said it did. But we didn't have to take their word for it—my team and I could test it in the lab and find out definitively.

We ran one basic attention study, then another just to be sure. In both, we gave participants computer tests that evaluated their attention, then sent them home with these devices and instructions to use them for thirty minutes per day for two weeks. When we brought the participants back in to retest, here's how much of an impact the device had had on their attentional performance: *zero*. There was no change, not even a hint of a directional trend.

The results from our other attempts weren't convincing either. Back in the early 2000s, it seemed that most brain-training games didn't work. By "didn't work," what I mean is that there was no solid scientific consensus that playing most of these kinds of games leads to any benefits beyond simply getting better at that particular game. Sure, you might get a higher score on the game after playing it for two weeks—but you won't perform better on a *new* game that also requires attention to excel. Any benefits were fleeting or constrained to only the specific game environment—they did not transfer or last. The reason? Well, the science on brain-training apps, and even on passive sensory devices, is steadily proliferating and the topic is still hotly debated. But my strong hunch is that they ask you to deploy attention in specific ways, and don't train a very important aspect of attention, which is the *awareness* of where your attention is, moment to moment.

We tried a lot of the new stuff. Maybe it was time to try something . . . old.

A short time after Richie Davidson's talk, I bought a book called

Meditation for Beginners, by Jack Kornfield, a longtime teacher and author of mindfulness books, which came with a CD of guided meditation practices. The first time I played it, I didn't expect much—I'd never done any kind of guided program before and didn't think it would really be my thing. But it wasn't at all what I thought meditation would be. I liked Kornfield's voice and style, as well as his running commentary directing me to pay attention to my breath and notice my mind-wandering. There were no special mantras, no chanting, no instructions to contort my body or visualize energy, as I'd feared and expected. And the striking thing was that he seemed to know my mind! He predicted that it would wander, resist, push away, criticize, and get bored. He advised that, when you notice the mind "doing what minds do, simply return your attention back to the breath." It wasn't overly earnest or spiritual; quite the opposite. It was ordinary, down-to-earth, matter-of-fact.

"Meditation" is a broad category of human activity. It's a general term, like "sports." If someone asked whether you have any hobbies, you wouldn't simply say, "I play sports." You'd tell them you play tennis, or basketball, or ultimate frisbee. Sure, they all require general physical fitness, but there are sport-specific physical skills and aptitude you'd also need to develop for the particular sport you play. And the training drills differ for gymnastics as opposed to, say, hockey. Meditation is similar. It involves engaging in a particular set of practices to cultivate specific mental qualities. There are many forms of meditation that have been offered up across human history from the world's wisdom traditions: philosophical, religious, and spiritual. The suite of practices—the mind's "workout"—differs based on the particular type of meditation you do—be it transcendental, compassion, mindfulness meditation, or something else. With transcendental meditation, for example, you aim to achieve a "transcendent" state, connecting with something larger than yourself, while compassion meditation is about cultivating concern for the suffering of others and acting on behalf of reducing this suffering. The Kornfield book I read focused on *mindfulness meditation*— anchoring your attention in the present moment and experiencing it without "editorializing": making up a story about what's happening or will happen.

Over the next month, I practiced daily, adding a couple of minutes each week, eventually working up to a twenty-minute practice every day. And I began to feel the slow return of sensation to my mouth. My jaw stopped aching all the time. I could feel my teeth again. I could talk with ease! It gave me enormous relief. And then I noticed that I could see my husband's face again. I mean *really* see it—notice his expressions, key in fast to what he was feeling or trying to communicate. It happened with my son, too. I felt so much more connected to both of them, almost effortlessly. And at work, I was feeling more present, more effective. I had a sense of being highly aware and anchored in my body, in my life. *Where had I been?*

Nothing else in my life had changed—I still had the same demanding job, the same grants to write and classes to teach, students to mentor, lab to run and colleagues to debate, the same nightly bedtime story to read to my son about the wumps (more like a cross between a camel and a donkey than a guinea pig, now that I was paying attention). But something *had* changed—I felt completely different. I had managed to close that gap, to move back into my body, into my mind, into my surroundings. I felt capable and in control, confident that I could face challenges and work to overcome them. I felt *powerfully alive.*

And I got curious about why this was happening. Through this meditation practice, I found myself feeling dramatically different after just a month or two. It seemed a little bit like I'd just miraculously landed into feeling better. Yet I knew it wasn't a miracle.

Something had happened to my attention system, and I needed to figure out what. I knew a lot about the brain science of attention, but I had not come across anything in the scientific literature on its link with mindfulness practice. I thought, *I need to take this to the lab*.

Road Testing Mindfulness

I knew that designing an actual scientific study would be quite a bit different from the small-yet-impactful experiment I had conducted on myself—committing to a daily mindfulness practice to "test" whether I could feel better, clearer, sharper. This study would have nothing to do with my personal feelings and everything to do with being rigorous in my methods to determine whether objective performance could improve in people I didn't even know. When we do a scientific study of attention, we set out to test specific questions, which are bound by detailed parameters and controls. The first thing we would need to know before asking specific research questions was how much time a person would need to engage in mindfulness exercises in order for us to be able to track the impact with objective metrics. Hours? Days? Weeks?

The best way to start, I decided, was to go big.

The Shambhala Mountain Center, outside of Denver, Colorado, is surrounded by the silver and green of aspen and birch, the ice blue of the Western sky, and the sharp purple ridges of the Rocky Mountains. The place is a retreat in the true sense of the word—removed from the rest of the world, from the usual business of life, even from cell phone service. Most important, for our purposes, the center conducts a monthlong intensive meditation retreat in which participants engage in a variety of activities mindfully for *twelve hours* per day, with most of those hours spent in formal meditation. If we were going to see an impact on our laboratory metrics of attention from mindfulness practice, we'd see it here—or it probably didn't exist.

Members of my research team flew to Denver with a suitcase full of laptops, each one loaded with the same kind of attention tests we used in the lab. At the retreat center, they set up a table at the check-in spot and, as people arrived, handed out flyers asking for volunteers. *"Participate in a study on attention and mindfulness meditation!"* the flyers said, and many people, most of whom had been meditators for years, perked up, intrigued. The next morning, before the retreat began, volunteers arrived in groups of five, sat down at the laptop stations, and were guided through a series of tasks designed to gather data and give us a baseline: What was their starting point? In terms of attentional functionality, what was their "normal"?

One of these tests was called the Sustained Attention to Response Task, or SART. This test was developed in the late 1990s, and, as the name suggests, it tests a person's ability to sustain attention. Here's how it works: participants sit in front of a computer screen where a number appears for half a second, then vanishes; a half second later, another number appears, then vanishes; and so on for twenty minutes. Their job: Press the space bar every time a number appears— *unless* the number is 3. Then, don't press. By design, the number 3 appears only 5 percent of the time—not a lot.

This test engages all three of your attentional subsystems. You *orient* attention, focusing on each number as it flickers; stay *alert* to the appearance of the number 3; and use *executive attention* to make sure you're following the instructions, pressing only when you should. Simple.

Simple, perhaps. But not easy. Most people are pretty terrible at this task. Why? Perhaps the numbers flicker by too quickly, making it difficult for them to actually see clearly? Nope. Half a second is plenty of time for the brain to process visual information. Maybe they look away from the screen? We checked. Tracking their eye movements by securing electrodes around their eyes, we learned that our participants were great at keeping their eyes on the screen. Here's what else we learned: although their eyes were on the screen, their attention was not. They were on autopilot, pressing the space bar no matter what number appeared. Their attentional flashlight was directed elsewhere, the floodlight was offline, the juggler dropped the ball.

I chose the SART for this exact reason. Before asking fine-grained questions about *which* subsystems of attention are strengthened, I wanted to know if mindfulness training could minimize a fundamental vulnerability suffered by *all* subsystems—attentional hijacking. Could a monthlong retreat boost attention to help keep it on the task-at-hand? To find out, I needed a test that would engage attention broadly, and also challenge it with distraction, boredom, and mind-wandering. The SART was perfect.

In follow-up tests, we'd ask more specific questions and isolate various subsystems of attention—to see if, for example, training improved the floodlight more so than the flashlight, which a later study confirmed.

Our study participants in the mountains of Colorado finished their initial tests and went off to spend the next four weeks immersed in mindfulness: living mindfully, and formally practicing mindfulness exercises for the majority of their waking hours each day. (I did a much shorter version of this type of retreat many months later, and the best way to describe it is "a bootcamp for the brain"—it was intense!) From the moment they woke early in the morning until they went to bed, they would practice—in silence—in thirty- to fifty-five-minute sessions. Even their meals were eaten in silence, and retreatants were given instruction on how to continue their practice while eating. At the end of that month, we'd be back to administer the SART again, and see what (if anything) had changed. It was a little bit like tagging fish and releasing them back into the ocean—off they swam with the rest of the group into the meditative waters of a retreat environment.

Meanwhile, we gave a group of nonmeditators the SART two times, a month apart as well. When we went back to Colorado a month later to catch those experienced meditators on their way out the door, what we found is that their attention had *improved*. They performed much better after the retreat. Before the retreat, participants were pressing that button when they shouldn't, about 40 percent of the time—that was their starting point. The nonmeditators also made errors 40 percent of the time, and their scores did not change when we tested them again a month later. But after the retreat, the meditators only mistakenly pressed the space bar *30* percent of the time. So, a 10 percent improvement overall.

If 10 percent doesn't sound like a lot—or if missing the number 3 doesn't seem like a big deal—consider the parallel real-world scenarios. A version of the SART was conducted with live-fire simulation. That means that instead of a number 3, a simulated human target would flash on the screen, and instead of pressing a space bar, the subject would fire a weapon with simulated ammunition. Participants' performance was not much different in the "live-fire" version of the SART, however. They were shooting when they shouldn't have—*a lot*. I was struck by this, as it suggests that attention—and improving it—could have life and death consequences in the real world.

Encouraged, we also conducted studies that let us dig into the subsystems of attention with mindfulness training. We used the attention network test to see how the flashlight, the floodlight, and the juggler responded to mindfulness. Here's what we found: meditators had better jugglers; executive attention was better in retreat participants *before* they even started the retreat. After the retreat, they improved in alerting—their floodlights were fast to detect new information.

We also offered the same test to medical and nursing students on campus. We found that after they took an eight-week mindfulness-based stress reduction course, like those offered at over 750 medical centers worldwide, they improved in orienting. They had a better grip on their flashlight.

In my own experience, in the very early days when I began mindfulness training, one of the first things I'd noticed was that I felt *worse.* I noticed the drop in my stomach—which, like the accompanying anxiety and sadness, would linger for hours—when I had to leave my son at day care and walk away; I noticed the dull ache in my clenched jaw, often synchronized with feeling overwhelmed by the parade of demands throughout my workday. My thoughts continued to whirl without stopping long after I got home from the lab. This stuff had always been there, of course, but now it seemed magnified *because I was paying attention to it.*

But then, because I was more aware of physical sensations and concurrent negative thoughts, I slowly began to catch the thought earlier. I could notice it, acknowledge it, and let it pass away on its own. This way of interacting with my mind gave me a stronger sense of control. Instead of feeling constantly hijacked and held hostage by distressing thoughts and emotions, I was aware of my body tightening and my attention drifting. Soon, I felt more capable of redirecting my mind if I chose to. I could step out of a loop of negative thinking, instead of getting caught in it, like in the churn at the bottom of a waterfall.

And now, the data from these initial studies seemed to corroborate my experience, suggesting that mindfulness meditation, unlike *anything else we'd studied so far,* could actually change the way our attention, our "brain's boss," behaved. But we needed to make sure.

Is Mindfulness Really the Secret Sauce?

Four days a week for four weeks we intercepted the University of Miami football team at the end of their weight-training workout. My lab assistants would hand out iPod Shuffles with headsets attached (it was back when iPod Shuffles were still a thing). A twelve-minute recording of the soothing yet confidently firm voice of my colleague Scott Rogers would guide players through one of two possible activities: a mindfulness exercise or a relaxation exercise. The players didn't know it, but they'd been separated into two groups: one group was receiving mindfulness training, while the other was receiving relaxation training. The exercises that both groups (unbeknownst to them) were asked to do at the same time *appeared* similar enough to the casual onlooker (for example, they were simply lying on their mats on the floor with eyes closed). But in fact their attention was being "instructed" in quite different ways—the mindfulness group was guided through exercises that honed their attention to be in an observational stance, like breath awareness and body scans (practices I'll lead you through soon), while the relaxation group instead used attention to manipulate thought and direct their muscle movements (as in progressive muscle relaxation exercises). And then, outside of the structured training sessions, we had all the participants download the same practice recordings onto their smartphones—instructing them to practice on their own on other days of the week we didn't see them.

We didn't have a no-training control group, as we typically would with a scientific study—everybody participated. The football players were in preseason training, a high-stress interval with high stakes: at the end of it, they'd all head to training camp, where their performance would determine the trajectory of their entire playing season, and maybe even their career. The head coach, cognizant that anyone who didn't get training of some kind could be at a disadvantage, insisted that everybody get something. This made for a stronger test anyway, because it asked an urgent question: If mindfulness training is helpful, is it *more* helpful than doing something else, like relaxation training?

We knew that those experienced meditators on retreat in Colorado as well as the medical and nursing students we'd trained back on campus had improved measurably. What we needed to figure out now was whether *mindfulness*, in particular, was the key piece of the equation that was helping, or whether relaxation exercises would have the same effect.

We were prepared to see our participants' attention decline over the course of the preseason interval. This is something we'd discovered about attention and high-demand periods: *everybody degrades.* Students, soldiers, elite athletes—everybody. So what we were asking was this: Could mindfulness training or relaxation help stave off that degradation of attention?

Here's what we found: Both types of training helped in some areas, like emotional well-being. But then, for attention, the two groups diverged—and they diverged the most for those who engaged in the daily exercises five or more days per week.

In the mindfulness group, attention skills *held steady* instead of degrading—mindfulness training had indeed worked to "protect" their attention, even through this high-demand period.

But in the relaxation group, attention got *worse.*

I'm absolutely not saying "don't relax." What I'm saying—and what the science is showing—is that trying to use relaxation as an antidote to attentional degradation *will not work*, because it doesn't actually address the *reasons* that attention is degrading.

As we discussed earlier, some tactics, while beneficial in many circumstances, can actively make things worse if they are used during high-demand intervals when attention is in short supply. Remember

"Don't think about a polar bear"? The common advice we hear is *suppress—don't think about it right now.* (Visualize something positive instead.) The new science of attention says no—instead, *accept and allow.* Trying to suppress has a paradoxical effect: it keeps the content in your working memory longer, because you have to actively remind yourself to keep suppressing. Many studies on mindfulness practice suggest that if you *accept and allow* instead of *resist* (which we'll be learning how to do in the coming chapters), stressful content will pass away.

We knew that mindfulness practice was the key to training attention. The next question was: *How* effective was it? Could it help us outside of a controlled university environment or a serene retreat locale? Could it help under extreme stress, under time pressure, under high demand? We'd tested mindfulness under ideal conditions—what about the opposite? In other words: *real life*?

Mindfulness Under Pressure

In the lab, when we started to consider how kryptonite conditions like stress impact attention, it seemed that there were many *different* ways. But one common factor was this: stress *hijacks your attention away from the present moment.*

Mental time travel takes us out of the current moment in time and, while doing so, monopolizes all our attention. The prevalence of attentional hijacking suggested to me that training the mind to stay in the present could be an important missing piece in *attention training*—a catalytic ingredient that the gadgets, brain-training apps, and other approaches we had tried were missing. To find out if I was on to something, we set our sights on one of the most high-stress, high-demand populations: the military.

I gripped my armrests as the plane circled above West Palm Beach, waiting to land. I was nervous, but it wasn't fear of flying: I was there to meet the leadership of a Marine Reserve unit. My colleague and I were pitching a pilot study on mindfulness training specifically for the military and I had no idea if they would accept it. Our liaisons, two captains in the Marine Reserves who'd tentatively agreed to let us on base, had gone out on a limb in allowing us to come out to run a mindfulness meditation program with their Marines. These were warriors. Mindfulness meditation was not exactly their *thing*.

The study at the retreat center in Colorado had yielded promising results. Those participants had *improved*, indicating that mindfulness could boost attention under ideal circumstances. But what about *less*-than-ideal circumstances? What about less than a full month of intensive, continuous meditation in a placid, remote place? Sounds great to be in an idyllic mountain retreat—but most of us need help with our attention while we're in the midst of our day-to-day lives, under pressure, juggling a million things. And further, meditating *twelve hours a day* is hardly realistic for the vast majority of people. Could mindfulness help the rest of us?

We'd been mulling over these questions at the lab when I got a phone call from a security studies professor from another university. A veteran who had turned to mindfulness after experiencing first-hand the difficulties associated with deployment, she was interested in offering it to other military service members. Since she didn't have a background in neuroscience or experimental research, she was look-ing for a research collaborator. Richie Davidson, who I had stayed in touch with since his lecture at Penn, suggested she try me.

I was intrigued and got to work poring over existing research on attention and military deployment. I was immediately engrossed and, frankly, quite concerned. The military represented a population that had to deal with extremely high-demand situations all the time, and it clearly took a toll. During predeployment, service members trained intensively, simulating scenarios in which lives were at stake all day, every day. Then they deployed into scenarios where lives were *actually* at stake. Those potent forces we've been discussing that degrade attention are a constant way of life for military service members. Add to that other factors that degrade attention, like sleep disturbances, uncertainty, extreme temperatures, and mortality salience (thinking about your own death). And to punch things up even further, this was in the post-9/11 era of the military surge in Iraq. The year was 2007 and, as a nation, the United States had been at war abroad for six years. Units were going out on back-to-back deployments. Rates of suicide and PTSD among service members were climbing. Not only was high stress causing warriors to spiral into psychological disorders, but many were suffering from moral injury, struggling with regret, remorse, and guilt when their own reactivity led to behavior that violated their ethical code.

Did I have any hesitations about working with the military? Sure. I thought long and hard about it. A lot of the problems that these warriors were suffering from stem from having to go to war. Wouldn't it be better not to have war?

Well, of course—wouldn't that be great? But that question is fundamentally similar to the questions of what the rest of us should do about stressors in our own lives: Should we change our lives, or our minds? I can't personally change the world and end war. But maybe I could help those serving in the military function better through incredible stress, protect their attention from degrading, regulate their emotions more effectively, and hold their own ethical code at the forefront of their minds even through the fog of war.

And finally, there was much to learn from this demographic. Could mindfulness help the attention of those under the most high-stress, high-pressure, and *time*-pressure situations imaginable? Could it give a boost to those who are compromised because of the job they have been asked to do, at the request of a nation? If so, it could probably help the rest of us, too. It was time to see if we could bring mindfulness down from the mountain and into the trenches.

This Is Never Going to Work

That's what then captain Jason Spitaletta said to me as we walked onto the Marine Corps Reserve Center in West Palm Beach, Florida. He sounded good-natured about it. He smiled when he shook my hand and cheerfully told me our study was probably doomed. Marines, he said, were just not going to go for it. *Mindfulness* wasn't something they'd invest in—it was too "soft" sounding. (This was 2007—it was very new to everybody back then.)

Nevertheless, Captain Spitaletta and his coleader on the reserve base had agreed to host the study. His coleader? Captain Jeff Davis, whom you might remember from chapter 2—this was my first time meeting with him, and I wasn't sure what to expect. When we'd spoken to Davis on the phone a few months before, he'd seemed skeptical yet open, acknowledging that they needed to try something new.

Spitaletta and Davis appeared exactly the way I figured Marines would look: jarheads. I admit that I had a moment of cognitive dissonance. It was hard to picture these two—stoic, brawny guys in desert camo—sitting and meditating. And if even I had trouble picturing it, military leadership would likely have its own doubts. At this early point in our research, there was no precedent for mindfulness meditation as "cognitive training." We were going to put this to the test and see what the data revealed. My main goal was to set the conditions for a strong experiment: asking the right questions and selecting evaluation metrics that would be sensitive enough to detect even small changes in attention. With thoughtful planning and luck on our side, we'd get a clear answer, one way or another.

I was fortunate to have Davis and Spitaletta as my collaborators. Although they were captains in the Marine Reserves, they could have been grad students in my lab. As we spoke, I found them whip-smart and curious, fascinated by neuroscience and experimental research. I could feel their compassionate leadership—that they truly cared and wanted to help their fellow Marines, who they were leading into difficult, complex, and dangerous situations. Davis, who had little kids at home, was about to go out on his fourth back-to-back deployment—talk about kryptonite!

It was true, what he'd said on the phone, about needing to try something new. We *all* needed to try something new.

On campus, our lab experiments had simulated high-stress situations by flashing disturbing images while research volunteers were in the middle of attention tasks. But here, in the Marine Corps Reserve Center, we had access to people who would be experiencing not just images in a lab but potent real-life stressors. This was no serene retreat center. Would mindfulness make a difference *here*?

My team and I set up our laptops and gave the Marines various cognitive tasks. We also probed their mood and stress levels. And then, for the eight weeks of predeployment training that followed, they were offered a twenty-four-hour program modeled off of the well-established, mindfulness-based stress reduction techniques that had been tested in medical settings, but contextualized for a military cohort. They were introduced to a foundational set of practices: attention to the breath, scanning the body, and so on—practices that entail bringing attention into the present moment, in a "non-editorializing" way. We knew we needed to deliver these practices in a way that would make sense to this demographic so that it would be accessible to them.

Their homework: thirty minutes of mindfulness practice every day.

Eight weeks later, we were back to test them again. Some had done the assigned thirty minutes daily on several days, but most did far less. They were all over the place. This was what data from the field can often look like: lots of variability across participants. It was quite a departure from the post-retreat meditators. To plot the results, we split the group in two. The "high-practice" group averaged about twelve minutes a day, while the "low-practice" group was made up of the participants who'd done significantly less. Here's what we saw: while the low-practice group got progressively worse in terms of attention, working memory, and mood over the eight weeks, the high-practice group remained stable. At the end of the training interval, the high-practice group performed better and reported feeling better than the low-practice group and a no-training control group. What we'd found in our earlier studies was holding true, even under higher demand: *mindfulness could indeed stabilize attention.*

After this phase of our study, the Marines were deployed. When they came back, we retested them. And again, the results were initially a mixed bag—nothing was reaching statistical significance. The group was small; some members had dropped out of the study, left the military, or moved on to a new post. Many had stopped doing the training practices during deployment.

Still, one pattern stood out. When we looked at those who had been in our low-practice group at predeployment, a subset of participants actually performed *better* than before they left. This result contradicted the earlier data and made no sense—why were they performing so well? After all, even before they were deployed, they'd done minimal practice compared to the others.

I called my colleague who had developed and delivered the training to try to get to the bottom of it. She didn't have an explanation either—until I read her the names of the participants in the low-practice group. That jogged her memory. It turned out they had emailed her from Iraq and said things like, "My buddy who did your program before we were deployed is sleeping through the night. I need you to help me learn to do what he's doing." From a distance, they were able to begin engaging in the mindfulness practices with the trainer's guidance.

Basically, this low-practice group had turned themselves into a *high*-practice group on their own. Mid-deployment in Iraq, with what I can only imagine were unpredictable schedules and very demanding circumstances, they'd taken it upon themselves to do *more* mindfulness practice, because it was blatantly apparent to them what a difference it made.

Now, it's important to note that this study—our first trial run of delivering mindfulness training in a military setting—was promising. Still, it didn't produce stunning results—it was small, and the data were variable. But even though the results were modest, the implications were *huge*. First: mindfulness-based training could be introduced to high-demand groups to protect attention. And second: it wasn't a situation where you could say "any exposure to training is helpful." It required regular practice to benefit.

All the hoops we'd jumped through to get the study off the ground had been worth it. We had right in front of us living, breathing proof that mindfulness training created a kind of "mental armor" that could effectively protect individuals' attentional resources, even in the most high-stress scenarios imaginable.

Time to Start Training

Imagine a moment that calls for physical strength. Say you're about to help a friend move a piece of furniture. You approach the heavy couch, realize you're not quite up to the task and . . . drop to the floor and begin to do push-ups in an effort to gain the strength you need.

If that sounds silly, consider that this is what so many of us do every day, constantly, when faced with cognitive challenges—instead of developing a training regimen, making it a habit, and doing a little bit each day to build up our capacities, we drop and try to eke out a "mental push-up" or two once we're under stress or in crisis, the whole time believing that it will help and that we'll be able to stand up and "lift that couch." Instead, we'll only be more depleted.

We need to start training *now*, both for the period of high demand we may be in currently, and for periods of demand we'll face in the future.

The good news is that you can start small. And you can start immediately. In fact, *you already have.* At this point, you're well on your way along your attention-training journey. You know your own strength (the power of attention). And you know your enemy (the chief forms of kryptonite, like stress, poor mood, and threat, and why they are so damaging). What we're going to talk about next are the ways in which our brains are built to wander, and why, and what we can do about it. It turns out that our attentional problems can't be pinned entirely on external types of stressors, like the ones we've discussed here. It's tempting to think of difficult circumstances as the main challenge—we think, *if we could just eliminate them, we'd be fine.*

But ultimately, factors that degrade attention are weeds on the *inner landscape,* or what I sometimes call the "mindscape": they have less to do with external forces working against you, and more to do with how attention works. If you whack these weeds down (by getting rid of stressors and "threats"), they'll just pop back up. Maybe you don't have any weeds creeping onto your mindscape during that weekend spa retreat or deep-sea fishing trip, but that doesn't mean they won't reappear as soon as you get back to regular life. In fact, your wish to return to your blissful vacation can be a weed itself, making your Monday a new type of miserable.

Through my crisis of attention, I discovered that I didn't know my own mindscape, really. Sure, I "knew myself" in the Socratic sense: my character, values, and preferences. But I didn't know, nor did I value knowing, what was happening in my mind moment by moment. Where was my attention in this moment? What thoughts, emotions, or memories were (pre)occupying me right now? What stories, assumptions, and mindsets were at play?

As someone who had always thought of myself as an action-oriented, results-focused, competitive go-getter with high ambitions and a driven edge, what I learned when I embarked on my mindfulness journey surprised me. For the first time, I experienced a way of engaging with my mind, and learning about my mindscape, that was not about striving harder, thinking better and faster, and *doing* more. It was about *being*—being receptive, being curious, being present for the moments of my life. Before, I'd always assumed I could "think" my way out of any difficult problem I was facing. My guess is that most of us believe this—that the only and best way to learn something, assess a situation, or manage a crisis is to think it through, puzzle it out, problem-solve with logic, and then do something about it. Psychologists call this "discursive thinking": judging, planning, strategizing, and so on. We don't know of any other way to operate. But thinking and doing, as it turns out, are simply not enough.

The science of attention emphasizes *action*. This stems from our understanding of why we evolved to have an attention system in the first place—to *constrain* our information processing and filter out irrelevant clutter so we can focus on a task and accomplish important goals. In other words, we need attention so we can act and interact with the world. This narrow emphasis in the literature is also why I came up empty-handed when I sought answers for my attention crisis. While it frustrated me at first, it also motivated me to investigate a different attentional mode, one that is receptive and entails *noticing, observing,* and *being.*

While Descartes resolved his existential angst by concluding "I think, therefore I am," most of us feel more angst *because* of our thinking: "I think, therefore I am—distracted." We are collectively and chronically addicted to thinking and doing, which is why shifting into a being mode does not come easily to most of us. It requires training. And a growing literature on the new science of attention suggests that with this training our thinking and doing become more effective and meaningful.

A peak mind is a mind that doesn't privilege thinking and doing over being. It masters both modes of attention. It is focused and receptive, and with this balance we can overcome and rise above our attentional challenges. This is how we win the unfair fight.

Captain Davis—whom we met in the middle of his own attentional crisis on that bridge in Florida—had another crisis recently, of a very different type.

At the age of forty-four, he had a heart attack while riding in an Uber. When he told me about it, he described drawing on the mindfulness training he'd started during our study, more than a decade ago now. Instead of panicking, he quickly observed and assessed the situation before launching into action—seeing himself as a man in a car in need of immediate medical care. He was focused and calm, directing the Uber driver to pull over. He called 911 himself, and even flagged down the ambulance as he saw it approaching. In fact, he seemed so unlike a man experiencing a life-threatening health crisis that the ambulance driver tried to brush him off, saying, "No, no, I'm here for a man having a heart attack!" Even though his body was in crisis, his attention was both receptive and focused. He was still able to access his peak mind.

When Captain Davis told me about the heart attack, I was so relieved to hear that he was all right. I also marveled at how he'd transformed his own attention. Here was a guy who went from having a really terrible "boss"—an attention system that almost drove him off a bridge—to having one that was an exquisite leader, guide, and ally: one that saved his life.

At this point, if you're ready to improve your own attention, you now have all the knowledge you need to move forward. You know now what we knew after our initial studies on mindfulness:

Attention is *powerful.*

Attention is *vulnerable.*

Attention is *trainable.*

And now we begin that training with a basic but essential skill: how to find focus in a world of distractions.

4

FIND YOUR FOCUS

On a recent trip to California, I flew into San Jose and drove a rental car south. The bright blue sky had a freshness that cleared away my jet lag. There was barely any traffic—the highway was four lanes, wide open, and my attention widened, too. I cruised along, having all kinds of thoughts. . . . I mentally worked on a paper I was writing, puzzled over an idea for a new experiment, made a mental checklist of the questions I needed to ask my kids when I called them in the evening. As I glimpsed the tall evergreen trees peeking above the concrete sound barriers, so different from the landscape at home in Miami, I sang along to my playlist. My mind shifted rapidly between these various currents of thought like a fish in a slipstream, from one to the next and then back, and that was fine—until I merged onto Highway 17, a narrow, curving, often dangerous road that winds through the foothills leading down to Santa Cruz on the Pacific Ocean. All of a sudden, it seemed, a veil of clouds slid over the sky. A fog surrounded my car; the rain started pouring and the asphalt got slick; the traffic thickened. The road pinched down to two lanes and a driver cut in front of me; at one point, a mudslide edged into the road. My thoughts narrowed with the road, down to a single intense point: *Get to where you're going alive!* But worry set in, and then, worry about being worried. I knew this would not serve me. I needed to funnel all my cognitive energy into navigating the road ahead. I had to *focus*.

Obviously, I made it past the mudslides and the daredevil drivers of Highway 17, or I wouldn't be reporting back to you now. The point of this story is that sometimes you need to be able to grab the flashlight of your attention, aim it, and hold it where you need it. Other times, your focus can meander, flitting about, occasionally taking hold of something in the landscape or your mindscape. Either way, your flashlight is affected, and that's something that most of us don't have much awareness of, or ability to control . . . just yet.

Your flashlight represents your *capacity to select a subset of information* from all that is out there. When I say *focus,* this is what I mean—that the information you've selected, whatever it may be, is being processed better and is of higher quality than everything else around it. Remember that "war" inside your brain: when attention is directed toward something, be it a place, person, or object, the neurons coding it temporarily win influence over the brain's activity. Focusing on something dials up its "brightness" while dimming down information that is irrelevant for our current goals. Without this capacity, we would often be frozen, confused, and overwhelmed.

We rarely notice the way our attention shape-shifts, from narrow to broad, depending on circumstances and the demands of the environment. But I'm betting you *do* notice when your flashlight isn't where you want it—the times when you need to focus on something important, yet struggle to stay on-task. It may be other thoughts, strong emotions, or personal preoccupations that are pulling you away. In an ironic twist, the pressure and stress of having to focus on a task or demand may be the very cause of your distractibility.

And when this happens, you may attempt to soothe or distract yourself in unproductive ways, leading to mindless mental scrolling and clicking, so to speak, that move you even further away from accomplishing your task. If you've had to fight your way back to focus, you are not alone. A recent survey of social media use in the workplace reported that while it can help provide a "mental break," 56 percent of employees said it distracts them from the work they need to do.

What we *are* aware of is that we're struggling to keep our thoughts from straying from the task-at-hand. How many times in a day do you look up, realizing that your mind is anywhere but on the work right in front of you? It can be incredibly frustrating—you *know* that there are real consequences for losing focus (a missed deadline, a car approaching that you don't notice, or something worse), and yet you simply can't seem to keep it where you need it.

How Steady Is Your Flashlight?

We conducted a study with undergraduate students at the University of Miami where we asked them to come into the lab, sit at one of our computers, and silently read chapters from a psychology textbook, presented one sentence at a time on the screen. Most of the text flowed normally. But then we'd throw in a completely out-of-context sentence. We did this infrequently—only about 5 percent of the time—but if you were paying attention, it'd be obvious that the sentence was out of place. The participants' job was simple: after each sentence, press the space bar to advance to the next sentence, or, if a sentence was out of context for the paragraph, tell us by pressing the shift key instead. I love eating tangerines. If you were in our lab for this experiment, you'd have pressed the shift key when you read that last sentence.

We encouraged them to pay close attention and gave them a clear incentive: there would be a quiz at the end, and they were receiving course credit for their time.

How did they do? Not well at all. They missed the out-of-context sentences most of the time. And naturally, the more sentences they missed, the worse they did on the quiz that came after—they were clearly not retaining the material.

You might protest that the experiment is too tough—textbooks can be so dry and dense, you say, and pressing a space bar often over twenty minutes sounds pretty darn boring. Perhaps. *But.* Other experiments have found the same thing with easier parameters: Read the text that appears on the screen, and if it's an actual word, press the space bar. If it's not, press the shift key. When participants read word after word, pressing the space bar ovet arp thj usult grept frew bramt. I have to ask—how many words did you read before you noticed that they weren't, well, words?

In the study, now repeated by many labs, people fail to immediately notice that the words are meaningless 30 percent of the time, and continue pressing the space bar an average of *seventeen times* before they realize the text they're reading is actually gibberish.

Maybe that wasn't fair—I didn't warn you it was coming! Let's try another exercise, with all the rules on the table. This one's very simple, and it won't take more than a few seconds. You don't even need to move from where you're sitting.

When I say "Go," I want you to close your eyes and take five breaths. If you already have a meditation practice, make it fifteen. Regular, even breaths. Your job is to focus on your breath—in, and then out—and *only* on your breath. As soon as you notice your thoughts moving to something else, or an intrusive thought popping in, stop and open your eyes.

Ready? *Go.*

All right, let's assess. How many breaths did you make it through before you experienced a distraction and stopped? I'm guessing not five. Not even close.

Admittedly, this was just a quick, low-pressure, on-the-page game—there weren't any stakes here. Perhaps if there were real consequences, you'd have been able to hold your focus on your breath (or any target) a bit longer. But what we've found in the lab, as well as in the field of attention research, is that it's the same when the stakes *are* high. People cannot hold their focus, no matter what. Not if they are paid. Not if their task is solely to enjoy an activity. Not even if the consequences for losing focus are disastrous.

The Neurosurgeon and the Mechanic

I got out of the cab on a cold, gray winter morning, coffee cup in hand, and headed into the looming hospital building on the campus of a major academic medical center. It was 6:30 a.m.—plenty of time to find the lecture hall for my 7:00 a.m. grand-rounds presentation. "Grand rounds," if you aren't familiar with the phrase, are a weekly event for medical teaching institutions, and usually involve a presentation on a particular malady or patient profile. Today, I would be the presenter, the audience would be a group of neurosurgery residents, and the topics would be mindfulness and attention.

I got my slides set up and waited patiently to begin. The clock *ticked ticked ticked.* Now it was 6:55 and not a soul was in the lecture hall. Had I gotten the day wrong? At 6:57, the doors burst open with a blast of noise and clamoring voices as some forty people rushed in to find a seat. Every chair in the room quickly filled. I was relieved—I hadn't gotten the day wrong, after all.

But as I began my talk, my relief faded. I wasn't sure what exactly was going on, but I definitely didn't feel that I had an interested audience. Phones buzzed. Chatter rippled through the room. People shifted about, rustled paper. There was a palpable restlessness in the air. I felt good about the material I presented, but when I finished I walked out of that lecture hall thinking it was the worst presentation I'd ever given. So I was dumbfounded to get a call, a week later, from the chief of neurosurgery. He told me my talk had been a hit. *Really?* I thought. *But they seemed so distracted!* Then he asked me if I could train all the residents in mindfulness.

"They need it," he said.

And, he added, he needed it too. He shared a recent experience. He regularly performed demanding, highly technical brain surgeries that could last up to eight hours at a time—a really long time to stand, tinkering with near-microscopic-precision inside an exposed human brain. The problem was that recently he was finding himself distracted. Not just during lectures, but during surgery. Hearing my talk helped him realize that his mind was wandering . . . a *lot*.

He described an episode that was emblematic of a larger pattern not just for him but for many surgeons. One night, he had a disagreement with his wife that got rather heated and went unresolved. The next day, in the middle of a surgery, one of the nurses came in to deliver a phone message to him. It was not unusual for him to receive messages or answer questions during the course of a surgery—brain surgeries like the ones he performed stretched through a whole day. But this time, the message was from his wife and was related to the argument they'd been having the night before. He could feel how difficult it was to return his full focus to the incredibly high-stakes surgery he was performing. The message was an intrusion. But even before the nurse walked in with that slip of paper, he'd been mentally traveling back in time to the disagreement. Why? Because of a very common need we all have, something referred to as a need for *cognitive closure*. This is that tug of wanting to achieve a resolution to something that is confusing, unsettling, or even ambiguous. While the surgery was properly in the foreground of his attention, whenever his mind would drift, it drifted to how to resolve the disagreement with his wife.

Very far from any operating rooms, Garrett, an engineer for the Washington State ferry system, started looking into mindfulness training as a potential tool for coping with long shifts when his focused attention is required but difficult to sustain. As chief engineer, he spends twelve-hour night shifts in the belly of an Olympic Class ferry. It gets up to speeds of almost twenty knots, carries as many as 1,500 passengers and a maximum of 144 vehicles, and weighs more than four thousand tons. Operating one requires both precision and advanced planning—it takes a great deal of lead time to turn or slow one of these white-and-green whales. Much of Garrett's job requires standing in front of gauges and other meters, monitoring every dial to ensure that everything is working correctly, and standing at the ready to receive orders from the captain to change course or speed. At 3:00 a.m., on the last of many sailings, this can get challenging, and the consequences of a mental lapse are extremely dangerous. Missing a problem could mean millions of dollars in damage, or even an accident resulting in loss of life. Garrett told me, "I'm doing repetitive menial tasks that have enormous consequences if I mess up."

Garrett was concerned that he couldn't sustain focus well enough to do his critical job safely. So he came up with his own system—he sets an alarm on his phone to go off every ten minutes. When it buzzes, he starts at the first display and works his way through a check of everything. Without it, he could easily get lost in thought, and the minutes would slip away like the water rushing under the hull.

To the chief of neurosurgery I said, "Well, first of all, ask your staff to stop giving you messages during surgery! But we can do more."

And to the chief ferry engineer, "It's good that you're aware of your attentional limits and set up a system to help. But we can do more."

It's not realistic to expect someone to stay focused through an eight-hour surgery or twelve-hour night shift on dark waters. It's not even realistic to expect them to do so for a single half-hour ferry crossing. Our focus—our *flashlight*—is very easily impacted. If you didn't get through all five breaths in that exercise above—if you didn't even get through *one*—don't feel bad. Your attention is built to behave this way. *Why?* The answer to that is rooted in some of the most basic ways the human brain's attention system functions, and will lead us through the major neuroscience concepts I'll unpack in this chapter, *load theory*, *mind-wandering*, and the *vigilance decrement*, along with the implications for each when it comes to training your attention. Learning about these will enable you to understand how your flashlight is working now, recognize the challenges it faces, and learn to control it with greater ease. The first thing to get clear about is what's happening when you start to become "mentally fatigued" and feel yourself losing the ability to focus. It can seem as if you're "leaking" attentional resources, as if your cognitive gas tank were running low. It makes sense intuitively—this notion that you've been burning cognitive fuel through your day, or through a task, and now you're running out. But that's not actually how it works.

Load Theory: Attention Is Not a Gas Tank

Attention never vanishes, even though it might feel as if it does when you're struggling to focus and simply can't. When attention begins to get fatigued or degraded, it makes it harder to place your attention where you want it. But it doesn't just fade away. In cognitive neuroscience, this is explained through *load theory*. What load theory boils down to is this: the amount of attention you have remains constant. It just gets used differently, and maybe not how you want it to be used.

Take the example of my navigating Highway 17 through the Santa Cruz mountains. The demands (or "load" in neuroscience-speak) were low during the leisurely part of my drive, while during the treacherous part my attention was distributed differently. During the low-load portion of the drive, I had attentional resources available to engage in other types of thought—planning, daydreaming, enjoying the scenery, listening to music. When the load was high, I didn't have the bandwidth for that—all my attentional resources were focused on the task-at-hand: driving safely toward my destination. Yet the total *amount* of attention did not change. You can think of it like this: You always use 100 percent of your attention. Attention always goes somewhere. So the question becomes: *Where?*

The Vigilance Decrement: You're Going to Get Worse at What You're Doing

Take any task that you might ask someone to do over a period of time and graph it: you'll find performance declines. Errors go up, responses become slower and more variable. In the lab, we've mapped this *vigilance decrement* with a test that requires accuracy during a long, repetitive task. Participants sit at a computer screen that shows them a different face every half second. They are given these instructions: When you see a face, press the space bar. But if you see an upside-down face, don't press.

The results?

Wow, people are terrible at this! During the first five minutes of the experiment, they catch themselves and don't press very often when the face is upside down. After that, they start pressing when they aren't supposed to. Over the forty-minute study, their performance gets worse and worse.

You might say, *Well, but that experiment is so boring—that's why they stopped paying attention.*

First of all: we see this pattern of decline in performance over time across many tasks, ones that vary in degrees of complexity and demand. Yes, it happens faster with simpler tasks, but with more-complex or varied activities, the vigilance decrement kicks in and performance begins to steadily decline, even during a short, twenty-minute task. When you think about how long we regularly need to be able to accomplish things that stretch across a much longer time frame (think about the eight-hour critical brain surgery, the twelve-hour ferry shift at night), twenty minutes is a very, *very* short window to achieve accuracy and good performance. And second: the word *boring* is subjective—is brain surgery inherently boring?

And finally: you're right. That experiment *was* boring. Or, in more accurate terms, it was designed to produce boredom as quickly as possible in the laboratory so that we could investigate what was really going on with our attention over time. We used to think that the vigilance decrement was due to a kind of mental fatigue—the brain got tired, just as a muscle would when asked to perform over a long period. If you were asked to do a hundred bicep curls in a row, your performance would most definitely decline. But this didn't mesh with what we knew about how the brain functions. It doesn't "get tired" like an overworked muscle—it doesn't work that way. Think of it in these terms: your eyes don't stop seeing if you've had them open for a while; your ears don't stop hearing after twenty minutes. The whole idea of the brain becoming fatigued didn't really make sense. And what we found was that as performance declined, mind-wandering went up.

Mind-Wandering: The Dark Matter of Information Processing

I call *mind-wandering* the "dark matter" of cognition because it's both invisible and ever-present—and it has consequences. We are in a constant state of mind-wandering, yet often we don't even notice. It's a category of brain activity that falls under the general umbrella of *spontaneous thought,* which is exactly what it sounds like: unconstrained thinking, leading to thoughts or ideas that pop up without your conscious, voluntary choice.

Now, spontaneous thought can be *great.* When there's nothing else you're supposed to be doing and you can go ahead and let your thoughts roam, it can be creative, energizing, and generative. Think of taking a walk and allowing your mind to wander, like a dog on a long leash, exploring some flowers or hedges. Some of the best, most innovative ideas come from this type of spontaneous thought, which we scientists call *conscious internal reflection,* or, more simply, daydreaming. And it can not only lead to ideas and solutions you might not have arrived at otherwise; it can also be beneficial to attention, by recharging your attentional capacities, boosting your mood, and relieving stress.

Mind-wandering is in the same category as daydreaming, though it's a quite different animal. It's the *other* type of spontaneous thought—the kind that happens when there's something you want or need to be doing, and yet your thoughts still veer away from that very task. In the lab, we classify it as any kind of *task-unrelated thought* (TUT for short). Think of the "taking your dog for a walk" example. On a leisurely stroll, letting your pup roam and explore is relaxing and harmless. But if you're trying to get somewhere, and you have to keep stopping to rein him back in, over and over, it's going to start getting problematic pretty quickly. It'll be harder to watch where you're going; it'll take you longer to get there; you're going to start getting irritated and stressed.

There's a big cost to task-unrelated thought. When we mind-wander, it rapidly becomes a problem in three major ways:

1. *You experience "perceptual decoupling."* This means you disconnect from your immediate environment. Remember the face/house study? We asked you to focus on the face, and in response your attention system amped up the face signal and dimmed everything else. Well, that's what happens here—except what's amplified is whatever you're thinking about (when mind-wandering, you're usually fast-forwarding into the future or rewinding into the past), while what's dimmed is, well, your actual surroundings. It's as if you can't see or hear as clearly. Which leads to the next problem . . .

2. *You make mistakes.* Along with perceptual decoupling come errors—a wandering mind is an error-prone mind. It makes sense: If your ability to perceive and process your surroundings is impaired, you're going to have lapses and slip-ups. If that doesn't seem like such a big problem, remember the number that kicked off this book: 50 percent, which is the amount of time we are mind-wandering and not fully present in what we're doing. With anything you're doing throughout your waking day, there's a fifty-fifty chance you're really there; anytime you're talking to someone, even if you're making direct eye contact, there's only a fifty-fifty chance they're hearing you. And remember all the studies that showed there were zero incentives or consequences that could persuade people to mind-wander

less? They were simply not able to stop themselves, even if the consequences were potentially high. Mind-wandering, it turns out, potentially happens at the same rate when someone's sitting on the couch reading a magazine as when they're performing brain surgery.

And finally . . .

3. *You amp up your stress.* Having off-task thoughts while we are trying to do something can have implications for our overall psychological health and mood. One thing we know is that regardless of what you're mind-wandering about—even if it's an amazing vacation you're looking forward to, or a happy memory you're reliving—the moment afterward is going to be riddled with a little bit of negativity. Let's call it the cost of "reentry," coming back into the present and having to orient yourself. There's a negative dip, which—the more we mind-wander—can start to affect mood and stress levels. And we know how kryptonite affects our attention: higher stress makes you vulnerable to even *more* mind-wandering, which leads to even more poor mood . . . you see the downward spiral of bad news we get caught in here?

To sum up: When you need your attention to accomplish a task, be it a work demand, a conversation with a child or partner, or time alone to read a book, having a mind that wanders off-leash is not a harmless little stroll. You miss stuff, you make mistakes, your mood sours. It's as if you just aren't there for the things you need to do, for others, even for yourself.

This all raises the question: Why on earth do we even *have* mind-wandering? When we consider that the brain is the success story of tens of thousands of years of evolution, we have to wonder: What possible reason could there be for us to have inherited this damaging, problematic tendency? *Why build a mind that wanders?*

Why We Wander

Let's rewind some twelve thousand years. Picture yourself in the forest. You're hunting for an animal, perhaps, or for edible berries—you need your focus to be able to find something to feed yourself today. We already know what happens to your attention system when you're scanning for something specific: your brain is now biased (selectively attuned) to a specific set of colors, sounds, and smells. When you spot the flash of movement behind a screen of leaves, or the specific hue and shape of a delicious fruit, your focus narrows and everything else falls away. You close in. And then . . . you get eaten by the tiger that you didn't even notice was there.

Would a mind that wandered have saved you? It's possible! Perhaps the early humans who toggled in and out of focus, those who *got distracted* and looked up every now and then—pulled out of their task by a wandering mind—were the ones who realized they were in danger of becoming prey themselves and acted appropriately, surviving to pass on their (distractible) genes.

In the lab, we'd observed across multiple studies how the human brain will *actively resist* staying focused on a task. The mind was determined, it seems, to roam. To figure out why, we needed to consider that, as destructive and problematic as we knew mind-wandering was, it could also be seen, paradoxically, as an asset.

To take you through how we investigated this, I first have to point out the difference between *voluntary attention* and *automatic attention*. Voluntary attention, as you can probably guess, is when you choose where to point your flashlight; automatic attention is when your attention is captured and pulled toward something without your active choice. *Attention-grabbing:* it's a figure of speech, but a very accurate one. Think of using a flashlight in the dark. You choose to point it ahead of you to illuminate your path: *voluntary attention. Now* think of what happens if you were to hear a sudden sound off to the side—the snap of a branch, for example. You'd instinctively swing the flashlight in that direction. You'd do it without even thinking: *automatic attention.*

Here's how we test this in the lab:

The computer shows a large blank screen with a plus sign (+) in the middle; we tell you to keep your eyes resting on that plus sign. The reason: your eyes and your attention are generally yoked together, but you can decouple them in certain situations (think of focusing on someone you're talking to at a party, while your attention shifts to the conversation behind you—eyes and attention decouple). For this experiment, we want to make sure the *only* thing that moves is your attention.

Your job: Press the space bar when you detect a large X on either the right or the left side of the screen. When you spot it, hit that bar as fast as you can. The twist: Sometimes there's a flash of light that appears *immediately* before the X does. And sometimes that flash happens in the same spot as where the X will appear; other times not. You're instructed not to worry about that flash. Just press when you spot the X, no matter where it happens. That's it.

Pretty simple, right? It is. But we're looking at how long it takes for participants to respond when they're cued by the flash of light versus when they're not. And as you can probably guess, when the flash of light precedes where the target will appear, the responses are much faster and more accurate.

Nothing may seem earth-shattering about this—obviously, the flash of light got their attention. Well, *exactly.* The flash "got" their attention. What this shows us is that attention can be drawn without our conscious or active choice. If somebody shouts your name on a busy street, your attention snaps to their voice. You didn't make the choice to place it there. And (crucially, for this discussion) there's nothing you can do to *stop* it. This is probably something you already know intuitively—you don't need me to tell you how it feels when you hear a distinctive buzz and your focus immediately flickers from whatever you were doing to the lit-up screen of your phone. What's important about this study is that it's demonstrably true that attention functions in this way. It doesn't just *feel* as if you can't easily stop your brain from attending to these distractions—you actually, literally, can't.

That gives us one level of understanding as to why your mind might wander away from a task: a distraction pops up, either from the environment (external) or from your own mind (internal), and your automatic attention bops right over to it. And that does explain some of the mind-wandering we do. But there's more to it than that. Let's go back to the screen with the flash and the target "X." I want to show you how we take it one step further—to investigate a really fascinating phenomenon in the brain—by making one teeny, tiny adjustment to this experiment.

Just as before, we show you the flash. And just as before, it appears exactly where the X is about to appear (cued) or not. But instead of presenting the target immediately after the flash, we pause *ever so slightly*—to the tune of a few hundred milliseconds—before we show you the target. And you're much slower. That advantage you got from the warning of the flash, that speedy edge? Gone.

But wait—*why*? If the flash pulled your automatic attention to the specific location where the target was about to appear, how on earth would you miss it now? What difference does a couple hundred milliseconds make?

Let's hit the slo-mo button and go through what happens, beat by beat:

1. The flash appears in the upper-left quadrant of the screen.

2. Your attention is drawn to the flash.

3. The X does *not* appear there.

4. Your attention now dismisses (in neuroscience-speak: "disadvantages") that side of the screen as an area of interest.

5. Your attention shifts to the other side of the screen . . .

6. . . . and when the target appears, late, in the original spot, you're slower at detecting it. You're faster, however, at detecting the X on the other side.

We call this phenomenon the *inhibition of return*: Your attention is, quite literally, inhibited from returning to that original location. If your attentional flashlight is drawn to a certain spot, and nothing happens or appears there, you'll automatically disadvantage that space. In other words, you eliminate it as an area of interest. And let me emphasize: this happens *fast*. It takes only five hundred milliseconds, total, for all these steps to occur in rapid succession, without your even being aware of them! And this happens across all types of sensory input. In the first study I published on this, we did it with sounds, and found the same.

Why does your brain do this? Well, it's likely a scanning strategy. Imagine yourself once again in the shoes of that imaginary ancestor in the long-ago woods. You're hunting or foraging, while also trying to be aware of *being* hunted. You hear something off to the left. Boom, your attention automatically goes there and scans the area. If you see/hear/smell nothing, your attention rapidly moves on and begins scanning the other areas around you—because whatever it was that made that sound is probably still close by, and it probably moved.

Obviously, we're no longer hunter-gatherers. You're not out there in your day-to-day life hunting for food or being stalked by a tiger. But it's important to recognize that while the *origins* of this brain activity might lie with our distant ancestors, this pattern isn't outdated—it still serves you in all kinds of situations. And while we contrive situations in the lab where we study either automatic attention or voluntary attention, in our everyday life we use both, and there is a constant dynamic interplay between them.

The human brain is efficient and strategic. It's always trying to maximize its activity for the greatest possible gain. Mind-wandering may have ultimately been selected for over the course of human evolution to maximize *opportunity costs*—the brain predicts that whatever it's giving up (focus and follow-through for the task-at-hand) is worth it in the long run for a larger potential gain (whether it be survival, protection, or finding out what else is out there that might be better). Boredom, as I said, is subjective—anything can get boring. Boredom might very well have evolved in order to simply force us to go find something else to do. We used to believe that the vigilance decrement was exclusively driven by mental fatigue, as we spend our cognitive resources. But I think (and others do, too) that it's actually more than just that. It's likely linked back to this essential survival mechanism. What this all means for you—a modern, twenty-first-century human—is that if you try to sustain your focus for a long time, you will begin to experience your attention resisting, and eventually scattering off in some way.

I've taken you through all this nitty-gritty cognitive science because I think of it as an opportunity—to realize that you're biologically predisposed to mind-wandering, and to embrace it (to a certain extent) as a necessary "capacity" you have. If you had a brain that wasn't susceptible to it, you could drive yourself in the wrong direction or no direction. Some people diagnosed with attention deficit hyperactivity disorder (ADHD) will often report that the problem is not that they can't focus—it's that they get focused on the *wrong thing*. When we get overly focused, we can lose track of our in-the-moment goals. We lose touch with whether our current behavior *aligns* with those goals. And we don't realize when we need to course-correct or address curveballs (*tigers!*) that come our way. There can be a real benefit to a waxing and waning of focus, and this is something we'll be talking about. But just because this mental behavior has potential benefits doesn't mean it's always the right way to be. And just because we're neurologically predisposed to it doesn't mean we have to simply accept it.

Let's Recap!

That was a fair amount of information we just whipped through. And as we already know, you might have missed a chunk of it. It's not your fault. Thank your savvy ancestors' survival instincts! Let's do a quick review.

Because you always use 100 percent of your attention (*load theory*), it always goes somewhere, so if you're not focused on your current demands, it may very well be because you are mind-wandering (experiencing *task-unrelated thought*) and are not mentally present in your current surroundings (*perceptual decoupling*). Mind-wandering is something your brain is predisposed to do, for various reasons involving, but not limited to, fast-moving saber-toothed tigers (*inhibition of return*), and it likely drives the *vigilance decrement*, which ensures that the longer you do something, the worse you'll perform. While mind-wandering may have its roots in something useful (*opportunity costs, attentional cycling*), it's bad for our ability to perform well on what we are trying to do (our "task-at-hand") and our mood.

Now that we know *why* we wander, we need to talk about what we can do about it. The first step is a simple one:

LEARN TO RECOGNIZE THAT YOU'RE MIND-WANDERING

A few years after I had my crisis of attention, my husband was plunged into one of his own. Since he'd started a demanding graduate program, both of us were doing our best juggling the demands of work and parenting one small child, and then two, after our daughter, Sophie, came along. Once he began his program's finite math sequence, Michael was having so much trouble focusing that he participated in a pilot program we ran on adults with ADHD, where we tested whether mindfulness training could help. We didn't ask participants to go off their prescribed medications if they were taking any—instead, we wanted to see whether mindfulness training could help strengthen attention wherever they were starting from, meds or no meds, so that we could measure any improvement from their baselines.

They *did* improve. The common feedback we got from partici-pants was that they didn't change their medication because of the training, but they reported being able to *use it more effectively.* What our participants reported was a better ability to notice where their flashlights were pointing and to be able to redirect them when nec-essary. One sample comment: "I'm not just sitting in front of the computer all day going from website to website. Instead, I'm aware of what I'm trying to do, and I'm *deciding* to use my attention to do it."

One of the activities we conducted was having a recording of a bell sound every five minutes. The idea was that people would use it during a formal mindfulness exercise to remind themselves to bring their focus back to the task-at-hand. But after the first few weeks, my husband brought that dinging bell recording home to use while he did his homework in the evenings. It helped so much that he started playing it all day long at work. He'd realized that he was off-task frequently and used that reminder, every five minutes, to come back to what he was trying to do.

It was a real wake-up call for me about how common this problem is, and how much help we need. Just a few years before, I was doing my own personalized mindfulness "case study" on myself, and one of the first things I noticed in my earliest sessions was how often my mind jumped like a grasshopper all over the place. Then I noticed that it wasn't only happening during those few minutes every morning when I sat down to do this still-unfamiliar practice. It was happening *constantly.* I was shocked by how much I was mind-wandering throughout my day. I started checking in with myself to see how often I was actually on-task.

The answer? Not very often.

For both Michael and me, the essential step was realizing how much of the time our flashlight was pointed somewhere we didn't want it. Try this: for the rest of the day, start checking in with yourself every so often and notice when you're on-task and when you're not. You might even set up your phone to ping you. If you don't want bells going off every five minutes all day long, as my husband did, you might set it for every hour. When the alert pops up on your phone, do a quick check-in, and be honest with yourself: What were you doing? What were you thinking about? *Where* were you, really?

If it works for you, use the chart on page 112 to keep track over the course of one day. (Or make one in a notebook you can carry, or even in the Notes app on your phone. This needs to be easily accessible so that it's quick and easy to accomplish.) Jot down the time, your task, and where your flashlight is. When you look back at the chart at the end of the day or week, you should get a fairly clear picture of not only how often you're off-task, but also where you tend to go.

Since we tend to engage in mental time travel whenever we

Time	Task	Flashlight
10 a.m.	Finishing grant application	Thinking about Sophie's dance competition this weekend and everything I need to do to get ready.
12 p.m.	Call with my sister	Listening to her describe her recent trip to Berkeley. Fully present. Excited about her successes and adventures.
2 p.m.	Giving a tour of the lab	I was very engaged at first, but started feeling distracted and worried about getting back to our grant.

mind-wander, you may find yourself in the future, planning and worrying—or you may get pulled into the past, into rumination loops. (Rest assured, I'll address this soon.) Either way, gathering data on *what* pulls you out of the present moment and *how often* it does so will be helpful moving forward. It's going to give you a leg up in terms of identifying and addressing any challenges you may be experiencing.

You might notice that you're frequently pulled off-task by digital distractions like email, texts and phone calls, social media, and so on. It's tempting to think that if we could just eliminate those distractions, we'd be all set.

Our Crisis of Attention: Is It Digital?

We're bombarded by the idea that at the root of our attention issues lies a single powerful culprit: modern technology. If we truly want to focus, it seems, we need to turn off all our devices, quit social media, and retreat into the woods for a digital detox.

Here's my resistance to that idea. At an elemental level, this particular era is no different than any other—there has always been a "crisis of attention." Historically, people have turned to meditation (and other forms of contemplative practice) to deal with feelings of being overwhelmed and scattered in focus, and to refocus and reflect on priorities—our inner values, intentions, purpose. This can certainly be a spiritual process, if that's how you define it. But we're discovering that mindfulness impacts the attention system and how it copes with the distractions that surround us—and those that are generated internally. In part, that's what meditation practitioners have always been pursuing. Think about life long ago: people in ancient India or medieval Europe didn't have smartphones and Facebook, but they were still suffering in their own minds. They still turned to any number of practices for relief. They still described the same challenge: *I'm not fully present for my life.*

A crisis of attention can happen anytime you don't allow yourself a break—when you don't allow your mind to "rest" without having any task-at-hand. Remember our distinction between *mind-wandering* (having off-task thoughts during a task) and *daydreaming* (task-free spontaneous thought and opportunity for conscious reflection, creativity, and the like)? Well, one problem today is that we are *always engaged* in something. With these digital tools at our fingertips, we have constant access to all these forms of communication, content, and interaction, and we don't tend to gravitate toward letting our thoughts meander, unconstrained. Of the two types of spontaneous thought we discussed earlier, it's the beneficial type—the daydreaming—that we barely get at all. When was the last time you stood in line at a store and just . . . looked around? Thought about whatever surfaced in your mind? Or did you pull out your phone, check your texts, read your email?

We all do it. I catch myself all the time, going from one type of mental engagement to the next. I call it *hypertasking*. Like surfing hyperlinks online (clicking from link to link as they grab your attention), we go from one task to the next and the next. You are probably doing it right now. We are "all task and no downtime." And we're asking an enormous amount—too much—from our attention systems. Your attentional capacity is not *less* than someone's from hundreds of years ago. It's only that right now, you're using your attention in a particular focused way, all the time. We're taxing our focused attention to the max. Hypertasking is hyper-taxing! Even something you might think of as relaxing (scrolling through Instagram, for example, or reading an article someone shared) is more engagement. It's *another task*. Checking your notifications may seem "fun," but it's work for your attention. Task: check to see who posted what in response to my post. Task: check how many likes I got. Task: check who shared my funny meme. Your attention was focused on task after task after task, with no attentional downtime, not a moment for the mind to roam free.

It's not always realistic to unplug. We can't just turn off our phones and pause our email. We cannot create a distraction-free world. The issue is not the existence of this technology; rather, it's how we're using it: we are not allowing our minds to pay attention *differently*. And this is where mindfulness comes in, as a way to steady your flashlight so you don't end up swinging it around at any and all possible distractions—digital or not.

Finding Your Flashlight

To find your focus, the first skill you need to develop is to *notice* when your attentional flashlight has wandered away from the task-at-hand. In this first "core exercise," your goal is to repeatedly find your flashlight. *This is the workout:* orient attention to a target object, notice when it wanders off-target, and then reorient it back to the target.

Think of this like training a puppy. Wandering around is just what puppies do. No need to be harsh or mean. But you should be consistent and clear with your instruction, over and over again. If the puppy does not follow a command, we don't indulge stories about how bad, flawed, untrainable, or unlovable the puppy is. Instead, we simply begin the training exercise again. Adopt a similar *supportive-yet-firm* attitude as you engage in this workout—and notice when old mental habits like justifying, chastising, or ruminating show up when you notice your mind-wandering. Now, reframe "mind-wandering" itself: it's not a failure or error, but rather a cue to begin again and reorient back to the target object. The more often you gently guide your attention back, the more easily it will follow—just as your puppy will learn to do. Your mind will begin to get more attuned to noticing when you've wandered off, as well: with more practice, you'll grow more able to notice the *initial* pull on your flashlight away from the target object, instead of becoming completely lost or hijacked before you do. All this will make bringing it back to the target easier, too. When we are able to find our focus more easily, we waste less time, experience fewer dips in mood and fewer spikes in stress, and worry less when we have something important to get done—whether for work, for others, or for yourself.

And interestingly, just as you improve your ability to notice when your mind has wandered, you begin to notice when you may need to truly let it freely roam. When we got our dog, Tashi, I loved taking him to the dog park for this very reason. Once the leash was removed, he was off, exploring, playing, running free. I felt like I was seeing a new part of him, his curious, exuberant-friendly-joyful side. And for those few minutes, I would choose not to take out my phone. I let myself get reacquainted with my mind without an agenda—no problem to ponder, no emails to answer. This small act was like a gift I gave myself. I noticed creative ideas bubbling up, a feeling of good-heartedness reemerging, and a buoyant energy returning back to me. Tashi and I would both return home with an extra little bounce in our steps. But I would not have been able to really let go of my flashlight if I didn't know where it was or how to hold it in the first place.

To find your flashlight, you'll draw on a foundational mindfulness practice often called *breath awareness*. This practice has been around for millennia. Contemplative traditions tell us that it cultivates concentrative focus. And now we know, after many studies, that it is also part of a suite of practices that can serve as cognitive training for attention. Breath awareness can seem deceptively simple: *focus your attention on your breath, and when the mind wanders, return it*. The instructions are quite basic, yet what the exercise is actually doing to your brain's attention system is anything but. The breath awareness exercise targets *all three* systems of attention, because it allows you to practice *focusing*—as you *orient* attention to the *breath; noticing*—staying *alert* and monitoring ongoing mental activity to detect mind-wandering; and *redirecting*—*executive* management of cognitive processes to make sure we return and remain on-task.

Why do we use the breath? We could potentially place our focus on any number of things. Training the flashlight of your attention on anything, and then bringing it back when it wobbles away, can certainly help you, and in fact I encourage you to try this during the day when there's something you want to bring your full attention to: listening to a lecture, briefing, or podcast; reading or writing a report; practicing a musical instrument. But for this daily practice, we use the breath for a couple of important reasons: It anchors us in the body. It allows us to experience the body sensations that are unfolding in real time as we breathe, in the here and now. This helps us more easily catch when our minds have wandered away from these sensations to thoughts about the past or future. And finally, our breath is always with us. It's the most natural built-in target for our attention that we can always return to.

Your breath is a changing, dynamic target, and in this exercise, your attention is to be constrained to a single, prominent, breath-related sensation in a specific body part (like your chest, nose, abdomen). The key is to select a specific target object and stick with it for the duration of the formal exercise. Remember that this is a concentrative practice—the flashlight's beam is narrow and steady on the target. One of the next practices will ask you to take that beam of your attention and sweep it through the body; later, we'll progress to a practice where you have no target to focus on, but will be monitoring the shifting contents of your moment-to-moment conscious experience—your memories, emotions, thoughts, and sensations—*without* getting caught up and swept away by them. To succeed at any of these later practices, you need to strengthen your flashlight first. And all these together are helping you learn how to *pay attention to your attention*.

CORE PRACTICE: FIND YOUR FLASHLIGHT

1. *Get ready* . . . **Sit in an upright, stable, and alert posture.** You want to be comfortable, but not overly relaxed. Think "upright," not "uptight." Sit up straight, shoulders back, chest open, in a posture that feels natural and embodies a sense of dignified presence. Let your hands rest on the armrest, or on the seat beside you, or on the tops of your legs. Close your eyes, or lower your eyelids to have a soft gaze in front of you, if that's more comfortable. Breathe, and follow your breath. You are *following* the breath moving at its natural pace—not controlling it.

2. *Get set . . .* **Tune in to breath-related sensations.** These may be the coolness of the air going in and out of your nostrils, the sensation of your lungs filling up your chest, your belly moving in and out. *Choose one area of the body—related to whichever breath-related sensations feel most prominent—to focus on for the rest of this exercise.* Direct and maintain your attentional focus here, like a flashlight with a strong, bright beam.

3. *Go!* **Notice when your flashlight has moved . . . and then move it back.** The real work of this exercise, after you've chosen the target for your flashlight and committed to resting your attention there, is to pay attention to what happens next. *Notice* when thoughts or sensations arise that pull your flashlight off-target. It could be a sudden reminder that there's something you need to do right after this. It might be a memory, floating up. It might be an itch! When you notice that your flashlight has been pulled away, re-direct it back to your breath. Nothing special to do other than this simple, gentle "nudge" that acts supportively to move *the flashlight back.*

That's it! That's your first practice. It's pretty simple. But in its simplicity lies its beauty *and* its utility: in that one basic exercise, we've figured out how to do two difficult things that we were most likely completely challenged by and largely unaware of before—noticing our mind-wandering, then redirecting our attention. As I hope you now know, mind-wandering is ubiquitous, it's common, and there's no reason to fight against it—it's just the nature of the mind. If you are conscious, mind-wandering will happen. But for the "formal" period of time you dedicate to doing the core breath awareness practice, during which you sit down to practice and point your flashlight intentionally at your breath, we do something different when mind-wandering occurs: we note it and then redirect our attention back.

The events in this sequence are:

- focus your flashlight,

- hold it steady,

- notice when it drifts, and

- then redirect it back to the breath.

This is what we might call the "push-up" of a mindfulness breathing exercise. I hope you're getting a sense of how doing this repeatedly over a period of time may not only engage attention, but strengthen it by exercising it over and over.

An important question: *How long should I practice?*

I told you earlier that twelve minutes was the "magic number," and in the final chapter of this book, "Feel the Burn," we'll be talking more about that "minimum dose" required for truly transforming your attention system. But just as you wouldn't start physical training by trying to bench-press your own weight, you're not going to start mental training by sitting down to a long mindfulness practice session right off the bat.

I recommend starting small. Try three minutes—set a timer on your phone. *Three minutes*: That's less time than it takes to boil water or make toast. Less time than even the quickest shower. I've waited for elevators that took longer than three minutes to arrive.

A heads-up: three minutes might be quick, but when you are new to mindfulness meditation practice, even a minute or two can feel like forever. You will probably have to move your flashlight back to your breath so many times, you'll wonder how you ever get anything done! Know this: *it will get better.* If you commit to daily practice—

starting with just *three minutes per day*—you'll be laying the groundwork for a potentially transformative mental workout regimen. So start small, but do it consistently. It will be easier to expand your workout once you already have a place for it in your day. If you find you would like to continue beyond the three minutes, of course feel free to continue practicing, but don't feel you "have" to go beyond the time you've set as your goal.

Now that you have a sense of the work involved in using your flashlight, here's a final, but very important, directive to keep at the front of your mind:

DON'T MULTITASK!

When Leo was in the fifth grade, he started to get bothered when he noticed people talking on their cell phones as they drove alongside our car. As a curious, smart kid, interested in lots of things, including what I was working on in the lab, he certainly knew more about brain science and attention than your average ten-year-old. He figured that trying to do two things at once, when each required a certain level of focus (talking, driving), was going to take a toll. So he set out to test it.

For a school science project, he set up an experiment: He had some friends come over and play car-racing video games on our Xbox 360 console in the living room. He'd call them on his phone from the next room and engage them in conversation while they were on speakerphone, asking them all kinds of questions. No surprise: the kids who were talking on the phone performed worse in the game than the ones who weren't.

I admit—this is a fifth-grade science fair project. But as it turns out, the science backs the kid up! Multitasking—or, more specifically, *task switching*—is terrible for our performance, accuracy, and mood. Leo was gratified but indignant: *Why was it legal to talk on the phone while driving?* To his credit, a lot of states now have strict laws prohibiting the use of handheld phones and sending or receiving texts while driving—but the reality is that, given what we know about attention, the laws don't go far enough. When we try to do two things at once that both require our attention, it's really hard to do either of them well. It doesn't matter if you're holding your phone or not. Hands-free or talk-to-text still require attentional engagement.

Think of it this way: You only have one flashlight. Not two. Not three. And your one flashlight can only ever be shining at one thing at a time. (To be clear: I'm speaking of tasks that require your active, focused attention—not "procedural" tasks like, say, *walking*, which doesn't demand attention in the same way.) When you're trying to accomplish multiple tasks at once that require your focused attention, what you're actually doing is moving your flashlight from one thing, then to the next, then back to the first . . . and you get it. Why is that a problem? This comes back to our conversation about *biasing*.

When you select and engage in a task—whether it's writing a legal brief, planning a budget, watching your child biking in the driveway, puzzling through the development of an app you're building, *anything*—your attention *calibrates information processing* to that specific task. What that means: everything that your brain is doing is now in service to that job, and it aligns all its activity to that goal. In the lab, I could show you this by having you identify dots (hit the space bar when you see a red one) or letters (hit the shift key when you see the letter "T") as fast as you can. If you get nothing but dots repeatedly, you're going to be really fast and accurate at identifying the red ones. Same with the letter "T." But when I interleave the two tasks, so that you have to do the dot task for less than a minute and then switch to the letter task and then go back to the dot task, back and forth repeatedly, your speed and accuracy take a huge hit. It's because your attention has to recalibrate after every switch.

In real life, of course, we're not exactly dealing with dots and letters. We're switching from crafting an email to taking a phone call; from taking the phone call to talking to the person who walked into the room and started speaking; from wrapping up that meeting to adding stuff to your calendar, and on and on and on. And recalibration to a new task-at-hand takes time and energy. There will always be a lag.

To get a sense of what this means for your cognition, imagine a studio apartment. There is only one room. Every time you want to use the room, you have to completely change out the furniture. Want to sleep? Set up a bed and nightstand. Want to host a party? Take down the bedroom and set up couches and coffee tables. Need to cook? Drag that all away and set up a stove, counter, and cooking supplies. Sound exhausting? *It is!* And it's the same for your cognition, when you switch from task to task.

In a day when you do a lot of task switching, you'll start having less integrity in *any* of the states your attention is in. That living room is going to look . . . disorganized. Your kitchen won't have the stove plugged in. You're going to become slower, more error prone, and emotionally worn down. What that will feel like to you is mental fatigue. And what it'll show if we brought you into the lab is that not only are you slower, but, worse, your mind-wandering is going way up. And to escalate everything, the mind-wandering itself will require more task switching, over and over, *back* to the task-at-hand. Which means things get even slower. Errors go up. And mood goes down.

The solution? Well, one is to start the mindfulness training exercises, which will help you in any instance when mind-wandering becomes an issue. But also: *monotask as much as possible.* Get rid of the problematic idea that "multitasking" is impressive, desirable, or superior. And when task switching seems unavoidable—as it sometimes is in real life!—realize that you're going to be slower. That you will need a moment to reengage. If you take your time, accepting and then facilitating the "recalibration lag" of task switching, you may very well be faster and more efficient in the long run. You'll miss less, make fewer errors, and (science suggests!) stay happier.

When she was president of the University of Miami, I remember walking into Dr. Donna Shalala's office for a meeting—I'm sure it was one of many she would have that day. She was deeply engaged in writing an email when I arrived. She didn't even look up. As I stood waiting, she continued typing, her focus seemingly unbroken. It probably only took a minute tops, but it felt much longer. Then she closed her laptop, took a brief pause before she looked up, and gave me what felt like her *full* attention. I have to say, the difference was palpable. It set the tone for the entire meeting—and I don't think she missed a word I said.

Several years later, I had the honor of speaking to a retired three-star general who had not only worked with many other senior military leaders, but also served as an advisor to them after he retired. I asked him what he noticed as a common feature across these incredibly successful individuals. He said that one thing stood out. He called it "pivot leadership." From what he observed, there was no residue from the last event, meeting, or gathering to the next one. The leader could completely pivot, with 100 percent of her or his full attention.

The moral of the story is: monotask when you can, accept the lag of task switching when you must, and do your best to reduce its effects. *Give yourself time so that you're not still trying to process the old task, and then fully shift your attention to the new task.* Of course, being able to do this requires becoming more *aware* of what's happening in the moment, including where your flashlight is focused.

Finally, realize that even if you do all this, and do your daily breath awareness practice diligently . . .

YOU WILL STILL NOT ACHIEVE
PERFECT, UNFLINCHING FOCUS

In the introduction of this book, I compared holding your attention steady for a long period of time to being asked to hold a heavy weight. It wouldn't be reasonable to expect yourself to have the endurance and muscle mass to hold up that weight without physical training. Yet somehow we seem to expect ourselves to be able to summon up mental stamina without similarly rigorous *mental* training. I stand by my point—though it was actually incomplete.

What *automatic attention* teaches us is that our focus *will* be pulled away from the task-at-hand—there's not much we can do to change that. And from observing *mind-wandering* we know that even if there isn't an external distraction yanking us away, our minds will periodically go searching for one. When you catch yourself off-task, it's not a failure or a reason to give up on attention training—*your brain was built to do this!* Even with training, we can't expect ourselves to hold our focus the way we would hold a weight for an extended period. Instead, I want you to picture yourself dribbling a basketball:

The ball drops away from your hand, and bounces right back.
Your focus shifts away from the task-at-hand, and then comes back.

Each time the ball falls away from your hand is either an opportunity (to reengage in your task, knowing you're still where you want to be) or a vulnerability (lose the ball, then spend effort and cognitive energy getting it back). The more you practice mindfulness exercises, the better you get at "dribbling." More and more, that ball will bounce back into your hand instead of rolling away. But you have to keep dribbling! Just as in basketball, there's no other way to effectively function. If you want to be, say, the Steph Curry of attention skills, you can't carry the ball across the court. You're going to have to dribble it effortlessly while some of the best athletes on the planet are trying to steal that ball from you—while you're getting exactly where you want to go.

I've been practicing mindfulness exercises nearly every day for a long time. At this point, I appreciate and accept that on some days I'm going to be more distracted than others, and that's fine. But at the very beginning, when I was starting out, I remember struggling through an especially unsuccessful session and feeling defeated. My thoughts were pulled in so many different directions, I felt as if I was going backward, getting worse. So I inquired with a colleague who ran the mindfulness clinic at a major medical center. He had been meditating for more than thirty years. By most measures, he was an *expert-level* meditator. I asked how long he was able to hold his focus so I could get an idea of what to aim for as a goal. I figured, after thirty years, it had to be something amazing—ten minutes? Longer?

"Hmm," he said. "The longest I can hold my attention without it drifting to something else? I'd guess about seven seconds."

Seven seconds? I was shocked. But then I quickly remembered one of the most important tenets of mindfulness training: the point is *not* that you're never going to get distracted. That's not possible. The goal, rather, is to be able to recognize where your attention is moment to moment so that when you *do* get distracted, you can easily and adeptly move your flashlight back to what it needs to be on.

And there's another vital reason why training our focus is so important. It determines what goes into your *working memory*, the dynamic mental workspace that allows you to hold, temporarily, information that you need to use for whatever you're doing. Think of it this way: whenever you're thinking about *anything*—remembering something, working out a problem, mulling over an idea, holding onto a point you want to make while someone else is talking, visualizing something—you're using your working memory to do that. We need working memory for nearly everything we want to do. Meanwhile, working memory is degraded by the very same forces that corrode attention—stress, threat, and poor mood. And at the root of most working memory failures is one of the more damaging habits of the mind: *mental time travel.*

5

STAY IN *PLAY*

I'm waiting for a phone call from a Pulitzer Prize–winning journalist. He's written articles and books about distraction and attention and has requested an interview. At our appointed time, my phone buzzes with a text from him: *Can we talk in ten minutes?*

I write back, *Sure*, and I wait.

Ten minutes later, he calls and starts to apologize. "It's been such a day," he says. "I—"

And then nothing. Silence. He clearly can't speak. I can tell that his brain has just—to use a technical term—glitched. Like when your computer freezes and that little spinning beach ball of death appears. I'm talking to a man who won a Pulitzer for his use of words, and he can't utter a single one.

He takes a deep breath and asks me if it's okay if we take thirty seconds to breathe. Again, I agree. The thirty seconds go by. But now he has another request.

"Can I write down a couple thoughts?" he wants to know.

By the time we finally start the interview, I'm feeling pangs of irritation at all this preamble that he could have just done alone, before calling me. As we launch in, now a bit short on time, I go right to the topic of *working memory*, because it's key to understanding attention and how to train it to work better.

Working memory, as we've discussed, is a dynamic cognitive workspace you use every waking moment of every day. Don't get thrown off by the word *memory*: this isn't only about the storage of information. It's a *temporary* "scratch space" that is, by necessity and evolutionary design, impermanent and fleeting.

"I always think of working memory as the mind's very own whiteboard," I explain to the writer when he can speak again. "But it's a whiteboard with disappearing ink. And that ink vanishes pretty fast. As soon as you 'write' something there, the ink basically starts to fade."

I describe how attention feeds into working memory: the flashlight of your attention selects key information from your surroundings, or internal environment, and that goes into working memory. Just like writing on a real-life whiteboard, you can scribble ideas, consider concepts, deliberate decisions, notice patterns, jot down something you want to say . . . and more. Unlike a real-life whiteboard, though, this one is peculiar: the ink only stays on the board for a few seconds.

A few seconds is pretty short. That's fine, even helpful, if you're moving quickly from one thing to another. But how do you keep important content on your whiteboard longer if you need more time? Simple: *keep paying attention to what's there.*

Directing the flashlight of your attention to the contents of your working memory essentially "refreshes" that content. It's as if you're tracing over the ink as it's fading, again and again. Stop paying attention—that is, move your flashlight to another target—and the ink dissipates and starts "writing" something else.

Because working memory is so deeply intertwined with attention, it's vulnerable to those very same forces that degrade attention—threat, poor mood, and stress. This is in addition to other corrosive factors like sleep deprivation and psychological disorders such as depression, anxiety, ADHD, and PTSD. Under these pressures, this critical capacity doesn't function so well. Your whiteboard rapidly becomes cluttered as your mind wanders, drawing in distracting content that fills up the space, leaving no room for what you actually want to do. As I'm explaining all this to the journalist, he suddenly cuts in.

"That's *exactly* what was happening when I called you!" he said. "I had just gotten off another call. I was switching between projects. I didn't want to leave you waiting. But my 'whiteboard' was completely full—there was no room to process anything."

He said he needed to "clear his mind," a common phrase that we've all probably used at some point or another. But there's actually no way to "clear" your mind—you can't wipe your whiteboard clean and keep it that way. It's impossible. As soon as the ink fades on one thing, it's replaced by something else.

The question is . . . what?

What's on Your Whiteboard?

Let's do a quick whiteboard assessment. You don't need anything for this but a pen, paper, and this book.

Here's your task. Think of someplace you visit regularly—a grocery store, your workplace, your child's school—that's about a fifteen-minute journey from your home. Picture it in your mind. Now, I want you to relive the path from your front door to this destination and count the number of times you have to turn. Doesn't matter if you walk, take a car, bus, subway, whatever—just try to accurately count the number of turns. If you lose track, no big deal, just start over.

If and when you do get distracted, take a minute to jot down what distracted you. If your phone buzzed because you got a text, email, or Twitter alert, write *phone*. If an anxious thought popped up about a meeting you have later, write *meeting*. If you find yourself thinking about the same distraction more than once, note the repetition. You may have had thoughts about the place you are journeying to (in your mind). Try to be as accurate as possible in getting the turn count, and as precise as possible in noting what got in the way of doing this. Don't skimp or skip over stuff—ideally, we want a lot of data here.

Remember that distraction can be *good* stuff. It doesn't have to be negative to qualify as mind-wandering. Your thoughts may shift back to something pleasant that happened this morning (*the stranger ahead of me in line bought my coffee; what a kind gesture!*) or something you're looking forward to (*three-day weekend coming up!*). No matter the category—positive vs. negative, productive to-do vs. unproductive rumination—simply jot it down.

This activity is similar to a mental activity I asked you to do in the introduction when I had you note the number of times your flashlight drifted from the page. In this case, you're noticing not only the *frequency* of your distraction, but also *what* was distracting you.

Now let's assess. What did you find yourself thinking about, over and over? Reading your list, you might notice that certain topics are "sticky," that they pop up repeatedly. You might have been fantasizing about the delicious lunch you're about to have or ruminating on an awkward comment you made at a gathering last weekend that you still feel embarrassed about. I have no idea. But I'm willing to bet that the vast majority, *if not all*, of the stuff on your chart isn't actually an external distraction like a phone call or a knock at the door. If you're like most of us, the biggest distraction culprit is actually *your own mind.*

We tend to think of distractions as external—the buzz of a phone, the *bing* of an email, a ringing doorbell, a colleague's voice inter-rupting your thought process. More often than not, the most irre-sistible distractions are *internally* generated. In the previous chapter, we talked about finding your focus in a world of distractions, which means noticing when your flashlight has strayed and how to quickly and smoothly move it back where you want it. This is an essential first step in training your attention. But one thing you're going to notice as you start paying attention to your attention is that even if you manage to eliminate potential external distractors (by silencing your phone, pausing your in-box, locking yourself in a quiet room—whatever it takes!), there's still always *something* popping up: a worry, a regret, a desire, a plan.

Where on earth do these thoughts come from? And why do they appear, unbidden, in our working memory, when we want to be us-ing it for something else?

Where Do Distracting Thoughts Come From?

Around two decades ago, those of us working in the field of neu-roscience pondered a mystery: A new and powerful technology—functional MRI (fMRI)—had just been invented, and a strange new pattern of brain activity was visualized for the first time. It didn't match any of the brain networks we already knew about—so what was it? The question lingered for years.

The new technology was thrilling for neuroscientists. We were able to see signals tied to brain activity while a research volunteer was actively doing things in the scanner, and we were able to track ex-actly *where* the action was happening. What we wanted to do most urgently was gather information about the brain regions that were ac-tivated during attentionally demanding tasks. In other words: Which parts of your brain "light up" when you pay attention in certain ways, and what does that tell us about how your attention system works? To do this, we needed to be able to compare the "at work" brain to the "at rest" brain.

First, we looked at the brain doing something demanding for attention and working memory, like the "3-back" working memory task: while in the scanner, you watch a screen as numbers go by one-by-one, and for each number you answer the question "Was it the same as the number you saw three slides back? Or not?" This is a tough one! It gives us a great snapshot of working memory *at work.*

Then, we needed an image of the brain *at rest* to compare it to. "Just rest," we told our study participants. No test, no task, nothing attentionally demanding to puzzle out.

As expected, certain prefrontal brain regions were much more active when participants were doing the 3-back task. In study after study, however, something odd kept happening when the participants were "at rest." A different network came online—a new combination of regions activated at the same time. Regions having to do with memory, planning, and emotion all came online together. We hadn't seen this before, and we couldn't immediately identify what it was. *Why would these regions get activated together during rest?* They even appeared to be yoked, so that their activity waxed and waned together.

We tried giving participants different, more-specific instructions, but it didn't matter what they did—when they were told to rest, we got a very specific activation profile in the middle of the brain (called the midline—think of the part of your brain that would be under the skull if you parted your hair right down the middle of your scalp). Every time we said "rest," this mystery network booted up.

So we started asking people as they came out of the scanner: *What did you think about during the rest period?*

Their answers:

"I thought about lunch."

"I thought about how uncomfortable I was."

"I thought about a fight I had with my roommate this morning."

"I thought about how I need to get a haircut."

The more participants we polled, the more we started to notice a pattern in their responses: they were all self-related topics. People weren't in the scanner thinking about world peace or politics—instead, they were turning inward, reflecting on recent episodes in their lives, making plans, analyzing their own feelings, thoughts, and sensations.

This led some research teams to try a twist. They showed participants a series of adjectives while they were in the scanner: *Tall. Funny. Smart. Attractive. Interesting. Friendly. Sad. Brave. Likable.* The instruction: rate how much each word described Bill Clinton (he was president at the time) on a scale from "not at all" to "quite a lot." Then: "Rate how much this word describes *you*." And boom, there it was again: the very same, unidentified network we'd seen during rest. As soon as participants were asked about themselves rather than the president, that same pattern of midline brain regions came online.

The researchers realized something: perhaps rest was never actually *restful.* Asked to "rest," the participants were instead defaulting to thinking about themselves. A new, somewhat playful acronym emerged and was jokingly used among brain researchers: Rapid Ever-present Self-related Thinking, or *R.E.S.T.*

Neuroscientists now call this once-mysterious network the "default mode network," because the brain is thought to default to this mode whenever it isn't otherwise occupied with attentionally demanding tasks (and, as we'll see here shortly, often even when it *is* occupied). Once we were able to isolate and identify the network, we started to see its fingerprint in all sorts of situations. When you're mind-wandering, the default mode is active. When you're performing a task and making errors—again, you're in the default mode. Many labs tested this and saw it consistently: when people got questions right, the attention network was "online"; when they got stuff wrong, the default mode network was active instead.

What all this tells us is that when mind-wandering directs both your attention and your working memory *inward,* your default mode is activated. Even in the absence of external distractions, your brain will produce its own salient, self-related content. And these internal distractions are just as "loud" as external distractions—emotionally charged thoughts can capture attention just as powerfully as someone shouting your name.

This might not be such a problem when you don't need your working memory for something else—as we discussed in the previous chapter, allowing space for spontaneous thought can be great. The problem is, this is happening all the time. And often you *do* need your working memory for something else. You need it for almost *everything.*

You Don't Work Without Working Memory

Using your working memory is how you learn and remember. It's a "portal" into more permanent storage: you need it to be able to *encode* information—an experience, new information, and much more—into your long-term memory. And when you want to get something *out* of long-term memory (retrieval), your working memory is where that information is "downloaded" for fast access so that you can use it.

Working memory is critical for social connection and communication. It's where you track and analyze the intentions and actions of other people and hold those observations in mind so that you can navigate social dynamics, like waiting your turn in conversation or listening even while you have something to say.

And it's where you experience emotion. When you recall a happy memory or something sad or upsetting, you're using your working memory to do so. You essentially "fill up" your whiteboard with the thoughts, feelings, and sensations associated with that memory as you construct a full, rich, emotional experience. Working memory is deeply connected to your capacity to feel.

It goes the other way, too: you need working memory to *regulate* emotions as they come along. Example: You're overcome by some feeling, and you need to get steady. What do you do? You think through the problem, or you distract yourself by focusing on some other topic, or you reframe the situation (*maybe it's not as bad as I think . . .*). All these tactics require the use of your working memory.

One study had participants come in and watch a disturbing movie. The only catch was that they were instructed to limit any overt expression of emotions while doing so. No shouting, crying, or facial expressions were allowed. Separately, researchers tested each participant's working memory capacity by asking them to remember letters in between completing simple math problems. Then they looked for a link: Was there any correspondence between people's success at suppressing their expression of emotion and their working memory capacity?

Yes. People who had *low* working memory capacity were expressing all over the place. They truly weren't able to control it, even though it was the one task they were given. Meanwhile, those who had *higher* working memory capacity were much better at modulating their responses. They may have been using working memory to keep the goal in mind ("My job right now is *not* to react") more strongly than those with low working memory, or perhaps they were *reappraising* the situation to shift their response ("It's just a movie; it's not real")—whatever their specific tactic was, the key was that they had the *cognitive capacity* to do it.

Finally, and critically, working memory plays a role in every single thing you *want* to do, every day, from making your lunch to thinking a thought. In neuroscience-speak, it's where you "maintain a goal."

Working Memory Is Your Portal to Your *Gooooaaaalllll!*

Working memory is where you *hold a goal in mind* so you can move toward it. By *goal,* I don't mean the kind that wins soccer games (though that is the goal of soccer). I mean the micro-intentions and deliberate aim of having a desired outcome for each and every task you engage in—all the decisions, planning, thinking, actions, and behaviors you do over the course of a day: anything you set out to do. Deciding to read a book, shopping for dinner supplies, thinking about your favorite memes, making your presentation slides, learning how to use a new gadget, waiting for traffic to clear before crossing the street. You lean on your working memory to maintain your goals and subgoals, update them, and scrap them for a different goal, on a continuous, moment-by-moment, task-by-task basis.

During the quarantine for the COVID-19 pandemic, my husband and I decided that we should really mix it up and do something exciting one evening. By "exciting" I mean that we decided to spend the evening playing cards with both our kids.

Sophie, our daughter, asked us all to play a card game called "Egyptian Slap." The rules go like this: players take turns rapidly playing a card from their hand, and when specific sequences of cards appear, you slap the pile and win the hand. The sequences you're looking for are things like: a *sandwich* (8–2–8), three of a kind (8-8-8), ordinal (7–8–9), and so on. The kids loved this game—Michael and I kind of hated it. There are *so many rules*. And you have to maintain constant access to them in order to win. You have to hold all these rules actively in working memory and take quick action in the moment.

Surprise, surprise, the kids wiped the floor with us. A couple of forty-something parents were no match for the lightning-fast mental and physical reflexes of our teenage offspring. Our kids, baffled by how poorly we were doing, kept trying to correct us. "No, no," they would say, "you have to slap as *fast* as you can." Adorably, they didn't realize that it wasn't that we didn't understand the rules, but that while their young frontal lobes were springing forward, en route to actualizing their full potential, ours were falling back, sadly on the decline. But it was interesting—as I was playing (and losing), it struck me that the game was the perfect example of a *pure working memory task*: we had to hold a goal in mind, and then take action based on that goal. That's how working memory works, and also why it impacts you so profoundly.

Working memory is the essential partner to attention: it's what allows you to actually *do* something with the information your flashlight focuses on. But if attention keeps piping in salient and distracting content, that will become a big problem for goal maintenance, let alone goal accomplishment. Why? Because you only have so much space to work with. Just like a real-life whiteboard, your working memory has limits.

Working Memory Is Limited

In the lab, we regularly run experiments that try to push the upper limits of working memory. We wanted to know: If working memory was so critical for every facet of our lives, exactly how much "space" do we possess in which to do all this important work?

We had participants come into the lab and look at an image of a face. We made it unremarkable—no unusual or striking features that would make it especially memorable. Then the face would disappear for three seconds, before being replaced by another face. Their job was to mentally compare the two faces and tell us if they were the same or different. Easy! So then, we increased the number of faces people had to hold in mind, to two, then three, then four, five, up to nine. It's a basic way to test working memory's capacity to maintain information: During those three seconds when those first faces are no longer available, the participants have to hold those images in working memory—that is, "draw" them over and over on that whiteboard. And when they start to answer incorrectly, we know they're reaching the upper limit of how much their whiteboard can hold.

So, how many faces can people remember before they "max out" their working memory? Take a guess. Five? Ten? More?

The answer is *three*.

Every time we did this experiment in the lab, people got worse with more and more faces. After three, their performance was no better than making a complete guess. They performed as poorly as they would have if they had never seen the faces in the first place.

"Well," you might say, "faces are complicated—they have so many little details!" But it turns out that three or four items are about the limit that can be held in working memory, even with very simple stimuli like colored shapes. Why? Well, one possibility is that each item you hold in working memory has a unique brain frequency signature—like a radio channel. And you can "open" three or four of those channels at once and still keep them separate from each other. But if you try to go past four, they start to scramble, or become "disambiguated."

The reason that local phone numbers have seven digits is actually directly related to the "size" of working memory: In 1956, a psychologist named George Miller published a paper on working memory titled "The Magical Number Seven, Plus or Minus Two." He'd found that seven (plus or minus two) was the sweet spot for memorizing a string of numbers—it was the upper limit of what most people could briefly hold or easily memorize, because the time it takes to say seven numbers in English is roughly the "time buffer" of our auditory working memory. Even a couple of seconds longer means that those numbers are already fading too fast for you to dial. (And if you remember rotary phones, you know how important this was at the time!)

You can use several strategies to assist you, now that you're empowered with the knowledge that your working memory is limited. For example, recall the journalist who had called to interview me. "Cognitive offloading" is what he utilized when he asked me if he could write down his thoughts at the beginning of our interview. Cognitive offloading is a great tactic—it's beneficial for task performance. Yet it doesn't address one of our core problems: *we don't always realize that we are overloaded.* We aren't aware, moment to moment, of all that is on our whiteboard, and we don't get clued in until we experience a failure.

When Working Memory Fails

The first story in this chapter is the perfect example of a common type of working memory failure: *overload.* You're trying to hang onto too much, and you push your working memory past its limits. You might also experience the opposite: *blanking.*

I just had it! you think as you walk into a room and have no idea why you're there. Or you've been called on to speak after sitting in class or in a meeting with your hand up, only to turn to your own mind, which moments ago had a brilliant, fully written speech, to find an empty white page. Why does this happen? The field of neuroscience suggests a few ideas. One is that we mind-wander with no awareness . . . the flashlight gets pulled away, whatever we were maintaining vanishes, and we return to a "blank" whiteboard. Another hypothesis is that there is a "sudden death" of neural activity for the information we were trying to hang onto: a whole symphony of brain activity is happening, and then all of it stops at the same time. You may have a sense that something was there, but now it's gone.

And finally: *distraction.*

You've learned by now how powerful salient distractors can be. Anything especially salient, or "loud" (literally or metaphorically), will definitely capture your attention, whether it's in your external environment (producing sights, sounds, or other sensations) or in your mindscape (thoughts, memories, emotions). One of the ramifications of this is that once the "loud" thing lands in your working memory, it may write over what you were trying to hang onto. Result: whatever previous content you were in the process of either *maintaining* (keeping the traces active for use) or *encoding* ("writing" more permanently into long-term memory) is disrupted. This form of disruption highlights again how deeply intertwined working memory and attention are.

Working Memory and the Three Subsystems of Attention

Working memory and attention are like dance partners: they must work together smoothly to accomplish any of your goals, whether large or small. Whether that's in service of a quarantine card game or a life-defining crisis, the mechanism is the same—and so are the key vulnerabilities:

- *The flashlight* encodes information and maintains it in working memory, "retracing" it on the whiteboard to keep it there for longer.

  — Key vulnerability: Bait and Switch

  When your attention is automatically "captured" or yanked by something salient, this more exciting (to your attention) content overwrites what was being maintained. Voluntary attention then starts retracing this new content. The prior information is lost forever, gone without a trace.

- *The floodlight* gains access to the whiteboard to accomplish an urgent goal. Under acute threat or stress, your alerting system temporarily *blocks access to* working memory to ensure that your brain's action systems prioritize basic survival behaviors (fight, flight, freeze) over any other goals or plans.

  — Key vulnerability: Road Block

  The alerting system can be set off by *feelings* of threat, even when there is no real danger. This temporarily cuts off access to working memory and impairs any functions that rely on it (like long-term memory, social connection, and emotion regulation).

- *The juggler* keeps your current goals active on the whiteboard, and updates these goals as circumstances change.

  — Key vulnerability: Ball Drop

  Overload, blanking, and distraction in working memory all derail the central executive's juggler, leading to lost goals and misguided behaviors. The juggler drops the ball.

Each point above represents an opportunity for that tight "dance" between working memory and attention to either work smoothly and fluidly in service of our goals, or to trip us up: Put the wrong thing on the whiteboard. Block important content. Derail goal accomplishment.

When we experience working memory failures—whether large or small—they can pile up over the course of a day, a week, and even a *lifetime*, and can set us far back from *where* we want to be and *who* we want to be.

"So," you ask, "what can we do about it?"

Decluttering the (Mental) Whiteboard

In 2013, our lab collaborated on a large-scale study with schoolteachers from around the United States and Canada to see whether mindfulness training would have any impact on cognitive performance and burnout, a particular concern for educators. The training was an eight-week mindfulness course taught by a qualified trainer. In addition to attending the class meetings, they had to do mindfulness homework exercises between classes. The teachers were all given a classic experiment to index their working memory capacity: Remember a short sequence of letters, say, M Z B. Then they were asked to do a simple math problem. We'd add another letter to the sequence, then give them another computation; then add another letter, assign another problem. We wanted to know this: How long of a string of letters could they remember accurately before their working memory started to fade and ultimately fail, all the while maintaining their ability to give correct answers to the math problems?

Half the group then participated in an eight-week mindfulness course, while the other half waited for their turn to take the course. (That's an important way to control for a potential study contaminant: differing motivation. Instead of having a control group that simply receives nothing or has no interest in receiving training, a

STAY IN PLAY | 143

wait-list control group, at least in theory, has a similar level of motivation and investment during the testing sessions, because eventually they too will get the training.) When we retested both groups after the first group finished their training, we found that those who'd already done their eight-week mindfulness course showed better working memory than the group that was still waiting.

These intriguing results led us to our next burning question: *How* was mindfulness training improving working memory? My hunch: It helped declutter the mental whiteboard.

Colleagues at the University of California, Santa Barbara, had the same hunch and tested it out in a clever experiment. They gave forty-eight undergraduate students the same working memory task we had provided teachers and those Marines we studied in West Palm Beach years before, but they added one important twist. After the experiment was over, they asked participants to report how often they were mind-wandering—were they having off-task thoughts often or not so often during the experiment?

After doing the working memory study, half of them were invited to receive mindfulness training for two weeks and the other half got nutrition education as "comparison training." They found that only mindfulness training improved working memory in these students, and it was most helpful to those who mind-wandered a lot before their training. This study also asked a practical question: Does improving working memory and reducing mind-wandering help students on academic tasks? The answer: Yes! Students who got the mindfulness training improved an average of sixteen percentile points on the reading comprehension section of the Graduate Record Exam (GRE), an important test for gaining entry into graduate programs.

Let's sum up and connect the dots: In high-stress groups, like teachers experiencing burnout, stress is kryptonite for attention—mental time travel is one of the main culprits. Instead of being able to keep your flashlight aimed where you need it, you're either in rewind (ruminating, regretting) or in fast-forward (catastrophizing or worrying . . . often about something imagined that may never come to pass). Working memory (your mental whiteboard) relies on this vary same attentional flashlight to encode and refresh its contents. But if stress-related mental time travel hijacks attention away, working memory gets filled up with irrelevant input. Any processes that rely on working memory will suffer as well. This means comprehension, planning, thinking, decision making, and experiencing and regulating emotions all become compromised.

In short:

STRESS-RELATED MENTAL TIME TRAVEL YANKS THE ATTENTIONAL FLASHLIGHT AWAY FROM OUR PRESENT-MOMENT EXPERIENCE AND INCREASES THE CLUTTER ON OUR MENTAL WHITEBOARD.

When it's present-centered, attention can encode and refresh the contents of working memory with task-relevant information. And in turn, working memory is able to successfully meet present-moment task demands. In other words:

MINDFULNESS TRAINING HELPS TO DECLUTTER THE MENTAL WHITEBOARD, SO THAT WORKING MEMORY WORKS BETTER.

The Loop of Doom

One Friday night, after a very long week of teaching, meetings, and deadlines, I told my husband, Michael, that I had really maxed out my decision-making powers. I asked if I could offload to him all decisions regarding our evening plans, but I had one request and one condition. The request: that we do something fun that would be "transportive" and entertaining. The condition: "I am not leaving this couch."

He announced that we would be streaming a show called *Lucifer*. It's a show about the Devil, who, bored with being in Hell, moves to Los Angeles (where else?) to become a nightclub owner. (I rolled my eyes in protest, but he pushed *play*. "You asked me to make the decisions!" he reminded me. Fair enough!) Lucifer partners up with a cop and dedicates himself to punishing people when they choose to use their free will to do bad things. And when they die? You guessed it— they get sent to Hell. And then the show started to elaborate on its version of Hell: basically, Lucifer was putting people in circumstances where they had to play out their biggest regret—the same time loop, over and over again. And I thought, *Ha! That's rumination!*

Rumination is one of the most potent forms of mental time travel. It involves getting stuck thinking about the same thing over and over. When we ruminate on something, we get caught in a loop: we go over events, wishing they could have gone differently; sometimes we imagine the alternate ways things might have gone, or we remember how they *actually* went, and we end up going over those events yet again. We can also ruminate by catastrophizing: imagining how events might unfold in the future, worrying about various potentialities that may never come to pass. These types of mental loops are magnetic—they become conflict states, and it's very hard to pull our flashlights away from them. When we do manage to, we tend to return immediately to the topic as soon as possible, like a tongue seeking a sore tooth.

It was kind of funny, to me, discovering that rumination is so terrible that somebody made a whole show about how it's *literally Hell*.

Mental time travel diminishes our working memory's ability to do the work needed for the demands of our present moment. And because when we're mentally writing and rewriting things over and over again, regardless of what we're looping on, it leaves no room for anything else. We don't have capacity available for either cognition or emotional regulation. You might find yourself, in this situation, making a hasty decision or snapping at your kids. Stress levels go up, mood goes down. That self-assisted stress wears on our attention, making it even more difficult to resist what I call the "loop of doom."

Whatever the contents of our working memory, highlighted and escorted there by our attention, they are the actual contents of our *moment-to-moment conscious experience*. Let's say your working memory is goal-focused, occupied and engaged in content aligned with both what you want to be doing and what you're actually doing, as in some external task. You're focused, engaged, responsive. You're noticing everything, from sensory details to the larger context of your experience—all the "information" about your surroundings and immediate environment that you need to accomplish your task is available to you.

In contrast, if there's something else on your whiteboard, then *that* becomes your experience in that moment. You are likely to lose the intention and purpose of the activity you embarked on in the first place. To use an example that's near and dear to my heart: if you're physically sitting with your child, reading a book together, but mentally mulling over a work-related problem, then you are, essentially, at work instead of on that couch with your child. You may even experience *perceptual decoupling*, where your flashlight is so focused on your whiteboard content that you aren't even able to process sensory input from your surroundings. (That, for the record, is how we get ourselves into situations where we've read a book a hundred times, and still don't know what a wump is.)

Here's how strong this effect is: if you're holding something in working memory, *your brain's computational resources shift to service that content.* This is what we call the *biasing* effect of working memory. In one experiment, we wanted to figure out the power of working memory's biasing effect on perception. How "strongly" does it influence *what you perceive?*

We ran an experiment similar to the one I described earlier that told us the upper limits of working memory. But this time, we put the brain cap on our participants while they did the experiment, and we only gave them one face to remember. What we found: when you're maintaining a face in your working memory, during those three seconds when there's no face on the screen, your face-processing neurons *stay active.* How did we know this? During the delay, we presented a small gray "probe" image—a sort of shapeless blob—which we made by taking all the pixels of the face image and randomly moving them around. We were intrigued to see a stronger N170 (the brainwave response generated when seeing a face) to these probes when participants were remembering faces than when they were remembering anything else (like scenes).

Let's break that down. Why was this an intriguing finding for us? Well, it told us that working memory performs the same type of "top-down" biasing that your attention system does: everything your brain does now becomes calibrated to what's on your whiteboard. It isn't just that it *seems* as if you're experiencing whatever you're thinking about instead of what's right in front of you. It's that neurally, that's exactly what's happening. Your brain is perceiving a face *internally*, even as your eyes are staring at a gray blob.

So: if you're reading about wumps on the couch, or driving across a long bridge in Florida, or sitting at the judge's bench while a defense attorney gives closing arguments, and your thoughts are elsewhere, then—as far as your brain knows—you *are* elsewhere.

Now, I want to take a minute here to make an important point. Everything we've been talking about so far regarding your working memory—its temporary nature, its susceptibility to threat and stress, and the way it can be hijacked by mind-wandering—all probably sounds like a litany of negatives. As if working memory is programmed solely for failure. Meanwhile, I'm telling you how important it is for all you want to accomplish. So, what gives? If this is such a critical brain capacity, why on earth would Mother Nature leave us with such a faulty, error-prone tool? Why are there so many "bugs" in this software?

It's a *Feature*, Not a Bug

My answer to that is: It's not a bug. It's a feature. Each of these apparent flaws has a purpose. Let's take a look.

Disappearing ink

If this fast-fading ink on our whiteboards is such a problem, why didn't we evolve to have ink that stuck around longer? Something more permanent?

Imagine what it would be like if your whiteboard didn't auto-clear every few seconds. Every passing thought, everything that caught your attention, every little intrusion or distraction would stick around. Even helpful stuff would turn into a burden. Forget maintaining goals or problem solving—you'd be overburdened by the weight and stagnation of any arising mental content. It would be hard to tell the difference between what is important or not, since no matter what, content would just stick around in your conscious mind, for longer than you might need it. Your working memory *had* to evolve to be fleeting. Your brain needs to automatically dump content at a rapid, constant pace, so that there is flexibility and choice in what you continue to focus on and, therefore, maintain.

Fragility

But why is my working memory *so* vulnerable to distractions?

Let's bring back our helpful assistant, your long-ago ancestor, to help us out with this one. Picture him in the forest. He has a goal he's holding in working memory: *find food.* He's scanning for the red pop of a particular berry that grows in this area—all his brain functions are now calibrated to achieving that goal. As he scans for *red*, his color-processing neurons are sizzling, active and ready. Then, he spots it: motion in the trees. Tiger. Working memory dumps the previous goal as fast as he could snap his fingers, and a new directive appears: *freeze.*

We still need this feature—though it can get us into trouble when we misperceive or imagine *threat*. We need to be able to *rapidly* act without a sluggish delay. And this feature allows us to perform this crucial, and sometimes lifesaving, pivot.

Capacity

But why are we so limited? Why can we only remember three things, instead of three hundred?

To be honest, we are still puzzling this one out, and frequency-based brain dynamics are likely to give us an answer. One explanation may be this: even if you *could* remember a million things, a big reason for having working memory, like attention, is to *be able to take action*, and you still only have two hands and two feet.

These features of working memory evolved so that we don't re-member everything and thereby become unresponsive to changing demands. They served our ancestors well thousands of years ago, and they continue to serve us well today, even in our mostly tiger-free world. It's just that these evolutionarily selected features come with their downsides. On the upside, though, we are learning rapidly, with more and more research studies suggesting that mindfulness training can help. With training, we can still have a peak mind—even with these tendencies.

To Reclaim Your Whiteboard, Press *Play*

I used to think mindfulness was about hitting the "pause" button, which to me always felt artificial or idealistic. Life has no *pause* button—why pretend it does? But when we're talking about stabilizing attention and developing a peak mind, what we're actually looking for is a *play* button. We need to stop holding down the rewind or fast-forward buttons and *stay in play*, to experience every note in the song of our lives, to *hear* and take in what's happening around us.

In the previous chapter, you tried out the first core practice, *Find Your Flashlight*. Now we're going to try a variation on that practice that helps pull us out of the loop of doom. It works because you must step outside your journey going around and around in those ruminative loops of doom to make a category judgment about the contents of your mind-wandering. And then, after labeling the content of your mind-wandering, you return back to the present moment. When you *do* get sucked into ruminative mind-wandering (which happens to the best of us), you start to recognize what's happening—and as you practice more, you recognize it *sooner*. You're not replaying an argument with a friend for the tenth time before you notice that you've been using your whiteboard for something else while you're trying to listen to your colleague talk to you. As you train yourself to monitor what's happening in the present moment, you'll default less and less to long, unproductive, and off-task bouts of mental time travel. You'll get better at noticing mind-wandering and asking: What are the contents of my working memory right now, and are they supporting me for what is needed right now? Or would shifting back to the present moment be best? If so, redirect your attention back to the sights, sounds, and demands of the present moment.

This is another "variation" of classical practices aiming to cultivate concentrative focus. It builds on the *Find Your Flashlight* exercise, and it will be great preparation for one of the more advanced practices coming up later in the book, where you'll need to develop the skill of observing and monitoring your mind, which begins by "watching" your own thoughts.

CORE PRACTICE BOOSTER: WATCH YOUR WHITEBOARD

1. ***Repeat the previous steps.*** We begin the same way we did with the basic *Find Your Flashlight* activity on page 117, by sitting in a chair, comfortable but upright, resting your hands in your lap, and closing or lowering your eyes (to limit visual distraction). Again, select prominent breath-related sensations. Remember the metaphor of your attention as a flashlight, the beam pointing toward your selected breath-related body sensation. When your flashlight drifts to something else . . .

2. ***Notice where it goes.*** This is a new step! In the first exercise, I asked you to notice if attention wandered away, and if so to immediately move your flashlight back to your breath. This time, I want you to pause for a moment and observe where the flashlight is now directed.

3. ***Give it a label.*** Identify what *type* of distraction has appeared on your whiteboard. Is it a thought, an emotion, or a sensation? A *thought* could be a worry, a reminder, a memory, an idea, an item on your to-do list. An *emotion* could be a feeling of frustra-

tion, an urge to stop doing the practice and do something else, a twinge of happiness, a swell of stress. A *sensation* is something in your physical body: An itch. A sore muscle. Noticing that your back hurts from sitting there, or noticing something you heard, smelled, touched, or saw (such as a door slamming, food cooking, the cat jumping in your lap, lights flashing).

4. **Make this a quick process.** Notice if you begin going down a rabbit hole of elaborating on the distraction, or asking why you are thinking about this particular topic, or defaulting to unsupportive habits like chastising yourself for getting distracted in the first place. It is not your job right now to answer these questions or reprimand yourself. Now is actually the time to notice what is on your whiteboard but *not to engage with it*. Just label the contents as best you can from these three categories: *thought, emotion, sensation.* And then . . .

5. **Move on.** Come back to the present moment, back to your breath, after every instance of labeling. If it's a strong experience, it might pop up repeatedly—then just label it again.

6. **Repeat.** Each time you notice yourself mind-wandering, tag the content of your mind-wandering (as thought, emotion, or sensation) and then come back to your breath.

An important point: I am absolutely not suggesting that the contents of your whiteboard should *always* match the contents of your immediate task-at-hand. Like the fallacy of having a "perfect unbroken focus," that's neither possible nor desirable. There's nothing inherently bad about having stuff on your whiteboard other than what's right in front of your nose. It's neither bad nor good—it's simply *how the brain works.* It happens. Spontaneous thought arises. We use working memory to work something out that has nothing to do with the present moment—puzzle out a logistical problem, figure out how we feel about something, or make a plan or a decision. There are plenty of situations where it's absolutely best to have the content of the whiteboard be information about the past or future—and in those moments, the present moment becomes enriched with the content that time traveling provides access to.

If spontaneous thought is not affecting your performance, then maybe it's not a problem. This could be a fine time to give yourself some "white space" and let your mind drag whatever it wants onto your whiteboard. (In fact, what your off-leash brain fetches for you can be quite informative—we'll be talking about that a bit later.) But this very well might be a moment when you *do* need your working memory for a current demand. And this is not just about some on-the-job type of performance—there are all kinds of reasons you don't want to be disconnected from your environment, like connection to others, learning, personal safety, and more. So ask yourself:

If I'm distracted, is there a cost?
If I miss this moment, is that important to me?

Managing your working memory, just like managing your attention, is not about being 100 percent present 100 percent of the time. The point is not that you become *only* about the present moment—you can't, and I wouldn't recommend it! What you *can* do is become aware of what's happening. That's the superpower that allows you to intervene.

The Power of Knowing What's on Your Whiteboard

In the show *Lucifer* (which I did keep watching after all), it was later revealed that Lucifer had one final trick up his sleeve. All the people who were "trapped" in Hell weren't really trapped at all. All the doors were unlocked. They could choose to leave at any time. They simply didn't, because they assumed they couldn't.

Ultimately, having a strong working memory is not about always using it for your goals and plans, every minute; or about always being in the present moment—this is neither realistic nor desirable. Instead, it's about becoming aware of what your working memory actually contains. It's about recognizing and heading off any interference (such as mental time travel) when there is a task to be done. It can even be about basking in the "nowness" of a refreshing morning shower. In the lab, we find that people who display better performance are better able to *drop the distractions*. They are able to allow the ink to fade when it's appropriate for it to do so, selectively making the decision: "I'm not going to rewrite that."

This is where the *new* science of attention has moved us forward in our understanding of how to reclaim this critical cognitive workspace. We have long understood the connections between working memory and attention, and between working memory and long-term memory. What we're understanding now is that working memory is far more than just a "holding cell" for information.

What's in your working memory will—as we'll see in the coming chapters—constrain your perception, your thinking, and your actions. So the first critical thing we need to work on is pointing the flashlight of our attention *at* that mental whiteboard, to see what's on it. This is an entirely new way to use the "flashlight beam" of our attention, but one that we are beginning to realize is critical to achieving the cognitive capacities we need to really thrive in the world we live in today.

However, you cannot just "decide" to be aware of what's on your whiteboard, moment to moment—as with any kind of training, you have to build up to that capacity. And this is why, at a certain point in my research, I had to push forward with exploring mindfulness practice even when I encountered resistance at every turn.

"Career Suicide"

That study with the Marines in West Palm Beach showed us that with mindfulness training, plus a commitment to daily practice, people under long-term, high-stress conditions could indeed keep their attention and working memory intact and have cognitive resilience. They could be trained to protect their attention and working memory from the damaging stressors surrounding them. It was a promising study, but small—too small. We needed a bigger sample group, and a more-honed experiment. I wanted to find out more about what type of mental training, specifically, worked best, and the "dosage" level required to make a real difference for someone operating under high-stress conditions.

Professionally, I was warned against pursuing this line of research. *Mindfulness* was a dead end, colleagues told me. It was too wishy-washy. Not rigorous enough. If I kept on this trajectory, they cautioned, I'd be "committing career suicide."

We wrote grants anyway. And we got funding: two million dollars to run the first-ever large-scale mindfulness training study with the US Army. I felt *ecstatic*. Maybe I was "committing career suicide," but at least I was going all-in.

There was only one problem: nobody in the military would accept the study. I shopped it around everywhere, but every door I knocked on stayed closed. It seemed we were asking for too much: we were asking for *time*, and a lot of it. This study had a brainwave component, and the setup for the electrode cap alone took one hour! And we were asking for their time during the worst-possible period:

predeployment, when soldiers train for some of the most intense and high-stakes conditions they will ever experience. But that was exactly when I needed them—during that high-stress interval when they'd have to perform at their peak, and then continue to do so as they were deployed. "No," everybody said. "No, no, no."

And then, after an entire year of asking, a *yes*.

That "yes" came from Walt Piatt, the lieutenant general we met in the introduction. At the time (more than a decade ago) he was a colonel, heading up a US Army brigade based in Hawaii that was in-between deployments. When my team and I flew out to meet Colonel Piatt about the study, I was briefed by his executive officer to keep our presentation short and to the point, as his time was extremely limited. I walked in ready for him to be stereotypically "military"— all business, stiff and stoic with a no-nonsense edge.

Instead, the first thing he did was take us to the base's "remembrance room," where the service members who didn't make it back alive were memorialized. We walked slowly around the room, looking at the names and boots of the fallen. He talked about the challenges of life in the military, before, during, and after deployment. He showed us photos of friends he'd lost, including Iraqi friends. And he told me that when he looked over our materials describing the study, he thought of something his wife, Cynthia, was always saying to him: "Don't deploy before you deploy." Through his multiple deployments, she'd noticed that before he had physically gone to a war zone halfway around the world, he would already be mentally gone. Immediately I thought of all the myriad ways so many of us might "deploy before we deploy," spending so much time in our heads planning and imagining the next upcoming thing that we completely miss our lives in the moment. I thought of myself earlier that week: standing on the sidelines at my son's soccer game, I was mentally already at the next day's faculty meeting. I barely remembered a thing about that game. (It still gets me.)

Driving back to the hotel, I went over the experience in my mind—it was not at all what I had expected. The colonel's decision to take us to the remembrance room first was telling. It occurred to me that in Sanskrit the word for *mindfulness* is *smriti*, which can be translated as "that which is remembered."

When we *stay in play*—when we are filling up our whiteboards with the present moment—we have a much greater chance of *encoding* that moment into long-term memory. We all want to "remember better." Can mindfulness help us also press the *record* button?

Yes. But pressing *record* isn't quite as straightforward as it may seem.

6

PRESS *RECORD*

The minute Richard walked into our training session, I could tell he was a skeptic. A gentle yet tough former active-duty soldier who now worked for a military research center, he hung back, quiet and reserved. He was unfailingly polite. But I could see it in his eyes—he wasn't on board, not at all.

This was a "training for trainers" program that my colleague Scott Rogers and I were leading. Richard had been sent by his bosses to learn how to deliver mindfulness training to military cohorts. His job in the Research Transition Office at the Walter Reed Army Institute of Research was to help adapt new science (like ours, on the attentional benefits of mindfulness practice) into training that the US Army could offer soldiers. But he had serious doubts. He was deeply concerned that mindfulness would clash with his religious beliefs. His Christianity was the bedrock of his life and beliefs, and he worried about the directive from his employer to train other soldiers in mindfulness, and to learn it for himself first. Would he be able to do his job?

When he walked into the session that first morning, he said he felt on edge. "My mindset was, *I'm going to find a way out of this.*"

But as we went through the material, his resistance started to melt. There was nothing religious in nature. The mission of mindfulness training, and the reasons it worked to strengthen attention, working memory, and mood, made a lot of sense to him. The message that soldiers often weren't able to respond to the demands of the moment because of other worries they carried really resonated. He started thinking, *This could really be helpful.* And he started to wonder: When he prayed—a practice that was deeply meaningful to him—was he there, mentally? Was he attending to the prayer? When he was with his kids, who were growing up fast, was he actually *with* them? His teenage children were always trying to share memories with him: "It was so funny when . . ." "Dad, remember that time when . . . ?" He'd think, *Oh wow, I don't remember that at all.*

He'd always written it off: *I just have a terrible memory.* Now he wondered—did he actually have a terrible memory, or was it something else? Every time his kids tried to connect with him over a shared experience, he felt a pang.

"I realized that I couldn't be part of those memories with them because I wasn't part of the moment to begin with. I was in another place, all the time."

Even though he'd been physically present for these events (he had the pictures to prove it), he hadn't actually experienced them. Busy, pressured, and driven, he felt that his attention was forever elsewhere, no matter what he was doing, no matter whom he was with.

"I wasn't there," he says now, "so I didn't remember it."

Memory can be tricky. We assume that we'll remember much more than we do. Then we run up against a moment like the one Richard experienced with his children, and we wonder how much of our lives we are fully taking in. What have we failed to record? Important moments with loved ones, essential knowledge—or more? You might make a mistake because something you do know doesn't surface in the moment you need it; you have a frustrating, fuzzy sense of *I should know that.* You want to listen and remember the content of an important meeting or a lovely moment with your family; meanwhile you're going over a regrettable incident from your past, something that's already *in* your long-term memory that you'd rather forget.

It's easy to wonder if there's something wrong with your memory— why experiences and learning seem to slip off instead of sink into your long-term storage. Yet for every single one of those examples— why some memories stick and others don't, why knowledge surfaces when you need it sometimes but not at other times—there's an explanation. And it probably doesn't have much to do with your actual memory. What we think is a memory problem is often an *attention* problem.

Are You Recording?

Take out your phone for a moment. Now open your camera roll and scroll back to the last event you photographed. It could be anything— maybe it's something big (a concert with your friends) or something small (a pic of your cat on your couch). Looking at the photos you took, ask yourself:

- What do you remember? Try to recall sensory details you remember experiencing, like the taste of the food, the smell of the air—anything not pictured in that little rectangle in your hand.

- What was said? What did you talk about?

- How did you feel?

- And finally: What did you miss? If you could go back in time
  to that moment, what would you turn your attention to first, in
  order to fill in the blanks?

When I popped open my camera roll just now and scrolled back
through time, the first event that grabbed my attention was the last
family dinner we had before Leo left for college—he was all grown
up and heading out into the world, and I'd wanted all four of us together at the table for one last special meal. Looking at the photo, I
vividly remember trying to get the angle just right, for everybody to
be smiling and looking at the camera. But I don't remember what we
talked about or much else about the meal.

If you're not a photo-taker, look through your text threads—have
you sent a screenshot or article to anyone recently? Do you remember why? Do you recall what it was about? Or have the context and
content utterly vanished?

It's tempting to think of memory as the brain's *record* button. And
indeed, I've been using the "press record" concept as a metaphor here
for how we remember. But we don't really "record" . . . not exactly.

Memory Isn't a Recording

Remembering is a complex, nuanced process. Memories are mutable,
not static. Unlike a photo on your camera roll, they don't stay the
same every time you pull them up. Memories morph and change.
And some things stick in our memories while others fall away. Rest
assured: there's probably nothing wrong with your memory. *This is
just how memory works.* Our memory privileges certain types of information, and we forget other things completely, by evolutionary

design. What you might say is "wrong" with your memory probably has an evolutionarily selected purpose.

Your memory is not a verbatim recorder of events. Your mind might be a fantastic time traveler, but you can't "rewind" and relive events exactly as they happened—because there is no "exactly as it happened." What you remember is filtered through your *experience* of what happened, as well as the experiences you had before and after. "Episodic memory," which is your memory for experiences, involves *selective encoding of only those aspects of experience that were most attended to and held in working memory*. Translation: you'll only remember what you focused on and "wrote" on your whiteboard—not everything that occurred. And further, your episodic memory doesn't merely involve the external aspects of events (who, what, where, and so forth) but is deeply wrapped up in your autobiographical take on what you experienced. So—was the experience happy? Sad? Interesting? Tense? Your emotional experience will influence what you focus on—and therefore what you remember.

"Semantic memory"—meaning your general world knowledge, for facts, ideas, concepts—is similarly selective. What you remember is based on what else you've previously learned.

Both these types of memory are not only inexorably linked with attention, but also a tightening circle: what we pay attention to is what we remember, and what we remember will influence what we pay attention to—and therefore what *else* we remember.

Why We Have Memory

A friend of mine who has little kids mentioned her concerns about the kinds of memories her kids are making—specifically, the memories they're making about *her.*

She described yelling at her son earlier that day about something small. This was a few months into the COVID-19 quarantine, and everybody's nerves were getting a little frayed.

"I thought, *Oh, I hope he doesn't remember this, out of all the good things we did today,*" she said. "And then I started thinking about it and realized that most of my very specific memories of my own mother from when I was a kid are the negative ones. I remember very vividly the times she was frustrated, or yelled, or when I was in trouble. There's only a handful of them, but I remember them very specifically, every detail. Meanwhile, it's hard to remember any of the good stuff in much detail. And it was mostly good stuff! She spent all day every day taking care of us, setting up art projects, being patient, listening to our stories—and all I remember are negative things? Is that what my kids are going to remember about me—only the bad stuff?"

When I responded, I started with the bad news: Yes, we remember negative information better than positive information. (Although the *good news* is that this bias *does* fade as we age into our sixties.) Our "record button," such as it is, does not record events comprehensively and with veracity—because the purpose of memory is not to allow us to savor the past, but rather to help us *act* in the world *now.* Memory, like attention itself, is a completely biased system that evolved to privilege survival. We are always "subsampling" experiences that are important to our survival—that's why scary or stressful experiences are more prominent.

Memory allows us to learn. It provides stability and continuity. The things that happen to us that are constant or "normal" tend to fade into the background, while the things that are outliers are more privileged—they become more salient in our memory. This feature of memory is once again yoked to attention, which privileges novel and outlier events.

Here's what I told my friend: that her negative memories of childhood stood out was, in fact, a great sign. It meant she'd had a happy, stable childhood. And the same would probably be true for her own children. Yes, they might remember certain episodes more than others. But if the backdrop of their lives is loving and positive, that too is part of their memory—specifically their semantic memory. We cannot remember every single episode—such a function wouldn't serve us.

Which is why we forget.

"Forget About It"

Forgetting is a highly evolved brain feature that we absolutely need in order to function. Just as you'd be overwhelmed without your attention system to filter and select, so it is with memory.

Long-term memory in most healthy individuals has a large capacity, but that also means it's prone to interference: information you remembered *before* messes up your ability to learn new information, while information you're learning *now* can mess up what you learned previously.

During the coronavirus pandemic, for a brief early period, we were told that face masks were unnecessary, and that it was irresponsible to wear them; at the time, it was believed the virus could not be easily passed from one person to the next unless you were in direct contact and that masks could best help medical professionals who were being exposed to severe cases up close. *Masks won't help you, so leave them for the doctors and nurses,* was the directive. But soon after, the Centers for Disease Control and Prevention guidelines quickly changed. Suddenly, we were required to wear masks at all times and it was irresponsible *not* to wear a mask. The old rule,

"Don't wear a mask," needed to be forgotten so that the new rule, "Always wear a mask," could be remembered.

Even remembering every single joyful moment in your life would be overwhelming—we need to filter and select with memory, just as with attention.

Forgetting is a good thing. It's a feature, not a flaw in our biological makeup. We need it—we rely on it, just as we rely on other "features" of memory, like negative experiences' becoming more salient, for survival, learning, and decision making. Another reason we *have* memory is for learning—for guiding us in how to act in the present moment and in the future. For that to work, it's every bit as important that we forget as it is that we remember. The mind works the way it does for good reason—we wouldn't want to fundamentally change any of these "features" of memory. And yet there are vulnerabilities within the system, and we do run into certain issues because of them.

A Picture Is Worth Very Few Words . . . Memory and Attention

Let's come back to your camera roll. When you opened it at the beginning of this chapter, did you happen to notice how many photos were in there? I just looked at mine: there are *thousands*.

We photograph and record information that's important to us because we know how shaky memory can be and we want to remember it. Ironically, it's often that very act of preservation that prevents us from doing just that.

A 2018 social media study set out to investigate an important question: Does documenting an event influence how you experience it? In the study, researchers designed a series of situations where people would be evaluated on their enjoyment of and engagement in an experience right in the moment, as well as their memory of it later. Participants were assigned to one of three groups: some were asked to document the experience for social media sharing, others were asked to document it simply for themselves, and the final group was asked to make no documentation whatsoever. One of the experiences was watching a TED talk, and another was a self-guided tour of Stanford University's Memorial Church in Palo Alto.

On the topic of enjoyment and engagement, the results were mixed. In some situations, participants seemed to really enjoy the experience of curating content for others to consume, viewing it as a source of connection and community, so it added to their enjoyment of the experience. Meanwhile, others worried about how their post would be perceived, or compared themselves to others on social media, detracting from their enjoyment. On the subject of *memory*, the results were consistent and clear: people who were asked to photograph events—either for others on social media, or just for themselves—were much worse at remembering details of those events later.

Why? First, documenting something requires multitasking—which, as we know, is actually *task switching*. You're not taking a picture *and* experiencing what you're photographing. You're taking the picture *or*. It's always a choice. When you're engaged in the task of taking the picture, you cannot simultaneously be focused on the activity you're documenting. This is as true if you're on vacation someplace gorgeous taking a picture (will you remember that sunset?) as it is in a classroom or conference room: studies have found that media use in the classroom (like using only a laptop to take notes) is linked with a decrease in academic success. This is partly because students get tempted to go online (their chat threads and shopping carts end up full, while their minds stay empty of much of the lecture-related content) but also because of the second reason: even when we *are* actually "paying attention" to what we're documenting, the way we use these devices affects how we process, and therefore remember, these experiences.

In the case of laptops in classrooms, even when students were dutifully typing out notes, they became a kind of typing robot, transcribing like Siri. The problem is, they weren't *synthesizing* that information. One of the things we do naturally when we take handwritten notes is synthesize—we pay attention while listening, then analyze what was said to pull out or summarize the most important points. We have to: we simply can't write fast enough to transcribe every word we hear, so we have to be strategic. And when we do this kind of synthesis, we're better able to encode that information in a richer, fuller, more integrated, and consequently more long-lasting way. Note-taking on laptops ends up being a great way to get a good transcription of a lecture into your computer, but a really bad way to get any of that lecture content into your long-term memory.

Using digital devices like phones and laptops to record what we most want to remember ends up having the *opposite* effect. The social media study's authors concluded that using media hinders us from later recalling the very events we are trying to preserve—because it gets in the way of really experiencing the event in the first place. We end up with a photo of something we can't actually remember, or a transcript of a lecture we didn't really "attend."

Nobody wants to be told to "put down your phone." Yet the study results were clear: people who documented their experiences remembered a lot less. It's simple, and there's no magical way around it: if an experience doesn't get on your mental whiteboard—where it can be organized and synthesized, where the elements of the experience can be integrated together—it doesn't go into long-term memory. It doesn't even stand a chance.

The Portal to Long-Term Memory

When I was an undergraduate, I learned about a famous patient in neuroscience history, known in the textbooks by the initials "H. M." In 1953, H. M. received an experimental brain surgery to treat his epilepsy. He'd been having seizures since he was ten years old, and by twenty-seven, they were so constant and debilitating that he couldn't work. His doctors had tried higher and higher doses of anticonvulsants, but nothing was working, so they took a drastic step: they removed most of H. M.'s temporal lobes, where the epileptic "storms" were happening, in an experimental procedure called a *bilateral medial-temporal lobectomy.* The surgery was a success—H. M.'s epileptic episodes declined dramatically. But the temporal lobes contain multiple brain structures involved in long-term memory. How much would the surgery affect H. M.'s memory?

As it turned out, H. M. retained all his long-term memories right up to a few years before the surgery. His working memory also appeared unscathed—in lab tests, he could hold number sequences in mind for as long as he kept his focus on them, just like any of us. When researchers distracted him, however, to briefly divert his attention away from whatever he was holding in working memory, it vanished—forever.

My teaching assistant had actually worked in the very lab that ran studies on H. M.'s memory function. One night, she was at the lab working with H. M. and had been given the errand of driving him home, back to his apartment at an assisted living facility. They were in the car, chatting, when she realized that she had no idea where he lived. H. M. began to confidently guide her, and so she followed each instruction as he successfully directed her to his home . . . his *childhood* home, on the other side of town.

Until he died in 2008, H. M. was the subject of decades of studies on memory and memory formation. Researchers found that his early memories from before the surgery were exquisitely vivid, possibly because there were no new memories being formed to compete with them. But study after study confirmed that he *only* had access to working memory—no new long-term memories (for episodes or new facts) could be created. What H. M. had lost in the bilateral medial-temporal lobectomy that cured his epilepsy was the *connection* between working memory and long-term memory. H. M. could *briefly* hold content on his whiteboard, just like anyone, but had no capacity to remember it in a more enduring way.

Your working memory is not only your cognitive "scratch space" where you do your creative thinking, ideation, focusing, and goal pursuit. It's also the portal into (and out of!) long-term memory. The stuff you want to remember gets *into* your long-term memory through working memory, and when we retrieve information *from* long-term memory, working memory is where it appears. To "remember" is in fact *both* of these functions—*encode* and *retrieve*—packed together: you encode something, and then fish it back up later. Each of these processes requires the effective use of *both* your attention *and* your working memory. And as we know, we encounter myriad opportunities for those systems to fail, get captured by something salient, lose track of the goal, go blank, or become distracted by competing information.

Problems Getting In: Failure to Encode

My mother-in-law called me recently, slightly panicked about her memory. As she has been getting older, lapses in her attention now upset her more—they could be indicators of a bigger problem, she believes, and that makes her nervous. I asked her to tell me exactly what happened.

She recounted her shopping trip the day before. She was driving to the supermarket. Halfway there she realized she'd forgotten her list, so she started running over everything she was intending to buy in her mind. She parked at the supermarket, got out of the car, and made a mental note about where she parked. She went in, bought her groceries, and pushed the cart back to her car. But as she was loading the groceries into the trunk, she noticed a scrape on the paint. She felt a rush of irritation at herself. When on earth had she sideswiped something? She hadn't even noticed!

She returned her cart, worrying about the scrape, and got in the driver's seat—only to realize that this car had a manual transmission. Hers was an automatic.

She was in the wrong car.

She located her own car—an identical model and color, without the scrape on the paint—just a couple of spots down in the same row, and sheepishly moved all her groceries. We both laughed together as she told me the story—to have gotten all the way into some stranger's car! I explained to her that I didn't think it was a problem with her memory—or, in fact, anything to do with the aging brain. Yes, our brains *do* age along with the rest of us. Parts of the brain get thinner and less dense, including the hippocampus and other medial-temporal lobe structures that we need to form explicit memories. And this can indeed cause memory issues. But in this episode, her whiteboard had simply been overloaded. As she was parking, she was rehearsing her forgotten list. She *thought* she was noting where she parked, but actually she was holding a ton of stuff on her whiteboard. She simply didn't have room.

A lot of the issues we see around memory and aging are actually misattributed. The problem is not "you're losing your memory." Rather, the problem is "you weren't paying attention and failed to encode."

A caveat to this story: where you parked your car isn't something you'd ever really want to remember long-term. In fact, this is an example of one of those times when you want to be able to forget—imagine if you could remember every single place you ever parked and had to sift through all the locations every time you walked out the sliding doors of a grocery store. Like attention, memory *must* serve as a filter, selecting what's relevant and what's not, what should be highlighted, and what should be dumped. I use this story simply as an example of how holding a lot in your working memory can get in the way of *anything* making its way into long-term memory in any kind of effective way.

And further: if your working memory is overloaded, knowledge from long-term memory can't always get *out* when you need it. This was the cause of one of the deadliest "friendly fire" incidents in recent US history.

Problems Getting Out: Failure to Retrieve

It was 2002, the height of the war in Afghanistan, and an American soldier was using a GPS system to guide a two-thousand-pound bomb to its intended target, an insurgent outpost. In this system, the soldier on the ground would input the coordinates for the airstrike into the handheld GPS device, and then the bomb would drop to hit that precise location. Before carrying out the strike, however, the soldier noticed that the batteries in the handheld GPS were low, so he switched them out for new ones. Then he sent the displayed coordinates to drop the bomb—which landed on his own battalion.

What happened? In that GPS system, when the batteries are replaced, the rebooted system defaults to displaying the coordinates of its own location. The soldier operating the system *knew* this—he'd been trained extensively on the procedures. After you change out batteries, you have to re-input the drop coordinates. This knowledge was in his long-term memory; he'd rehearsed it many times. But for some reason, it didn't "load" onto his whiteboard when he needed it. He looked at the faulty coordinates and sent them. A lot of people died that day. And it was because of a problem between one soldier's long-term and working memory. I can only guess at the explanation, but it may be a tragically simple one: if working memory is overwhelmed by stress-induced mind-wandering, then knowledge may not surface when it's most urgently needed.

This is an extreme example, but any of us can experience breakdowns like these during processes of memory encoding and retrieval. Multiple steps are required in the process of encoding and retrieving memories, and all of them require your attention *and* your working memory.

How to Make a Memory

To *remember*, you do three critical things. The first: *rehearsal.* You trace over information—the name you just heard as a new colleague introduced herself; the most important facts from the work training you're in; the details of a good experience you just had. In school, when you studied with flashcards, that was rehearsal; when you go over the nuances of a joyful moment (your child's wedding—the toasts, the taste of the cake), that too is rehearsal; when you find yourself reliving a painful or embarrassing moment, even that (unfortunately) also becomes rehearsal.

Then: *elaboration.* Similar to rehearsal, this involves relating new experiences or facts to knowledge or memories you already have. You can store a much stronger memory for things when you already have a base of knowledge. Example: picture an octopus. Now I tell you: *An octopus has three hearts.* If you didn't already know that, you are—right now as you read this—*tethering* that new knowledge to that existing image you have of an octopus. The next time you see one in an aquarium or in a nature show on TV, you might suddenly remember, turn to your companion, and say, *Did you know that an octopus has three hearts?*

And finally: *consolidation.* This is what happens *as you're performing* the above two functions, and it ultimately leads to the memory being *stored.* As the brain replays information, it's laying down new neural pathways and then going over them, strengthening those new connections. This is, essentially, how information gets from working memory into long-term memory: the brain *structurally changes* to solidify a particular neural representation—and it needs time for unconstrained, spontaneous thought to do that. That's why we think that mental downtime and sleep are both important: they're opportunities for *memory consolidation.* It's also part of the reason we experience mind-wandering—one thing that can fuel that mental roaming about is neural activity related to replaying experiences we've had. With more replays, all the noise fades away and the clear signal remains, which is what comprises the memory trace in the brain. If your attention is constantly engaged, with zero mental downtime for you to experience the emergence of conscious spontaneous thought, you may be degrading the link between working memory and long-term memory. You're disabling vital consolidation processes.

The process of remembering—already subject to your framing, biases, experience, and previous knowledge—is fragile and easily disrupted. It gets derailed when your attention is hijacked away. When something other than what you want to remember takes over your working memory, the memory-making process is interrupted. And ironically, that "something" is often long-term memory itself.

The "Raw Material" for Mind-Wandering

Memory can fail if, during the process of encoding, attention does exactly what it often does: *wanders*. When it's grabbed by some salient thing. When it strays back to the hot topics and preoccupations that have become *conflict states*. Those attention-grabbing thoughts have as their raw materials long-term memory traces. These are concepts and experiences that can be reconfigured in new ways to create a new worry or they may comprise existing memories that are already fully formed. They become the content for mind-wandering.

When I spoke earlier about *mental time travel*, what I meant was: you've been hijacked by content created by your own mind, using the raw materials from your long-term memory. This content can interfere with your ability to pay attention to what is taking place in the actual moment. And this makes it difficult for you to form new memories of your current experience.

Remember the *default mode network*—the brain network seen in study after study of mind-wandering? It turns out that this network is made up of smaller subnetworks. One of these subnetworks has nodes comprising the medial-temporal long-term memory system we've been talking about. I think of this subnetwork like a *thought pump*. It pumps out content like memory traces and other mental chatter generated by raw memory input. It does this even without our conscious awareness.

And sometimes, this pump spits out salient information that grabs our attentional flashlight. It's no different than the pull on our flashlight when threatening, novel, shiny, or self-related stimuli happens in our external environment. In fact, a second subnetwork of the default mode network functions like a flashlight for the inner landscape— sometimes this is called the "core default mode network." This term seems appropriate, given that self-relatedness is at the *core* of what grabs our attention by default.

Salient in your inner landscape are things that are:

- *Self-related*

- *Emotional*

- *Threatening*

- *Novel*

Not only will these things grab your attention—they may also *keep* your attention, filling your working memory with this content to further elaborate on. Unlike some attentional captures that grab you and let go quickly, salient content from the "thought pump" tends to really suck you in. It becomes the gateway for the loop of doom. And it informs other types of mind-wandering too—it's your past experiences that you use to decide what you should worry about and plan for.

The great irony of long-term memory is that it supplies the raw materials for what may pull you away from forming *new* memories.

Eric Schoomaker was serving as Surgeon General of the US Army when his father died suddenly. It was completely unexpected—he was healthy and vibrant, so nobody saw it coming. It also came at a furiously busy time in Eric's career.

Two years later, in the middle of dinner, he looked up at his wife and said, "Dad died."

She stared at him. "Yes," she said. "*Two years ago.*" And he replied, "Well, I guess the tape finally caught up."

We know by now that we need to *stay in play.* One of the reasons is that for the most part, you can only "record" in play-mode. The memory-making process begins in the present moment. Yes, there's work that your brain does after that to make a memory a memory—but it starts with the raw input (from either the environment or your own mind) that you get from the *now*. You can't do it later or put it off. *Now* is the only time you can record.

We have so much to think about: past events to process; future events to plan for and anticipate. Our time is so precious, so valuable, so often slipping through our fingers like sand. We can be in the middle of something that we need or want to remember, and we think, *I'll come back to this later. I'll think about it later. I'll remember it later. . . .* But attention can't be saved. *You have to use it now.* And when you realize that, it changes the way you orient to experiences—and the way you remember them.

If you feel that you can't participate in shared memories (like Richard from the Army Institute of Research did), or if you feel out of step with the events in your life (like Eric Schoomaker did, experiencing the "lag" in his tape), it may be an *embodied* attention problem. Our memories are strongly tied to our senses. So, one way to boost our chances of remembering the things we care about is to use mindfulness training to root ourselves *in the body.*

Remember Better

Our memories for experiences, or episodic memory, involve vivid contextual details—sensory details like sounds and smells, how we felt, and what thoughts we had in the moment. Episodic memory has a highly specific state of consciousness associated with it, called *autonoetic consciousness.* This term describes the embodied fullness—the richness, the detail, the three-dimensional depth—we have when we recall an episode from our lives with self-awareness. Try it out now: think of a specific favorite childhood memory. Maybe it's a memory of getting ice cream with your grandmother on a hot summer day, or washing your family car with your siblings. Autonoetic consciousness is that feeling of having experienced the event from the inside. You might remember the tastes, sounds, smells, expressions on others' faces. You might remember feeling joy or happiness. And recalling it may actually produce a small jolt of joy right now.

How we remember episodic memory also gives us a clue as to *how to encode* episodic memory. For more detail and richness, we fill up our whiteboards with all those granular elements.

Your working memory is a great tool for memory, and also a major point of vulnerability—if it's occupied with other content besides the experience you want to encode or the information you're trying to learn, there won't be effective memory-making. Simply being physically present for something doesn't mean you'll absorb it. You need to intentionally place your focus (flashlight) on what you want to encode. And further: you need to make sure both your mind *and body* show up for the stuff you want to remember.

In our next core practice, you'll anchor yourself in your physical sensations. You may begin to notice discomfort, or even pain. It might be a breeze on your skin or an itch on your forehead. It might be hunger. It might even be the complete *absence* of sensation. Regardless of what's there, you place your flashlight on it. Use your flashlight like a searchlight and move it slowly through the body—in doing so, you practice *being in the body* in the present moment. You practice being in the present moment in an *embodied* way.

CORE PRACTICE: BODY SCAN

1. As with the other practices, begin by sitting comfortably, closing your eyes, and finding your flashlight: bring your attention to your breath sensations.

2. But now, we're not going to keep it there, on the breath. We're going to move it through the body. We're going to keep that focus—

that beam of attention—concentrated, though the focus will move, sweeping slowly, like a searchlight through the body.

3. Start by directing your attention to one of your toes. Take note of whatever sensations you notice there. Cold? Warm? Tingling? Tightness in your shoes? Nothing? Notice it, then move on to the other toes, and the other foot.

4. Go slowly! If you're trying this for three minutes, as with the last exercise, think of your body in thirds and take about a minute with each section. Gradually move your attention up from your lower body—your lower legs and then your upper legs—to your core: the pelvic area, lower torso, upper torso; to your upper body: your shoulders, upper arms, lower arms, and hands. Then finally move attention up to your neck, your face, the back of your head, and finally the top of your head.

5. Pay attention to each sensation—or lack of sensation—rising and falling away, moment by moment, but don't fixate on it. Move the flashlight along.

6. Throughout this practice, as you are moving your attention slowly up your body, whenever your mind wanders simply return it to the area of the body where your attention was directed before the mind-wandering occurred, then continue.

As you do this "searchlight sweep" you'll also start to see how stress, worries, and emotions are showing up in the body. You can start to observe your own emotions, and how they show up there. If it starts to feel difficult, like you're having trouble holding focus through this practice, you can always default to the *Find Your Flashlight* practice on page 117 as an anchor. That's your foundation. It's a good landing pad if you feel as if you're getting off-track by having a moving target as you guide your attention through the body. But once you've stabilized the flashlight back on your breath, resume the body sweep if you can. This practice is perhaps better tailored to memory-making because it roots you not only in the present moment, but also *in the body*.

When you train your mind to pay attention in this way, you are setting yourself up to acquire and retain more and better data. You are able to encode experiences more richly. You can learn new information more thoroughly. You might not be able to remember *everything*, but you can certainly remember better.

For Better Memory, Live Mindfully

My daughter is a dancer. I was annoyed the first time I went to one of her recitals and discovered their hard and fast rule: *no video or photography.* I put my phone back in my purse, a little upset that I wouldn't be able to record Sophie's performance for posterity. Then, as I sat there watching her on stage, illuminated in the spotlight, I felt my attention begin to focus and intensify. I mentally zoomed in on her. I remember trying my best to *feel* her dance. To notice the way she moved, the soft thumping sounds of her feet on the stage coming through under the music, the tight look on her face when she began and the satisfied look when she finished, knowing she'd done well. The fullness of the experience felt really good to me. In that instance, I simply had no choice but to fully pay attention. And my memory of that recital is still vivid.

At the beginning of this chapter, we looked at how using devices like phones and laptops to preserve stuff we want to remember can massively backfire, making it *less* likely that we'll remember what we most want to. So, do you need to put down the phone?

Not necessarily. Another study involving participants taking photographs of artwork in a museum initially found the same as the one we discussed earlier: photographing the artwork left people remembering less. As before, when they "offloaded" into the camera, they also forgot the content. But here there was a twist. They were then asked to use the camera's ability to zoom in on a particular segment of a painting as they photographed it. In that instance, their ability to recall details of the experience rocketed back up. The simple act of zooming in—deciding what to focus on and then doing it—allowed people to remember more depth and detail of the experience.

I'm not saying that you shouldn't photograph things that are important to you. But the next time you do take out your phone to capture something you want to remember, take a minute. Take in the scene outside the rectangle of the phone. Hold in your mind what you really want to remember. Notice the details, the sights and smells and colors; notice your own emotions. What you're doing is maximizing and integrating the elements of the experience in your working memory in order to encode the fullness of the experience. Imagine viewing a scene in color instead of in black and white, or in 3D instead of 2D. Mindfulness exercises help train your attention to be more fully in the moment as it's happening—which can add that fullness to your episodic memories.

You don't need to make every photograph you take a huge exercise in mindfulness—sometimes a photo can just be a photo! But it's very easy to live our lives behind these devices and to create a stream of digital memories without making *actual* memories. And combating this need not be a time-intensive process. Simply taking a moment to mindfully notice and to fully experience events or surroundings could make a big difference in our ability to remember them. When there's something you really want to remember, *zoom in*.

And finally: if you want to remember the things you experience and the things you learn, you need to allow for the free flow of spontaneous thought. If your days are all engagement, all the time, you're skipping a critical step we discussed earlier: opportunities for *consolidation.*

At the grocery store, you fill your cart and head to the checkout. Bummer—there's a long line at every station. You get in the shortest line and pull out your phone. There's a work email and a personal one—you read both, then start drafting a response to the work one with your thumb. A notification pings and you click it; the email draft autosaves and you swipe over to Twitter, where someone in your field has replied to something you posted earlier. You want to be supportive, so you click the heart and retweet, then scroll—a news article about climate change catches your eye and you tap it. You're halfway through skimming the article when the checker announces your total, loading plastic bags into your cart—the eco-friendly canvas bags you brought are still tucked under your arm.

Sound familiar? I know it does to me. We live busy lives. The urge to pack as much as possible into every pocket of time is intense. If I didn't draft that work email while standing in line, I'd have had to do it later, in the lab, when I could have been doing . . . something else.

It often seems necessary to use our time in this way—we think of time as a commodity; it has a price, and it's generally quite valuable. We don't want to waste it. And we don't see mental downtime, when we purposefully disengage from finding, gripping, and tightly pointing our attentional flashlight to some urgent and occupying task, as a valuable thing to do. But that's only because most of us don't realize how critically necessary it is. Ever had a great idea in the shower? It's not because the scent of your shampoo is oh, so inspiring— the shower is forced mental downtime. You can't take your phone in there, or your laptop, or a book. You're trapped in a small, wet box with nothing in particular demanding your attention. It can become a creative, generative time where you make connections, or have ideas, or maybe sink into daydreams that actually have the vital function of assisting in memory formation and solidifying learning.

We need white space in order to reflect on what we hear and experience. For those in leadership roles, this can feel like a challenge, but also a chance to do something innovative. Memory-making and learning are benefits of mindfulness training, yes, but you need both: to be *mentally present in the moment*, and then to have *space to let the mind roam free, unconstrained by any task or demand.*

Is the answer to take more showers? Well, sure, if you can spare the time and water! But now that you know, you can create micro-moments and even *nano*-moments for unconstrained spontaneous thought throughout the day. Try this: Leave your phone in your pocket or purse. If you are up for it, leave it hidden in the car. At work, walking from one meeting to the next, feel your feet walking and let whatever comes to mind come and go. Remind yourself that these unconstrained mind moments are valuable—more valuable than filling every second with tasks.

What to Remember About Remembering . . .

We fail to remember when we fail to *notice* what our attention is up to. We don't bring our attention into the present moment. We forget to point our flashlight. We don't keep that selection in working memory long enough—we get hijacked away by distraction in the outer landscape or the inner one. We privilege all engagement, all the time.

Mindfulness practice as attention training allows us to notice when we are no longer *in* the moment we want to remember. We now have a choice, and we can choose to intervene. To notice when highly salient, highly "sticky" content is circulating in working memory, and to intervene by coming back to the present moment in an embodied way. This can be especially important when we encounter a particularly potent "loop of doom" with memories that are really damaging or upsetting—as with trauma.

Traumatic memories can feel indelibly written, as if etched into metal. Are they unique? Like many important topics, this one is under active debate. What we do know is that trauma leads to: reexperiencing the stressful event, avoiding reminders of the trauma, and over-activating the alerting system. These symptoms lessen and resolve over time. But when they don't and people continue to suffer, it becomes a clinical disorder—*post-traumatic stress disorder* (PTSD). There is growing evidence that clinical treatments involving mindfulness can help PTSD patients. And here I want to bring up an important caveat: self-guided *mindfulness training is NOT a replacement for a clinical treatment*. Trauma can be extremely complicated, and people experiencing clinical levels of PTSD should seek treatment by a competent therapist.

I'm not a clinician—I'm a neuroscientist and a researcher—so I don't treat PTSD. But a lot of us have experienced trauma, or have upsetting memories or thoughts that can become intrusive or distracting, even without a diagnosis of PTSD. In my opinion, it's pretty hard to go through life without accumulating some of those. And we all need tools to deal with that. A big part of that is knowing when, and *how*, to address the stuff that's coming up repeatedly on your whiteboard. We've practiced noticing the *types* of mental content that can arise (thoughts, feelings, sensations), and then letting them pass away instead of engaging with them. This skill can certainly help you with intrusive, upsetting memories. And in the coming chapters, we'll be adding more practices to our toolkit.

Certain things may become "sticky" on our whiteboards because of *generalization*. We can make generalizations about the behavior and intentions of others ("She never supports me") or regarding ourselves

("I will never amount to anything"). An incident where you made a mistake becomes "I always get this stuff wrong—I'm such an idiot!" It's not the incident itself that takes center stage on your whiteboard: it's the generalization you derived from it. The oversimplified packaging allows it to remain in working memory with minimal effort: it's short, it's clear, and it probably isn't accurate.

The generalizations we come up with can be helpful because they efficiently condense information we need to remember. Yet generalizations can be harmful when they're wrong, and whenever you're dealing with complex emotional states they *are* often wrong, or at least form only part of the picture. This becomes critical when we use the raw materials from our long-term memory for *simulations*, which we do all day, every day, every minute we're awake.

Your mind is an incredible virtual-reality machine—the best there is. It can create entire worlds by drawing on your memory and knowledge, worlds full of sights and sounds and even emotions both experienced and imagined. You create simulations all the time—and you need to. It's how you plan and strategize and innovate: You imagine the future. You spool out various possibilities. Our knowledge and experiences are what allow us to forecast events in the future, to be prepared and high-performing.

The problem we run into is that these detailed simulations that we create are by necessity—like all virtual reality—incredibly transportive stories spooled by our own minds. They grab our attention and then *keep us there*. So, what happens when our stories turn out to be just . . . *wrong*?

7

DROP THE STORY

Afghanistan, 2004. Walt Piatt, then a lieutenant colonel, and his unit received intel that a large group of Taliban fighters had amassed on a nearby mountain. This was a group they'd been tracking for months. They had received imagery of the site; they'd visualized the camp and everything checked out. It was the insurgent encampment. Piatt had already been given approval to bomb; the planes were in position. All parties had intelligence from the top levels that this was *it*. All he had to do was give the okay, and the camp would be obliterated.

Piatt and his soldiers, though, were already on the mountain. They were close enough to be able to hike up. It would be a tough climb— the camp was at eleven thousand feet, and it was starting to snow. But Piatt felt strongly that someone in the vicinity should get a good physical look at the camp. So on that cold morning, with whipping snow filling the air, a team of scouts headed further up, looking for final confirmation that this indeed was the Taliban cell.

As the team of scouts ascended, Piatt was getting messages from his leadership reminding him over and over that he had authority to engage—that the scouts weren't necessary. But he waited. Finally, the radio clicked on and the lead scout called in to report. His team was close enough to see for themselves that everything checked out: encampment, tents, a young bearded man circling the camp, obviously standing guard. Then another guy, walking along with him: a pair of patrols.

"So that was it—game on," Piatt recalls. "We had a camp, a couple of guards—it all confirmed what we already knew."

Piatt was about to launch the ground assault when the scout's voice came over the radio again.

"Wait a minute, wait a minute," he said. "I don't see a weapon on this guy. Repeat. *No weapons!*"

There was a moment of frozen silence.

"We're so close," the soldier said. "We can just tackle them!"

The soldiers rushed out of the snowy fog and took the guys to the ground. The rest of the patrol came in behind them with their weapons drawn, ready for a deluge of Taliban fighters to come swarming out of the tents. Instead: a very aggravated, tall, and imposing woman burst out of one of the tents, shouting. They couldn't understand her, but the gist was: *Let go of my men!*

The intel had been wrong. The "insurgent encampment" was in fact the winter camp of a Bedouin tribe. The tents were filled with families. They had been making their way to this land for centuries, to let their animals graze. They had absolutely no affiliation with the Taliban.

In this situation, what we call "confirmation bias" could have killed a whole tribe of people. Confirmation bias is common—it happens when people essentially "see what they expect to see," discounting any information that doesn't line up with their expectation. The team of soldiers sent up the mountain expected to see a Taliban camp, so at first, that's what they "saw." It took only one person who was able to see things clearly to avert disaster.

Walt Piatt thought about that day on the mountain for years after it happened. He reflected on what a valuable skill it was to be able to quickly and flexibly drop expectations, and instead to see what was *really happening* right in front of you. It wasn't something that typical military training covered—and that struck him as a big problem. He wondered: What gave *that* soldier the ability to see the scene so accurately, when everyone around him was viewing it through a biased lens? And was there any way to train other service members to acquire that ability?

The Power of a Story

One of the motivating reasons I wanted to work with military service members was exactly that: I wanted to know if we could help them not only to *pay attention* better, but also to be more discerning and *situationally aware*. Situational awareness—the mental state of constantly knowing what's going on around you—is critical for people in a variety of professions, including police and first responders. Could mindfulness training, I wondered, help soldiers (or anyone) come into situations less susceptible to biased thinking so they could see more clearly, be less reactive, and respond appropriately and proportionately?

Our prediction was *yes*, because of how mindfulness practice guides you to use your attention: in the present moment, without judgment, elaboration, or reactivity. In other words: *without making up a story about what you're experiencing.*

Sometimes a story is given to us and we quickly accept it—like the soldiers and the expected insurgent camp. Other times we arrive at the story ourselves, through our own mental simulation. We are incessantly concocting narratives about what might happen in an hour, or tomorrow, or about what others are thinking or feeling, or about their motivations. We visualize options and courses of action. We imagine how events might play out so that we can be more prepared;

we troubleshoot various possibilities: *If she says x, should I reply y or z? If that road is closed, what detour will I take? If the schools reopen while COVID cases are still high and new variants are emerging, will we send our kids?* To visualize the possible answers to such questions, you create a whole world in your mind, with sensory details, characters, plot lines, and sometimes even dialogue. You experience emotions in response to this world you've created—it makes you feel sad, or anxious, or satisfied—and those feelings help you make decisions about what you may choose to do next.

We use simulations to arrive at *mental models* that guide our thinking, decision making, and actions. This is really what I mean when I say "story." You come up with these mental models, or "stories," rapidly and constantly—you simulate, arrive at one, then use it and move on; or you receive new information that causes you to update or dump that story and simulate a different one. The key ingredients for your simulations? Memories of episodes you have experienced in your life, fragments of these memories, plus everything else you have learned and remember. Add to the mix your capacity to think, reason, and forecast, and voilà—a freshly simulated new story!

The simulation process is vivid, detail-rich, and captivating, and the mental model requires our attention and working memory to come alive. But it also puts heavy demands on these limited capacity systems. That's part of the reason stories are so powerful: they can become a kind of "shorthand" for efficiently framing and maintaining a situation, problem, or plan in mind—and this efficiency helps free up cognitive resources to do other things. But (there's always a *but*) stories also constrain information processing. They *capture and keep* our attention locked onto a subset of data. Now our perceptions, our thinking, even our decisions are constrained. So when the story you come up with is *wrong*, then your actions and decisions after that can skew wrong, too—*because of the way the story interacts with attention.*

Remember that famous experiment with the dancing gorilla that I described to you earlier in this book? To refresh your memory: There are two teams on a basketball court, one dressed in black T-shirts and the other in white, and study participants are asked to count the number of passes that occur between players on the white-shirted team. In the middle of the "game," a guy dressed as a gorilla walks through the scene, does a little dance, and then strolls off. And the people counting passes *completely miss it*. Why? Because they were asked to watch the white-shirted players, they (very appropriately and skillfully!) screened out everything dark—including that gorilla.

I presented that study to you to highlight the incredible *power* of attention, and it certainly does. But it also highlights a potentially catastrophic weak spot. The people in the study had a clear-cut, simple mission: *filter out the color black, focus on the color white*. Yet in a real-life situation, we usually don't know ahead of time what we should focus on and what we should filter out. And in a real-life situation, the stakes for "missing the gorilla" can be a lot higher.

Why It's So Hard to Drop the Story

The mind's job when it's in "simulation mode" is to *transport you*.

Think of things that transport you so that you're completely absorbed in another world and lose track of time: movies, books, video games. What are the qualities of these media? They draw you in because of their compelling narrative, their vivid detail, their rich emotional meaning. The end result of all this is that your attention is transfixed and doesn't waver—that's what a good story does. It's all-consuming. And so is a simulation that you generate in your own mind. Your mind is a *great* simulator. It's capable of that exact type of intensive, immersive, *all-consuming* story creation.

Our own minds are wildly versatile simulation generators: we can create "movies" on the screen of our whiteboards, reliving past experiences, predicting future ones, and more. Our simulations give us the capacity to *relive* and *pre-live*. We believe this is a unique capacity of the human mind—this ability to "try out" multiple different possibilities and time lines, to imagine scenarios before we enter into them. You don't have to drive five different routes to figure out which is the best one: you simulate them mentally and then choose one and drive it, based on expected traffic congestion and maybe even the scenery. The ability to produce—in vivid detail—an imagined future based on our past experiences and knowledge is incredibly useful and powerful. This is a desirable *feature* of the brain—not a flaw. You would not ever want to be without it.

Simulations allow us to:

• try out various options;

• project ourselves into the past, the future, or even into other people's minds; and

• create vivid versions of reality that guide decision making.

Let's look at that last one. Over the past week, how many times have you imagined a potential outcome, just to see how you might feel about it? An outdated (yet still common) view is that feelings are a nuisance—a distraction that gets in the way of logical and efficient decision making. In fact, having an emotional reaction *during* the decision-making process is indispensable. Without emotion, we'd be left floundering. Emotion is how the brain determines the value of something (say, an event or a choice). If you choose A over B, do you feel: angry, happy, disgusted, sad, fearful? Your simulation—and the feelings that arise—allows you to come to a decision.

In the lead-up to the 2020 US presidential election, voters across the entire country were likely simulating what it would feel like to have a particular candidate win. And our simulations continued as the votes slowly came in, as projections shifted, as social media opined, and as lawsuits were filed. Simulations can be powerful not only in guiding decision making, but also in helping us emotionally prepare to accept particular outcomes.

Your brain is quite possibly the best, most robust "virtual-reality" machine there is. We can create entire worlds. We can project ourselves through time and geography and into the minds of others. We need this capacity for everything we are able to successfully do as humans: for imagining, for strategizing and planning, for decision making and problem solving, for innovating and creating, for connecting, and much more.

The problem? Our virtual-reality capabilities are a double-edged sword: our simulations can be *too good*.

To have your simulation inform your eventual decisions, plans, and actions, you need to feel as if you are there—to really see, hear, and feel it. To this end, the brain mobilizes its powers of perception, conceptualization, elaboration, and narration to create the most vivid, detailed, and realistic world that it can. And "vivid" in the internal landscape of your mind is the same as "salient" in the external landscape: think of it as *very loud*. It grabs your attention and holds it. Your flashlight snaps to it without any effort at all.

Remember *perceptual decoupling*? We talked about this earlier in the book when I introduced mind-wandering. When you're mind-wandering, you sort of "unhook" from your actual immediate environment. Well, that's exactly what happens when you have a simulation running. The simulation is salient and loud; everything else gets dimmed down. Sensory input becomes degraded and inconsistent; this effect gets even worse when we're dealing with stress, threat, poor mood, or fatigue. When you're deep in a simulation (aka "deep in thought"), someone could be calling your name and you would not hear them. Even *touch* may become dulled.

Our simulations are so effective that we get immersed and *fused with them*, and *persuaded by them*. Studies on the impact of advertising have shown that *vividness* is what grabs people's attention and convinces them to buy. With simulations, we create our own persuasive content. So persuasive, in fact, that our bodies physically respond: When presented with an image of a slice of cake, people's mouths will water; show a smoker a picture of a cigarette and they will experience intense craving. With a stressful memory or a stressful simulation, we'll experience the release of stress hormones. Our minds and bodies begin to believe we are really experiencing the simulated event.

And finally: *we are simulating all the time.*

A Simulation Is Always Running

So far, I've been talking about simulating as something we do on purpose, for active decision making and planning. In fact, you are simulating all the time.

Remember that 50 percent of the time when you're mind-wandering? As we discussed, when your mind wanders, your *default mode network* is activated. The default mode is massively involved in simulation: your attention and working memory are mobilized inward and you begin simulating versions of reality, projecting yourself into the past or future, or even into other people's minds and lives. Much of the time that you're mind-wandering, *you're simulating*.

I was struck by a recent quote I read by the actor Jim Carrey: "Our eyes are not only viewers, but projectors that are running a second story over the picture we see in front of us all the time."

I don't know if Carrey has ever taken a basic neuroscience class, but I'll say this: he's spot on. And therein lies the problem. Our simulations happen even when we don't actively choose to engage in them. They can constrain our information processing in confounding and unhelpful ways, affect our well-being, impair our judgment, and hinder our decision making.

This incessant simulating we do (largely by default) quickly becomes a problem when:

1. *You're simulating "kryptonite."* If you're transporting yourself to a sad, negative, threatening, or stressful scenario (whether remembered or imagined), it's going to lay claim to your attention and working memory bandwidth, make you more error prone, and tank your mood. Repeated simulations of this sort, referred to as *maladaptive repetitive thought*, are considered a "transdiagnostic vulnerability," meaning they are a hallmark of many serious clinical disorders, including depression, anxiety, and PTSD.

2. *Your simulation causes you to make decisions that don't align with your longer-term goals or sense of civility.* You eat the piece of cake even though you've vowed to change your eating habits. You smoke the cigarette when you desperately want to quit. You send a nasty text message accusing and vilifying someone without knowing all the details. You hoard toilet paper and cut in line during a global pandemic. All these outcomes can result from your mind's simulations, compelling you to act.

3. *Your simulations lead you to a mental model that is wholly wrong . . . causing your course of action to skew wrong.* Remember: simulations *constrain perception.* They dampen the information that doesn't align. They literally make the stuff that

isn't consistent with your imagined scenario *harder to see, hear, and feel.* That means that if your simulation is off-base, so will your thinking, your decisions, and your *actions.*

When the Story Is Wrong

My family and I recently traveled to my mom's house to celebrate a milestone birthday with her. On the day of her big birthday party, the house was crowded with longtime family friends, most of them Indian men and women in their sixties and seventies. As the party wore on, my sister and I rushed to replace platters of food and serve drinks. When the time came to serve the cake, I was at a loss—my daughter was nowhere to be found, and my sister was busy cutting and plating the cake while I ran frantically back and forth with two plates, trying to get to all the guests. Finally, I felt a hand on my arm. My husband, Michael, was standing there with our son and my nephew.

"Can we help you?" he asked, looking a little baffled that I hadn't asked already.

I was startled and immediately felt silly: *of course* they could help! They'd been sitting right there, in front of me the entire time. I asked them each to grab some plates and, within minutes, everyone in the room had cake in hand.

Why didn't I think to ask them? I reflected on it later, bothered by my inability in the moment to see the males in the room as helpers. Why had I only thought of my daughter and sister as "servers"?

Because men don't serve food in Indian households!

I was shocked at the sexism in my own mental model. Yet I could not deny that my attention was biased, entirely on the basis of sex. My flashlight was only scanning for females who could help me. It was as if the males were blanked out of my field of view. My actions were then biased, too—with no females in sight, I felt compelled to serve the cake on my own. It took Michael's gentle question for me to snap out of my own story. With the blinders suddenly off, my attention broadened to more easily see additional options on how to maneuver through the situation.

As a woman in the sciences, I'm acutely aware of the casual and constant ways that unnoticed biases can manifest, every day. It's not uncommon for me to receive an email addressed "Sir," or to answer my office phone and be asked "Is Dr. Jha available? When will he be in?" I still hear older relatives refer to seeing a "lady doctor" during a medical appointment.

As I reflect on my own biases, I want to shout, *"But I'm not sexist!"* Yet here's the reality: our mental models rely on our memories and knowledge for their inputs. So if sexism exists in the world, it exists in my lived experience of the world. And this means that it also exists in the memory traces of this lived experience in my brain. Accepting this frees me up in a useful way. I can be on the lookout for sexist influences in my own mental models. And when I see them, knowing that they will bias my attention *and* my behavior, I can intervene. I can build a new, better-informed model.

However, when we're *unaware* of the mental models that are guiding us, we may not be able to pivot away from them. The decisions and actions we make, while perhaps sensible under our model, may be inappropriate in reality and can have consequences for ourselves—as well as for others. The science of bias and attention has clear implications for the training of police and first responders, for physicians, for teachers, for lawyers and judges . . . well, for all of us. We all have a sphere of influence in the world. And we all have deeply seated biases that can show up in mental models, which means we have a responsibility to become more aware of the mental models we each hold.

A flawed mental model can affect us in all kinds of ways—*bias* is a big one, but any time we simulate a certain outcome and can't drop it, we can suffer because of it. If you go into a conversation with someone expecting it to be contentious, that mental model can ensure that you selectively focus on the aspects of the interaction that reinforce that story, and dim down competing information that might have offered a better way forward.

Because mental models are made from fragments of our own knowledge and experience, along with our observations in the moment, they can be *constrained* in ways that can end up being limiting instead of helpful. Making predictions based on what has happened in your past experience can allow you to plan and prepare. Yet things don't always unfold the way they have in the past or even the way you think they will based on information you've been given—like those soldiers going up the mountain in Afghanistan who'd received flawed intel. That day, after the dust settled (literally and metaphorically), Walt Piatt was invited into the tribe leaders' tent to sit with the elders and share some of the hot chai they were pouring. The Army's interpreter didn't speak the tribe's dialect, but they were able to communicate in some basic ways. As he sipped the hot liquid, Piatt looked around the dim room at all the people who would have lost their lives had someone on his team not been able to "drop the story" and allow in the contradictory information: *the man was not carrying a weapon.* Had they mistakenly obliterated the camp, they might never have come to realize their error. They might have carried on, believing the story that they'd successfully bombed a Taliban camp and achieved their mission.

Nuanced, flawed, and incomplete content is often the raw material feeding our simulations, from both long-term memory and the world around us, and the current brain science suggests that we have little to no conscious awareness of it. This is the content that scaffolds what we simulate in the stories we generate. So, what can we do about it? How do we use our incredible virtual-reality powers to imagine, plan, and strategize, without being limited and constrained?

How *do* we "drop the story"?

Unbias Your Mind

You've practiced *finding your flashlight.* That exercise was about identifying where your brain's attentional orienting system is directing its "beam" and then moving it where you want it. You've practiced *watching your whiteboard*, noticing what's occupying your working memory, and *content labeling*, which helps because when you do the work of "categorizing" that mental content, you cease to be lost in it.

The specific skills you've been practicing are already setting you up to "drop the story." And keeping your attention in a mindful mode—that is, in the present moment, *without conceptual elaboration*—increases *situational awareness*: your ability to observe and see clearly what's happening in any given situation you find yourself in. You're not elaborating on what you see or think or feel. You're not analyzing or extrapolating from thoughts or feelings. You're not taking what's happening in one moment and spooling it out into the future, imagining what might happen next, or connecting back to similar situations you've encountered in the past, expecting them to be the same. In this mindful mode, you *don't* try to predict or strategize or analyze—you merely, but mindfully, observe.

You're not simulating.

You may have noticed that there are many books, apps, and entire programs and workshops out in the world dealing with mindfulness. They describe a "mindful mode" as having specific qualities, many of which begin with "non"—as in non-elaborative, nonjudgmental, non-narrative. For many years, I wondered how these qualities hang together. But when we look at what it takes to have vivid, rich simulations, we see how they do. Simulation mode requires default mode activity. Meanwhile, mindfulness reduces default mode activity.

In short: mindfulness becomes an "antidote" to relentless simulation.

Looking at the table below, you might wonder: Why do I want to be in the left-hand column? The right-hand column seems like so much more fun!

My answer to that: It's not that you want to live an entire life where you're always in the "perpetual now"—that's not what I'm advocating. But training the mind to be able to shift into a mindful mode vs. the highly prevalent simulation mode is a necessary safety

"Mindful Mode" vs. "Simulation Mode"

Mindfulness is . . .	Simulations are . . .
Present-centered (*this* moment)	Past- and future-focused (mental time travel)
Direct experience (not imagined)	Imagined, remembered, hypothetical, or projecting into someone else's experience
Embodied, sensory	Conceptual
Curious; no expectations	Planning, expecting, anticipating
Non-elaborative (not associating or "hyperlinking")	Elaborative, associative, conceptually rich
Non-narrative (no story)	Narrative (strong story)
Non-evaluative; nonjudgmental (no assessing of good or bad, nor of other labels)	Emotional evaluation (positive or negative; rewarding or not rewarding)
No (or low) emotional reactivity	High emotional reactivity (immersed)

net—because your mind is so prone to doing everything listed in the right-hand column.

Without intervention, we live our lives almost entirely in simulation mode. We default to it automatically—we do it constantly, effortlessly, and often unwittingly. It's very difficult for us to not simulate, not elaborate, not generate, which is exactly why we need to train for this capacity. We need to be able to shift out of a simulation mode into a mindful one so that we can open our eyes and see what is actually around us vs. the virtual reality of our making. This capacity is becoming more and more essential as our world becomes more unpredictable. In recent years, we've faced unprecedented challenges, from pandemics to politics and many more, and the future holds more uncertainty. We cannot live in simulation mode through this. To be resilient and capable, to preserve our attentional and cognitive powers, we have to be able to access the mindful mode.

Both of the columns in the table will lead you to a mental model, and both have their utility. The difference is, the mental model you arrive at by using the mindful mode, instead of the simulation mode, has a much better chance of being unbiased.

Ultimately, though, the goal is not to rely solely on a single mode all the time. Both modes are valuable. We can gather critical information from both. The goal is to have the capacity to shift into a mindful mode when you need it. We need to be able to toggle—to drop the story, for a few minutes at least, in order to create mental models that are the most accurate depictions of the situation we are in. If we can train ourselves to more quickly and effectively move into a mindful mode, that short break from the simulation mode will then allow us to reenter it with a better idea of which of the many possibilities we can choose from is the best one. So here's a peak mind "cheat sheet" on how to use some of the skills you've already practiced . . . plus a new one.

1. *Know that you will have a story.* No matter the situation, you will arrive at it with some kind of expectation. A story, a plan, a framework, a mental model. Step one is realizing this and noticing it whenever you can. Asking yourself "What story do I have about this?" is a good habit to get into.

2. *Stay in "play."* You've already learned this one—you should be a pro by now! Just kidding—this takes *practice.* But the point is, the skills you are already working on are going to help you here, as well. The more you stay in play and pull your mind back from leaping into predicting mode, or reliving mode, the more agile you'll be when it's time to drop a story and pivot. Just because you've been in a past situation that had 80 percent in common with your current situation isn't a good reason to dismiss that 20 percent of new information.

3. *Remind yourself: thoughts aren't facts!* When we trace over stories in our minds, they become essentially "engraved." This is a lot of what's happening when we ruminate, or "loop"—we're reifying a story. In most situations, consider that any thought, prediction, or other simulation you have is only one of many possibilities— not an immutable fact. The way that you do this is by putting some distance between yourself and the current contents of your mind.

Getting Some Distance

In psychology, as well as in mindfulness practice, we call this practice of stepping *out* of your simulations and mental models "decentering." Decentering emphasizes a perspective in which the experiential "I" is not at the center. From a decentered perspective, it's easier to determine how well our simulations represent reality. They are only a guess—one of many possible mental models. When you can step outside of a constrained mode of thinking, you're able to recognize a story that's not serving you and can drop it quickly and flexibly instead of remaining locked in.

During the spring of 2020, in the early months of the COVID-19 crisis, we ran a study offering mindfulness training to older adults—a particularly at-risk population during the pandemic—specifically to help them manage fear, stress, and loneliness. Going into the study, we wanted to know if people were finding their own thoughts and worries about the pandemic to be disruptive, and if so, at what level.

To answer this, we used a "COVID Intrusion Scale." We asked our participants—fifty-two individuals between the ages of sixty and eighty-five—how often they found themselves thinking about COVID, and when they did, how distressing those thoughts were. Did their thoughts come out of the blue? Were they unwanted? We also asked questions about their mood, their stress level, and their *capacity to decenter*, by which I mean that we probed their ability to *see thoughts and feelings as separate from themselves*. Did they naturally and automatically distance themselves from unwanted or intrusive thoughts? Or were they highly identified (fused) with them? Did they have the capacity to "sit with" unpleasant feelings and let them pass away, or did they get swept into a ruminative loop?

We found that those with *higher* decentering scores reported fewer intrusive thoughts, better mood, sounder sleep, less loneliness, and greater well-being. Their capacity to distance themselves from their mental content—to see their reactions to events and their internal stories as mental content that arises and fades away—benefited them in all these important ways.

Now, these participants weren't guided by us in any way when these data were collected—we hadn't put them through any kind of mindfulness class or instruction. We simply evaluated the mental tendencies they'd walked in the door with. But many other studies that have offered participants specific instructions on how to decenter found the same beneficial effects and more.

In one study, researchers prompted people to call up negative memories from their past—personally experienced events that they could vividly recall. Each memory was assigned a cue word. (If the negative memory had to do with being bullied at school, the cue word might be "bully.") Then, during an fMRI brain scanning session, each participant was shown pairs of words while researchers monitored their brain activity. One was the memory cue word (*bully*) and the other had the *cognitive stance* they were to take toward the memory:

1. *Reexperience:* Simulate the event by immersing yourself in the memory. Relive the event as if seeing it from your own eyes; revisit the thoughts and feelings you had then.

2. *Analyze:* Remember the event and think about all the possible reasons you felt the way you did.

3. *Decenter:* Take a distanced, observational view. Watch the memory unfold from an "audience" perspective. Accept any feelings associated with the memory, letting them arise and pass away.

After each pair of words, participants rated the intensity of their negative mood on a scale of 1 (not at all) to 5 (very negative). Unsurprisingly, they felt the most negative after the *reexperience* instruction, followed by *analyze,* and the least negative after *decenter*—decentering was the most protective of their mood. But interestingly, their reports also corresponded with the fMRI results, specifically with the *amount of activity in the default mode.*

The study showed that decentering *reduced* default mode network activity—the network most involved in mind-wandering and simulation. And it revealed how powerful the impact of how we relate to our memories is on our mood. The interpretation of the brain imaging findings was that people had the least amount of default mode activity and negative mood during decentering because they weren't transporting themselves back through time into the negative memory. *They weren't simulating.*

Weakening the "Pull" of Simulations

I've been asked why I don't emphasize "stress reduction" when I discuss the topic of mindfulness. My answer to that? I study attention, and mindfulness training entered my laboratory's research in our search to find effective cognitive training tools to improve attention. Most of the groups we approach are not primarily interested in reducing stress—that is not their goal. Rather, their goal, like ours, is to strengthen attention and optimize attention-related performance. The great thing, though, is that mindfulness training does both: it reduces stress *and* improves attention. And being able to weaken the pull of simulations by *decentering* is key to achieving both of these benefits.

Some mindfulness exercises emphasize *voluntarily paying attention, noticing mind-wandering,* and *redirecting it as needed* (like the *Find Your Flashlight* practice), while other exercises target the *capacity to decenter* (you'll learn such a practice up ahead). With greater control over the flashlight and awareness of where it is directed, we can catch our mind-wandering more often to get attention back on track. And with greater decentering, we can dial down the strong hold that our mind-wandering episodes have on us, especially for those that are filled with powerful, emotionally charged negative and worry-filled simulations. These are the ones that not only grab us but *hook* us. They capture our attention and keep it there to loop on, as in rumination.

Decentering is a powerful technique because it weakens the hold that mind-wandering episodes can have on our attention. You're able to "drop the story" when it isn't serving you or when it's causing you distress. By unhooking attention in this way, decentering leads to reduced stress and even reduced symptoms of disorders like anxiety and depression.

Decentering On Demand

Over the years, I've had the opportunity to give a lot of lectures. But when I got the request to come and speak at the Pentagon, I was . . . a little daunted.

I prepared meticulously, working on my slides in advance. I made sure I had our most recent science incorporated and fine-tuned the flow from slide to slide. I was ready. I packed up my laptop with the presentation loaded and prepared—backups for everything, just in case—and flew to DC the night before my talk. I arrived, had a nice dinner, and was preparing to turn in for the night so I would be fresh and ready. But when I popped open my laptop to quickly peek at my email and make sure there wasn't anything urgent from the lab, a message grabbed my attention. It was from a colleague, an Army colonel and a professor at the Army War College. I'd sent him my PowerPoint slides the day before, asking if he had any thoughts or advice on how to optimize it for an audience of strategic military leaders. I imagined that if he had the time to take a look at all (given his busy teaching schedule), he might offer a few minor tweaks. But when I opened the email, my stomach sank—he'd run the presentation past a focus group of his students, and there were extensive notes on nearly every slide.

The suggestions were sweeping: *Cut here, elaborate here, they didn't like this, or this . . .* My mind scrambled around, trying to work out how I could possibly make all these changes so last-minute. I was grateful for the time and thoughtfulness of his feedback, but with so little time, I also felt overwhelmed and worried. I could feel the swell of unhelpful and very negative thoughts fill up my mind. *I'm never going to be able to get this done. I'm going to fail!*

I closed the laptop and decided to take five minutes to do a mini-practice. I knew that what I needed to do was zoom out and get a bird's-eye view of the situation. As always, I began by finding my breath. And then:

On-Demand Practice: "Bird's-Eye View"

1. *Get the data.* Observe yourself and the situation at a distance. Get the raw data of what you are experiencing, not an analysis of it.

2. *Replace.* Watch your inner dialogue and distance yourself from it. It helps to replace "I" statements with "you" or your name. Better yet, just notice what is coming up: *Amishi thinks she can't get this done. She's afraid her talk won't go well.*

3. *Remember that thoughts come and go.* As thoughts bubble up, remember that thoughts are merely constructions in your mind; they will appear and they will fade away. I pictured each thought as a bubble, floating away into the sky.

It was only five minutes. But what that mini-practice allowed me to do was *decouple from* the story that I had started narrating, one filled with worry and doubt. I was watching what was on my whiteboard, at a distance. I noticed thoughts, feelings, and bodily sensations arising and passing away without being overtaken by them. I quickly dropped the story and stopped drafting up worst-case scenarios. And seeing myself "in the third person" made me want to encourage Amishi instead of tear her down. I wanted to be supportive of myself, as I would be for a good friend. By the end of the mini-practice, I felt clearer and less reactive. Decentering in this way, for only a few minutes, allowed me to reconnect with my intention: to give my audience a successful learning experience.

And to do so, I needed to reach them, which was exactly what my colleague's feedback would help me do. I returned to the presentation, curious about his suggestions instead of daunted and overwhelmed. As I opened my presentation file, I thought, *In this file, there is useful guidance to help me educate and inform my audience. Let's see what I can learn and apply in the time I have.*

The day after my presentation, I got a text from the same colleague who had provided the feedback on my slides. He'd watched the livestream of my talk. It said: *You nailed it!*

"Don't Believe Everything You Think"

A lot of people whom I work with have an initial resistance to the idea of "dropping the story." They exist in worlds where planning, strategizing, visioning, and imagining next steps is absolutely critical for success. After that talk I presented at the Pentagon, during which I discussed my team's research findings on offering a program called Mindfulness-Based Attention Training (MBAT) to conventional and special operations forces within the US Army, there was a short Q and A session with the audience. When it began, retired Lieutenant General Eric Schoomaker, the 42nd Surgeon General of the Army, raised his hand first.

"Why are you telling us not to engage in narrative?" he asked. "We need to build stories in order to be prepared for the future."

"Absolutely," I replied. "And there is nothing within mindfulness practice that instructs you not to build stories. It's simply that you should be aware, in all circumstances, *that* you are building a story. And you should be aware that any story you have, at any point in time, is just one of many possible outcomes or interpretations. It's not the only one, and it may not be correct."

I conveyed to him what I convey to many who ask similar questions: "Don't believe everything you think."

You can cultivate an awareness of which simulations or elaborations are filling up your working memory without sacrificing decisiveness and action. In fact, having that awareness enhances those abilities by giving you the flexibility not only to reframe a situation, but to *de-frame* it based on the raw data that emerge.

"Dropping the Story"

Dropping the story is NOT about . . .	Dropping the story IS about . . .
Second-guessing yourself	Reorienting to the present moment with agility
Hesitating	Observing what's *really* happening
Being indecisive	Flexibly responding

Returning to an important question we discussed earlier: Can mindfulness practice combat the strong biases that we all carry within us, based on the world in which we were raised?

The best answer I can give to that right now is: *Maybe*. Research is unfolding about whether or not mindfulness practice can help reduce implicit biases—this could have huge implications for all of us and for our institutions, for example our justice system. It's promising, but we just don't have the data yet. What we have looked at is the intersection of mindfulness and discriminatory behavior. Studies are finding that mindfulness training can indeed help people *act* in less-biased ways, perhaps because they are more aware of the mental models they hold and more able to drop the story.

Watching the Mind

A group of psychologists came to the lab to discuss incorporating mindfulness practice into their own training. They weren't ordinary psychologists—they were operational psychologists with the US military, which means that they provide mission support to deployed units and are, on occasion, embedded in those units. One of their responsibilities is supporting service members who regularly spend long, twelve-hour shifts watching drone footage. The psychologists wanted to know what they could do to support the service members in that role.

To best answer that question, I needed an answer to one of my own first: When these service members are watching drone footage for a dozen hours straight, what is the purpose of their watching? Why are they doing it?

The reply: "They are a key part of the 'kill chain.'"

It was a startling statement. I realized immediately what he meant: that they were in charge of spotting targets and relaying that information up the chain of command. Even with all the work I've done with the military, this made me pause. It's easy to assume that it's the people in charge who wield most of the power and carry most of the weight for the decisions that are made, and for the actions taken by our military. But every single person in our military carries the weight of every decision they make. It reminds me of why I do this work—to help them make the right ones. And in a situation like this one, it's absolutely crucial for these people to be aware of what kind of biases they are bringing to the job. This is the place where the story you have is going to influence what you're seeing—if you think someone's a terrorist versus a civilian, every action you see is going to be interpreted through that lens. The operational psychologists reported that for these drone operators, it was very difficult to maintain mental resilience and flexibility over such long shifts. Their ability to do so was compromised by how long they were there and how tired they were. Meanwhile, they have somebody's life in their hands.

What's so interesting about this group of people is that they have the bird's-eye perspective all the time. They view the landscape below through that distant perspective. But does that automatically offer them a clear view? Only if they are aware not solely of what they are viewing below them, but also of their own mental model.

Most of us, of course, aren't military drone operators. We still need to be able to surveil our own mind. The stories we make up about other people's intentions and motivations can do a lot of damage. They can derail a friendship. They can cause political divisiveness. They can even start wars.

This highlights the most important feature of going to the distanced perspective: the most important thing to include in the scope of your viewing is *your own mind.*

It's one thing to practice decentering in your formal practice; being able to actually do it in your life, and under tough circumstances, requires using your attention in a different way altogether. In order to intervene in your own cognitive processes when they get off-track, you need to realize that you require intervention. In other words: the first critical step to *dropping the story* is to know that you *have* one. And that is one of the most challenging attentional skills to build.

8

GO BIG

Leaders across every field often think that to be successful, they need to use their attention in specific ways: By multitasking. By constantly planning. By having a future-oriented mindset. By simulating outcomes to strategize and prepare.

They also tend to believe they should be unemotional, disconnected, or stoic—especially in the military, first-responder, and business communities. I recently briefed a group of leaders at a large tech company on mindfulness training for attention, and why it was critical for them as leaders and innovators in a highly competitive industry. I also told them that these common assumptions about what constitutes strong leadership and clear strategic thinking are wrong. Instead:

To get more done, monotask—don't multitask. Task switching slows you down.

To best plan for the future, don't just simulate possible scenarios—observe and be in the present moment to gather better data.

To lead well, become more aware of your own emotions and those of others.

To do any of this, you have to be fully in the here and now. You need to observe. You need to be aware of what's going on *right now*—around you in your environment, and inside your mind, in your *inner environment,* which is just as dynamic, distracting, and informationally rich as the world around you.

We're used to living in action mode: *thinking and doing.*

Mindfulness training unlocks a new mode: *noticing, observing, and being.*

This observational stance is an elixir that allows you to do everything better: Accomplish tasks. Plan. Strategize. Lead. Innovate, Connect. All from a capacity to fully access the present moment and to know, moment to moment, what's happening *in your own mind.*

Engulfed

When a bushfire starts in the Australian wilderness, it can grow quickly, decimating wildlife and racing toward population centers. It needs to be contained before it gets out of control. But much of the Australian bush is difficult to reach, inaccessible by road or any other form of land-based route. Specialized firefighters must be sent in by helicopter, where they rappel directly into the wildfire area. These rappel crews land right smack in the middle of a dynamic, dangerous, and rapidly changing situation. Job descriptions for roles like these—like "smoke jumpers" in the US—often explicitly state that you must not only be in excellent physical condition, but also *possess a high degree of emotional stability and mental alertness.*

Steven is a heli-rappeller who visited my lab all the way from Australia, driven to seek our help because of a recent incident. He and his fellow crew members were deployed to a particularly challenging terrain in the Australian bush to contain a blaze that threatened to grow out of control. Weighed down with heavy gear—each carried a personal kit with hand tools like rakes and shovels and firefighting equipment—they fanned out, each taking a sector; a support helicopter would soon arrive to drop foam or water from the air. Steven began working on a section of fire right in front of him. He was very focused and meticulous in his methodology. And then he heard a distinctive sound behind him, a roar like the loudest vacuum, the sound of the air being sucked up—the sound of the fire taking over. He was being engulfed by a wall of fire approaching from behind.

Now, firefighting rappel crews—along with first responders, pilots, health care teams, military personnel, judges, lawyers, and a broad range of leaders across various fields—are often highly trained in situational awareness. Situational awareness training in these professions usually takes the form of a decision-making model—a way to make sure that the choices you make in fast-moving circumstances are based on your real-time, present-moment observations, as well as your knowledge and experience, and are of course in service of your goal. Steven's goal was to *control the fire*, which he was actively working toward; under pressure and surrounded by salient distractors, he had exquisite focus. His attention was strongly deployed to the fire he was fighting to control. And his training had involved simulating and practicing this *exact* scenario. But in that moment, something critical was missing.

In the previous chapter, we talked about how we use *simulations* to arrive at a mental model. We *perceive, process, predict;* this allows us to *decide, act, communicate.* These steps aren't typically linear, but instead dynamic and interactive: Simulations create mental models that lead to decisions, which then influence the next simulation, and so on. This is a shifting, fluid, constantly unfolding process, not a static one. *Dropping the story*, then, is not a single action, but rather an *ongoing process*—one that requires you to become aware, over and over, of what's happening not only around you, but also *inside your own mind.*

Steven got so focused on putting out that smaller fire right in front of him that he stopped monitoring the larger fire event. In cognitive psychology, we call this *goal neglect*: a failure to execute the demands of a particular task, even though you can recall the instructions. He *knew* that his broader mission was to monitor an unpredictable situation that could unfold in any number of ways, but he still got overly focused and lost track of the main goal.

Obviously, Steven lived to tell the tale—he was able to successfully navigate his way out of danger. However, the close call lingered with him. He started using the story to train new firefighters, to communicate that even with impeccable preparation, their situational awareness could still be incomplete. He now tells them that *situational* awareness isn't enough. Surveilling the external landscape—even if you do it well, and mindfully, and with your attention in the present moment—isn't enough.

Beyond Situational Awareness

Steven faced a particularly challenging instance—a high-demand situation that also required close-field focus. And yet, you don't have to be rappelling into a literal wildfire to experience something like goal neglect and to suffer because of it. Think of any time you've drifted off course from an important goal—and remember that *goals* show up in our lives in different ways. We could be talking about something at work: you get focused on one aspect of a project and sidetracked, losing sight of how it fits into the larger mission of your organization. We could even be talking about parenting.

My daughter, Sophie, gently summoned me to her room one night, frustrated. She was stuck on a particularly difficult math problem. She asked for my help.

I went in and sat down next to her and took a look at the problem. I started by trying to talk her through it, asking, "Okay, tell me what the problem is saying," and other leading questions. But I was confused, too—I couldn't quite remember how to tackle this particular formula. *I should know this!* I felt a surge of determination. And for the next forty-five minutes I worked furiously on the problem, completely driven: *I'm going to dominate this math problem. I am going to crush sixth-grade math!*

It worked: I solved the problem! I looked up triumphantly—to see Sophie leaning back in her chair, reading a book.

Oops.

My goal, always, is to raise independent, self-motivated kids who can problem-solve on their own. When I sat down next to my daughter and started talking her through the problem, that was absolutely my mission. I rapidly got sidetracked, even though I *felt* focused and on-task.

One of the reasons we get sidetracked in moments like these is that it feels good. You see a smaller goal you can accomplish—*put out that fire; solve this problem*—and you lose awareness of your larger purpose: *control the unfolding fire event; raise an independent thinker.* Solving that math problem was very satisfying for me, but as soon as I looked up I realized, *This is not the best use of my energy with my child.* Certainly a good realization, but how much better would it have been to catch those moments earlier, *before* I sank most of an hour into the task? *Before* the wall of fire raged up behind you?

Of course, we want to be able to focus. And we started this book by working on that important skill. But we also need to be able to pull out of focus when necessary—to be intentional about how and when we focus, and on what. In that moment I was *highly* focused—completely immersed, in fact. If you'd walked into that room, you'd have thought I had no problem with attention. The problem: this wasn't a time for me to be highly focused. I lost track of that, and I lost track of what my mind was up to. I was off course and completely unaware of it.

So here is the next major way that we go wrong: We *are* paying attention. But our attention is too narrow or too wide, too stable or too unstable. You're paying attention in some way successfully—but it's not *appropriate for the moment.*

To correct that, you need *meta-awareness.*

Surveilling the Inner Landscape

Meta-awareness is the ability to take explicit note of and monitor the current contents or processes of your conscious experience. Basically, it's an awareness of your awareness. When I say "pay attention to your attention," what I mean is apply your meta-awareness. That day in the Australian bush, Steven was focused on the fire. But paying attention to his attention would have offered something more: the realization that he was fixated on it and needed to expand his attention.

If situational awareness in high-demand professions means "surveilling the external landscape," then you can think of meta-awareness like this: situational awareness for the internal landscape.

My colleague and friend Scott Rogers, whom I've been working with for the past decade to bring mindfulness training to all different types of populations, is a wizard at describing meta-awareness. It can be a tough concept to grasp, but Scott has a knack for coming up with phrases that really make difficult mindfulness concepts more easily accessible. When we worked with the University of Miami football team, he put it this way: "You are scanning the field."

He asked the players to picture the football field and all the dynamic elements that go into it: the sidelines, the goal lines, the moving players, the ball in play, the roar of the crowd, the constant chirping from opposing players, the Jumbotrons in every corner . . . everything. He invited them to think about how they navigate that complex landscape, full of salient elements that want to yank at their focus. Then he asked them to visualize their mind the same way: as a field, with the same kind of salient moving pieces that might grab your attention and suck it in. He suggested that just as players choose how to navigate the football field, and how and when to engage other players, they think of the "field" of their mind the same way.

You can hover above yourself—observe from a distance, as we practiced in the last chapter with the "Bird's-Eye View" decentering practice. And there are other important cues you can notice, as you build an "awareness of your awareness" that will clue you in.

Some of these cues happen in the body. When I went into Sophie's room to help her understand a math problem and instead emerged an hour later a heroine in my epic battle with middle school math, I became hyperfocused. I wondered why that had happened, when I went in with such a clear goal. As I thought back to the incident, I remembered feeling gripped by a desire to win—to "beat" the math problem. I understood that I was driven by the feeling of satisfaction I get from "winning," and that it fueled my hyperfocus. For me, that "gripping" feeling is a red flag. I'm much more aware of that sensation now—when I feel it, I check in: Is my attention where it needs to be?

It's not always a "satisfaction" feeling—sometimes we get tripped up and sucked into hyperfocus (or another attentional state that isn't appropriate to the moment) by anxiety, fear, or worry. Sometimes, "seeing" the mind is actually about feeling mind-states in the body. These might show up as restlessness in your legs, nervousness in your stomach, tension in your jaw. All those years ago, when I lost feeling in my teeth? I was completely unaware. That's why it got so bad. I had no meta-awareness, no sense of what was happening in my mind and body, no ability to course-correct until it got to a crisis point.

With more awareness of my inner landscape, these days I am able to intervene earlier and more effectively in my own attention issues. I'm attuned to how my mind and body are relating to each other when I'm hyperfocused or stressed. I can notice now when I'm starting to clench my jaw; I do a three-minute practice, I take a walk, I relax my mouth—any number of things to stop the mindless teeth clenching. And the last time I wrote a grant application on a crazy deadline, I knew I wasn't going to be great at staying meta-aware. So . . . I wore a mouth guard. (Sometimes, we just have to accept our limitations!)

When I talked to Steven in the lab about his instance of "goal neglect," he described feeling "enticed" by putting out the small fire—that's what led to his hyperfocus. Now, he watches for (as he calls it) "that delicious satisfaction feeling" in his upper arms and stomach. That's what tips him off that he may be sinking into hyperfocus. He can respond by broadening his attention as needed.

He described meta-awareness, from a firefighter's perspective, as "watchstanding": taking a position where you can see what's happening more clearly. That's an important part of what having a peak mind really means: it's being able to get that "peak" perspective and take in the entire landscape of your mind. With meta-awareness, we are aware of the current contents of our conscious experience, and we monitor to see if those contents are aligned with our goals. We're asking ourselves:

What am I perceiving?

How am I processing it?

And is the form my attention is taking aligned with my goals?

It's easy to confuse meta-awareness with another thought process we call *metacognition*. The difference is this: Metacognition is thoughts about how you think. It's knowing that you have certain mental tendencies. Metacognition is, in part, self-awareness. "I have a tendency to assume the worst," is an example of metacognition. Or: "I take a long time making decisions." Metacognition is certainly helpful—this kind of incisive self-awareness of your own cognitive tendencies can clearly support you. But it's not the same as meta-awareness, and it can't replace it. While you might know that you tend to think in certain ways, that doesn't mean you'll be able to be aware of problems as they're happening. When you're mind-wandering and simulating, it doesn't matter if you're the most "metacognitively" savvy person on the planet—you'll still get caught up in these mental processes in the moment.

You're Unaware that You're Unaware

We brought 143 undergraduate students into the lab to test their *awareness* of their own mind-wandering. We knew people were mind-wandering about 50 percent of the time, but did they realize it? We gave them a standard "working memory task": remember two faces, compare them to a test face, do this multiple times over a twenty-minute period. We tracked their accuracy and speed as usual, but this time we stopped them in the middle of the test at various points and asked two questions: How "on-task" were you—very, somewhat, or not at all? And how *aware* were you of it?

The results? There were four main clusters of responses: (1) reports that participants were *on-task* and *aware* of it; (2) reports that they were *on-task* and *unaware* (this would look like a deeply immersed "flow state"); (3) reports that they were *off-task* and *aware* (choosing not to pay attention anymore because they thought the task was boring, which researchers call "tuning out"); and (4) reports that they were *off-task* and *unaware* ("zoning out").

In addition to all these response clusters, we found that participants' performance got worse and worse, they mind-wandered more and more, and they became less meta-aware over the twenty-minute task.

The drop in performance over the course of the twenty minutes was not surprising—we've already discussed the *vigilance decrement*: performance gets worse over time when continuous attention is required on a task. What these results pointed out is that mind-wandering was increasing as performance was getting worse. When we first talked about mind-wandering, we talked about all the evolutionary reasons the brain might be "wired to wander," like opportunity costs, scanning, looking for something better to do, and so forth. The human brain may simply be designed to cyclically pull away from the task-at-hand. We are *built* to have these cyclical patterns in our attention. And that might be fine—if you can notice the pulling away. But what we found here is that *we do not notice.*

This is what the meta-awareness responses conveyed—as mind-wandering was going up, meta-awareness was going down. We are mind-wandering more and more over time, and growing less and less able to catch ourselves doing it. And when we don't catch ourselves, we cannot course-correct to get attention back on task.

I started this book by telling you that you spend 50 percent of your time mind-wandering, and that's true—that statistic has held up across many studies. It's easy to conclude, looking at that number, that mind-wandering lies at the root of our problems with attention. The surprise, though—from this study and others—is that mind-wandering itself may not be the real culprit. After all, there are plenty of instances where it's fine to wander. Think of how you allow your thoughts to roam while watching your child's or grandchild's favorite movie for the third time, or while doing something automatic and easy, like vacuuming a room—"tuning out," on purpose, as opposed to "zoning out."

The difference? *Meta-awareness.*

With tuning out, meta-awareness of the situation lets you make sure that your current behavior is aligned with task goals before you decide to shift your attention away—no adjustments of attention are needed. But if the task demands suddenly rise, and performance starts slipping, attentional resources will be diverted back to the task-at-hand. Your own mind cues you—you don't need an external cue, which, as we know, usually come too late anyway. Without meta-awareness, no monitoring occurs—no noticing of the task demands growing, no noticing of the current state of attention, and no redirection of attention.

ADHD patients tend to have high mind-wandering—so high that it can lead to detrimental real-life outcomes. A recent study found that even though mind-wandering is higher in these patients compared to those who don't suffer from ADHD, the "costs" of mind-wandering were abated in patients who were more *meta-aware of their mind-wandering versus those who were not.* Meta-awareness "protected" them from making mind-wandering–related errors.

The problem is not mind-wandering—the problem is mind-wandering without *meta-awareness.*

The very young field of contemplative neuroscience is pushing us toward the new science of attention: *meta-awareness may be the key to improving attentional performance.*

Get Meta

Chris McAliley, a federal judge in the State of Florida, was inspired to start a mindfulness practice "like a lot of people do—when I was beset by unwelcome events in my life." She was going through a divorce. Her children were teenagers, "with all that that entails," she says now, with a sigh.

"I was in a complete mental battle with my 'now,'" she says. "I didn't want it. I was judgmental with myself, with others; I was mad at the universe. I was at the mercy of repetitive thoughts. And I was trying to work through it all. I had to go to court and make all these decisions—decisions that affected people. Meanwhile, there's this constant rat race of thoughts in my head. I was exhausted by it."

Chris and I met at a conference for female judges where we were both panelists invited to speak on the topic of mindfulness and judging. We shook hands waiting backstage before the event. Chris joked that attendance might be sparse, that we'd only have the other panelists as our audience—would anybody come to a panel on mindfulness and judging? Perhaps it was too niche a topic for the judiciary world. But when we walked on stage to take our places at the table, the cavernous room was packed with people. Every one of the five hundred seats was filled; women were standing in a crowd at the back of the great ballroom. It appeared there was indeed a need for mindfulness in judging.

A courtroom is actually the perfect example of a space where you would need both *situational awareness* and *meta-awareness.* Sitting on the bench, Chris is required to engage and sustain multiple types of attention. There's a lawyer questioning a witness the judge must attend to. Meanwhile, the judge is holding in mind the testimonies she's just heard, the laws that apply to the facts of the case, and the rules and standards that govern what the lawyer is saying in the moment: she is listening to what is being said, while being ready to respond if the opposing lawyer objects (will she sustain or overrule?). At the same time, she's monitoring *other* people's attention: Is that juror in the back row asleep? Is the court reporter keeping up? Judge McAliley needs to make sure that every word is captured, so if the reporter looks harried, she should slow things down. There might be an interpreter she needs to be aware of, as well; there might be a baby crying in the gallery.

"There is so much to attend to," she says, "and then on top of it, there's your *own mind* to attend to. If the lawyer is making his closing arguments, and I'm thinking about my divorce, or what I want for lunch, I'm not doing a good job. I'm not there! And it's consequential."

She needs an awareness of what's going on in the courtroom *and* what's going on in her mind. Mindfulness training has given Chris greater insight into the kind of stuff that gets her off-track. Frustration, anxiousness, worry—they all show up in the body. She often does a mini-practice in the courtroom: *be still, sense the body, sense the breath.*

"I have to get below my neck," she says. "It's so amazing, to notice what happens to the body when we have emotional feelings. We ignore them, but there's great information there."

For her, these feelings will show up as anxiousness or frustration—the lawyers don't seem prepared; she notices her own voice rising; she realizes she's been ruminating. *Should I call them out for not being prepared? What impact will that have on them, or on the case, or on the defendant?* Mindfulness practice has helped her use her own emotions as information.

"This is supposed to be a rational system," she says, "so I don't want my emotions—without my understanding or decision—to lead me to a decision. But I'm a judge, not a robot. I need to be able to experience emotion and be informed by it . . . not ruled by it."

Meta-awareness allows her an awareness and understanding not only of her own thoughts and emotions, but also of her implicit biases. It's something she has to think about in every case. If there's a police officer testifying against a previously convicted felon, Chris asks herself: What are her personal assumptions? What's her drop-down menu of biases when it comes to gender, profession, class, race? Can she notice them, but not be constrained by them?

"A lot of this practice is simply trying to notice our assumptions in life," she says. "When you actually pay attention to them, you understand: they are *rapid-fire.*"

For her, the big revelation was paying attention *without judgment.* Without judgment of herself, or of others, or of circumstances. Ironic, because *judging* is quite literally Chris's profession. But being able to *pay attention to the present moment, without judgment or elaboration,* is what now allows her to be more effective when she's making decisions that shape people's lives.

"It's such a privilege to be a judge," she remarks. "Our society picks people like me to resolve disputes. I'm sitting there, hearing people testify to completely opposite versions of events, and it's my job to determine who's credible. Sometimes it's clear, but sometimes it's not. And I have to try to get it right."

Why It Works

In the lab, it's really hard to "see" meta-awareness directly through people's behavior alone. So (as in the working memory study I mentioned above) we have to give people attention and working memory tasks *and* ask them to then self-report on it. Study after study shows that the more *aware* people are of where their attention is, the better their performance is. We also know that when they are more aware, they can catch themselves mind-wandering (without being asked). And we know that some things cause meta-awareness to tank—like cigarette cravings and drinking alcohol.

With experienced mindfulness practitioners—and even with people who've taken an eight-week mindfulness-based stress reduction class—we see something else, too: *reduced default mode activity.* You remember what that is: reduced activity in the brain network, sometimes called the "me" network, that's most involved during internal attention, self-focus, mental simulations, and mind-wandering. Why would mindfulness training, compared to no training or some comparison training, reduce default mode activity? As we've discussed, there is growing evidence that mindfulness training increases attention and decentering, and decreases mind-wandering. Mental simulations that can hijack attention are less frequent and less capable of keeping you locked-in. But all of this may hinge on mindfulness training's power to increase meta-awareness.

When you're meta-aware, you're looking at yourself. You're the object! You can't be simultaneously immersed in self-related thinking (mind-wandering, simulating) *and* reflecting on the self. This is why, as meta-awareness goes up, mind-wandering goes down. It makes sense that these would be antagonistic processes: the self can't be outside and inside at the same time. Think back to the decentering technique you practiced in the previous chapter, which asked you to step outside, or "de-fuse," from the self for a moment. You were already practicing meta-awareness in that moment—now, we need to be able to do it even more often, as a mental habit.

We want greater meta-awareness . . . and mindfulness practice is what gets us there.

Noticing: Your Attentional Powerup

Think back to your first time doing a mindfulness exercise, like *Find Your Flashlight*. You might have been surprised at how much your attention moved around. Attention is like a ball in motion. To effectively dribble it, you have to keep engaging and reengaging it over and over. If you "zone out" (mind-wander without realizing it), the ball will roll away. And the ball rolls away often. You only become meta-aware when you completely lose the ball: You walk out of a meeting and realize you have no idea what has been said. During an important conversation, you hear someone ask "Are you even listening?" and you realize you've been nodding along, but hearing nothing. You hear yourself shout, angrily, "I'm NOT angry!" You realize: *Oops. I'm angry.*

In each of these examples, that moment of realization of *where your attention actually is and what your mind is doing*—that's meta-awareness. That's it—that's what it feels like. Those "meta moments" are what we want. But we want them much earlier, when they can truly be effective and protective.

Our goal with mindfulness training is to *increase* our meta moments so that we can actually execute the attentional pivots that are so critical for our success and well-being. Even if you have the strongest attention system in the world, you could direct it to the wrong place. To be able to implement any of the tactics you've been learning, you have to realize that you need to do so.

In *The Art of War*, which I used to introduce this book, Sun Tzu offers up a second approach one can use in an unfair fight:

The force applied is minute but the results enormous.

Don't struggle against a brick wall. Find a way to apply the minimum amount of force with the maximum amount of impact. The skill we want to cultivate is not only the capacity to pay better attention, focus more, concentrate harder: this is equivalent to going to battle and training for the fight—helpful but incomplete. We need to build something beyond this. We need a *force multiplier*, like a power-up in a video game. The attentional force multiplier you need to acquire is your capacity to be meta-aware, to *notice*.

To *notice* when we are not focused or *too* focused.

To *notice* when we are mentally elsewhere and not in the here and now.

To *notice* what is happening around us and within us.

Noticing is what unlocks our capacity to intervene in these pervasive attentional problems.

It's simple: To know if you're getting grabbed by something and need to intervene, you have to be watching.

The good news: You've already been practicing this the whole time. Meta-awareness has been part of every practice you've done so far.

Meta-Tate

In the *Find Your Flashlight* practice, the moment you noticed that your flashlight had drifted away from breath-related sensations—that was meta-awareness. During the *Watch Your Whiteboard* practice with labeling, when you noticed a thought, feeling, or sensation and labeled it—that was meta-awareness. During the decentering practice, when you took the bird's-eye perspective and scanned your mind for biases, simulations, and mental models—that was meta-awareness. Even during the body scan, when you directed your attention to a particular bodily sensation, you were noticing which sensations were there and becoming aware of mind-wandering.

Up to this point, our goal has been to make sure that your attention was on a target object, like your breath. Now, the target of your attention . . . *is* your attention.

Ultimately, all the practices you've been working on in this book will build meta-awareness—and practicing any of them regularly supports your ability to *observe and monitor your own mind*. This next practice is specifically designed to notice the moment-to-moment contents of your conscious experience, without getting caught up in the thoughts, emotions, and sensations that arise.

This is a variation on a traditional "open monitoring" practice that asks you to observe the contents of your moment-to-moment conscious experience *without engaging with it.* While the prior formal practices have aimed to cultivate concentrative focus, this practice is instead about having receptive, broad, and stable attention.

CORE PRACTICE: RIVER OF THOUGHT

1. *Get ready . . .* This time, stand up! You can always sit if you prefer, in the same way as with the previous practices. But I usually recommend doing this practice in what is commonly known as Mountain Pose. Stand comfortably, your feet shoulder-distance apart. Let your arms relax at your sides, palms out. Close your eyes or lower your gaze.

2. *Get set . . .* Find your flashlight and direct it toward prominent breath-related sensations for several breaths. This is always where we'll start with any practice. And at any point in this exercise if you feel yourself getting drawn away (for example, getting caught in a ruminative loop), you can always anchor back on the breath. *Flashlight on the breath* is your home base—return to it whenever necessary, and reset.

3. *Go!* Now broaden your awareness so that you are not selecting any target object. Instead, use the metaphor of your mind being like a river. You're standing on the riverbank, watching the water flow by. Imagine your thoughts, memories, sensations, emotions—whatever arises—as if they are flowing past you. Notice what appears there, but don't engage with it. Don't fish it up, chase it, or elaborate on it. Just let it flow by.

4. *Keep going.* Unlike in the *Watch Your Whiteboard* activity we did, you're not going to be actively "labeling" the stuff that you notice on your whiteboard, nor returning to your breath once you do.

Your job right now is not to be making distinctions between which content is useful or relevant, and what's mind-wandering. You're not even going to try to *stop* your mind from wandering. The river will keep flowing—there isn't anything you can or need to do about that. This is the key to open monitoring: *you allow your mind to do what it will do.* Your job is simply to observe that flow, at a distance, without engagement or participation.

5. ***Troubleshooting.*** If you have difficulty letting things pass you by, come back to your breath. Imagine your breath sensations as a boulder in the middle of all that flowing water. Rest your attention on that stable, steady object; when you feel ready, broaden your attention again and go back to monitoring.

I'll be honest with you: participants often report open monitoring to be the most challenging of the core practices. So here's a way to think about what we're doing in this practice, from an experience I had recently while practicing it myself.

I had set myself up to practice in my living room. It was a beautiful autumn day, breezy and warm, and I had all the windows open. My dog was in the room with me, lying by the window and gazing out at the street. Tashi is a Lhasa Apso. If you aren't familiar with them, Lhasa Apsos are small dogs with long white hair that sweeps the floor if you don't cut it. I find mine adorable, but I'm willing to acknowledge that they look a little bit like a floor mop. Lhasa Apsos came from Tibet and were historically kept in monasteries—their job was to monitor the common areas of the monastery and alert the monks of any intruders by barking. And they are *very* good at barking.

I was a few minutes into my practice when Tashi was already yapping at something. He does this all the time—he loves to go and stare out the window and then if anybody walks by, he'll bark. Actually, it doesn't even have to be a person. It could be a car, a squirrel, a small branch falling off a tree—anything will get him going. I tried to forge ahead with my practice—after all, I figured, the barking was just a sensation like anything else—but he simply would not stop. I was getting *so* irritated—and then it dawned on me: *I'm doing the exact same thing that he is.* I'm sitting here, watching for what's different on my whiteboard. He's watching for what's different in that rectangle of window available to him—that's exactly what open monitoring is! Sure, maybe I'm not actually *barking* at stuff, but it's kind of the same thing. Tashi barks when he notices something, while I might get stuck and emotionally reactive about something I notice. I got up and closed the curtain. He stopped barking and lay down.

We can't just "close the curtain" on our thoughts. We also can't sit at the window and bark at every passing thing. But we *can* learn to notice it—and let it go.

My dog doesn't have that ability—but you do! Think of it this way: Would you run outside to talk to every person who walks by your house? No. So treat the thoughts that arise for you throughout the day in the same way. You can't stop them from coming any more than you can stop people from walking down your street. But you *can* change the way that you interact with them. You can decide when to engage with them, and when not to, and instead allow them to pass by.

Using "Choice Points" to Improve Your Practice

When offering the president of the University of Miami and his leadership cabinet MBAT, the program my colleague Scott Rogers and I codeveloped for high-demand professionals, we set up shop in a conference room. After a bit of discussion, we got into the practices. We had been working with this group regularly, and were in the part of the program that introduced them to the open monitoring practice.

We all took a seated Mountain Pose, and we talked them through "watching mental content pass, like clouds in the sky." At a certain point before beginning the formal practice, one member of the group loudly sighed.

"This noise is driving me crazy!" she said. Indeed, the air conditioner was making a persistent, irregular rattle. "I don't think I can do this practice with this thing going. It's *so* irritating!"

She was right—the air conditioner *was* very hard to ignore. It was also a great opportunity to point out why engaging in open monitoring practice can be helpful for precisely these types of irritating, annoying, or anger-provoking moments in our lives: we can recognize *choice points*.

I conveyed to the group that I didn't know her direct experience in that moment, but I have similarly been irritated by annoying sounds during my practice on other occasions. If I could have watched her mental whiteboard, or mine, in such moments, here's what I might have seen: A sound was noticed—a sensory experience registered on the mental whiteboard. Then, a concept showed up—the thought *It's so irritating*. Next, an emotion—*feeling* that irritation. And finally, the expression of emotion aloud—"It's so irritating!"

It may feel a bit contrived to break it down as a linear sequence— sensation, thought, emotion, action—especially when it feels so packed together, like a big jumble of irritation. But as we learn to watch what is unfolding in our minds with a practice like open monitoring, we can see the sequence of mental events flowing by with greater precision and granularity. And we may notice the small gaps between events—where we are making choices. Linking the sensory experience of the sound with the concept of *irritating* is a choice. Feeling irritation is a choice. Expressing that feeling is also a choice.

With practice, we get better at noticing mental events and identifying opportunities to intervene—to make *different* choices. Think of instances in your own life when your reaction felt ballistically driven by an instigating event, like getting cut off in traffic and flipping someone off. It may seem very difficult to break down such episodes to see choice points. But we can get better at this, and open monitoring practice helps. It tunes up our meta-awareness. With more practice, we might even be able to experience events as spacious, appreciating the infinite possibilities before us in any moment. My favorite expression of this insight comes from Velvet Underground front man Lou Reed: "Between thought and expression lies a lifetime."

There wasn't anything we could do about the sound—we couldn't adjust the thermostat to turn it off, and there really wasn't time to try to find someone to fix it. The sound was going to be there as we tried to practice. However, thinking about our experience of it in terms of choice points, noticing the space between the thought and expression, offered an opportunity: when the thought *This is so irritating* occurs, you can make a different choice. Instead of feeling and then expressing anger, you could choose not to hang onto it. Just let it fade and allow your whiteboard to remain "receptive" to whatever arises next.

Whether it's a thought tied to the rattling of an air conditioner or a fear or worry that loudly presents itself in your mind, you can use this same strategy. Thoughts, memories, and anxieties may appear in the mind unbidden. We can remember that we have a choice on what we do next. Think of Tashi, and make a different choice. No need to bark: let them walk on by.

There is a concept in Buddhism called the "Second Arrow." It comes from a famous parable: the Buddha asked one of his students, "If you are struck by an arrow, does it hurt?"

"Yes!" the student replied.

"If you are struck by a second arrow," the Buddha asked, "does it hurt even more?"

"It does," the student replied.

The Buddha explained: In life, we can't control whether we're hit by an arrow or not. But the second arrow is our *reaction* to the first. The first arrow causes pain—the second arrow is our distress about that pain.

I love this parable because it very simply encapsulates the connection between mindfulness and attention: The first arrow happens. There are arrows every day. But the second arrow—your response to the first—is what sucks up your attentional bandwidth. And that *is* within your control. This is another choice point you can access—if you have an awareness of your own mind.

Choice points become especially important in another arena: *relationships.*

Whether an interaction you're having is with a loved one, someone you've just met, or a nemesis, the "packaged" story you're carrying in your working memory about that person, or about how the interaction will go, can determine how events flow . . . not only between you and this other person, but also with others. The ripple effects of our relationships, and whether they're effective, compassionate, and communicative or closed off and full of misunderstandings, can have a far reach.

One important node in the brain network for meta-awareness is located at the very front of the prefrontal cortex—it also happens to be part of the brain network for social connection. It's activated when we are meta-aware and also when we connect with others by simulating their reality and seeing things from their point of view. Meta-awareness offers us a window into our own minds as if we are watching it from someone else's perspective, but it also allows us insight into others. Using your attention, you can not only time travel, but *mind travel.*

GET CONNECTED

When Congressman Tim Ryan of Ohio invited me to travel to Washington, DC, to share our research on mindfulness training for active-duty service members, I immediately thought of Major Jason Spitaletta and Major Jeff Davis, the Marines I'd met back when they were both captains, during our very first study on mindfulness in the military. Jason was the one who'd warned "This is never going to work," but who'd then thrown himself wholeheartedly into practice. Jeff, who was attentionally hijacked while on that bridge in Florida, says that mindfulness practice "saved his life." I asked them to join me for the meeting with Congressman Ryan.

We met up outside a Metro stop near the National Mall. I hadn't seen them in years, but they were as boisterous as I remembered, and launched right into catching me up on their lives. Jason, who had been midway through a PhD program in psychology when he deployed to Iraq, was so impacted by the mindfulness study he participated in with us that he changed his research focus when he returned. He was now studying *distress tolerance*—the ability to withstand aversive mental states. Jeff, now retired from the military, was pursuing his MBA at George Washington University. Their lively stories, zig-zagging from training in Florida and grad school in DC to deploying to Baghdad, both captivated and transported me. Before I knew it, I was looking straight ahead at that iconic white building, the US Capitol. And then I noticed something odd. People were peering in our direction. At one point, two women in business suits powerwalking our way just stopped and stared right at us from across the street. What was going on?

I turned around, curious to see who might be behind us. No one. Jason laughed and said, "They think we're your Secret Service detail." Jeff chimed in, "Amishi, they're trying to figure out who *you* are." The sight of two brawny dudes in sport coats flanking a 5'2" Indian woman was apparently odd enough to draw attention, even in DC. For the rest of our walk up Independence Avenue, they did not hold back razzing me about my "terrible situational awareness." I had to take it on the chin.

We made our way to the congressman's office in the Rayburn Building, and were led right in to see him.

"Please call me Tim," Congressman Ryan said, towering over me as he shook my hand.

From the moment we all sat down together, I was struck by Tim's full and unwavering attention. He was direct and probing, wanting to know about Jason's and Jeff's military experience, their journey with mindfulness, and thoughts on how mindfulness could be made more accessible to both active-duty and veteran service members. We discussed the results from the study with their unit and my lab's ongoing research efforts. Twenty minutes later, a staffer knocked on his office door.

"They're calling a vote on the House floor," she said.

Soon after he disappeared from his office, Tim reappeared on the wall-mounted TV screen, delivering a short yet impassioned speech on trade. Then, in no time at all, he was back with us, excited to continue our discussion.

What stood out most that day was when Tim described the value of mindfulness practice in his own life. He humbly acknowledged that the battles he faced in DC were nothing like those that Jason and Jeff had endured during their military deployments. He conveyed that he had come to lean heavily on his daily mindfulness practice as *mental armor*. And it showed—his commitment to serving the public good was contagious.

On my flight back to Miami, many thoughts bubbled up. The congressman's capacity to make us feel motivated, heard, and understood—even while he juggled other critical responsibilities— was remarkable. I hadn't earlier made the connection that, exactly like warriors and first responders, leaders' pressures and demands eat away at the very qualities they need most. Tim had learned for himself that clarity, connection, and compassion were trainable, and he trained daily. How, I wondered, could we get these tools to other leaders? How could we study their effects? As the plane landed, I felt energized—it was time to get back to work.

Sharing a "Mental Model"

During the COVID-19 pandemic, guidelines from the Centers for Disease Control and Prevention have constantly encouraged Americans to practice social distancing, keeping at least six feet of distance between ourselves and others to limit the spread of the highly contagious and potentially deadly SARS-CoV-2 virus. As many social psychologists were quick to point out, "social distancing" is a misnomer. More important for our physical and psychological health is that we remain *physically* distant while staying *socially* connected.

As human beings, we need social connection from infancy, and we'll keep needing it for the rest of our lives. I'm not being dramatic when I say that without social connection we die *faster*. Loneliness and social isolation are risk factors for poor health as well as accelerated mortality. Social connection has been scientifically studied for decades across multiple fields and many perspectives, ranging from mother-child bonding and romantic attachment to team dynamics and social networks. And *attention* is one of the fundamental building blocks for all social relationships: it's what shapes our moment-to-moment interactions with other people. In fact, the Latin root for the word "attention" is *attendere*, which means "to stretch toward." In this sense, attention is connection.

Imagine yourself speaking to someone on the phone. If the cell phone signal is glitchy, perceptual details will be lost. If you get distracted, your attention may be diverted. You'll have both a poor mental model and poor situational awareness of the conversation.

Conversations rely on *shared mental models*. These are cocreated by both speakers, and dynamically updated as the conversation progresses. So, on your imagined call: lousy input and processing may have led to a lousy shared model, and most likely a lousy experience for you both. We've all been there! Contrast this with speaking to an attentive and undistracted conversation partner on a good cell phone connection. Her words are crisp and clear, her attention is locked on you, and there is a long and rich shared history of content and warmth during the call. Under these conditions, our shared mental models will be stable and vivid, heightening our feeling of connection. We will feel cognitively attuned as we are transported into a (mental) space of our own shared making.

High-quality interactions require high-integrity mental models. And to make them, we need to draw on all our attentional skills: *Pushing* the flashlight where we want it to be. *Resisting or correcting* the pull of salient distractors. *Simulating* but also *dropping the story* when the mental model is wrong—when it doesn't match up with the other person's. (If you've ever used the phrase "not on the same page," you know what that feels like.) And finally, you need that meta-awareness piece to implement it all.

All the skills we've been practicing come into play here: Directing the flashlight. Simulating the other person's reality. And watching to make sure the entire interaction stays on track.

Distraction = Disconnection

Human interactions are nuanced and complex. They can be fun, stress-relieving, entertaining, rewarding, productive. They can also be tense, challenging, adversarial. Every day, we have interactions with people that we look forward to, and ones we may dread. Yet we have to show up for all of them. And when things go astray with these interactions, it can seem as if the problem is insurmountable, or foundational, or maybe "just the way people are."

Like so many of the other challenges of living, a lot of the problems we run into in these interactions come down to something more basic and more fixable, or, as we have been discussing throughout this book, *trainable*. Think about a recent challenge you experienced connecting, communicating, or collaborating effectively—I'm willing to bet that distraction, dysregulation, or disconnection were at play, with one or both of you. How does this relate to your attention and working memory?

Distracted

- You can't keep your attentional flashlight pointing to one or more conversation partners.

- Your mental whiteboard is cluttered—you have failed to let distracting content fade from your working memory.

- You keep time traveling, unable to stay in the present moment of the conversation as it unfolds.

Dysregulated

- You can't regulate your emotions.

- You are reactive or display volatile behavior during the interaction.

Disconnected

- You incorrectly believe that thoughts are facts.

- You fail to have a *shared* mental model of the situation.

- You apply the wrong mental model to the situation.

While I said "you," I'm not suggesting that you blame yourself. It takes two to tango. It's entirely possible, in fact, likely, that in any moment failures of attention are not yours alone.

Many of these issues arise due to challenges we experience when trying to direct our voluntary attention or when we suffer from depleted working memory. There are many deleterious consequences of having depleted working memory. There are fewer mental resources to engage in emotion regulation strategies (for example, to reframe or to reappraise). Our whiteboards function as if they are "smaller" because we are more prone to distraction, leaving fewer cognitive resources to engage in the kind of mental work we need to do in emotionally challenging circumstances. Sadly, a recent study examining parental behavior and working memory capacity found that parents with lower (vs. higher) working memory capacity were more likely to engage in verbally or emotionally abusive behavior toward their children.

In addition, lapses in meta-awareness can get us into hot water when it comes to our interactions with others. We can make assumptions and have stories (mental models) that are not shared by others or are entirely inaccurate. This can lead to a cascade of errors, including wrong-headed decisions and actions. No matter the cause of challenging interpersonal interactions, the result will be the same: the interaction is unfulfilling and unsatisfying at best, and aversive or damaging at worst.

The Benefits of Regulating and Responding vs. Reacting

Some people hear the term "regulation" and think "robotic"—that's not what we mean at all. We mean *having a proportionate response.* This entails having emotional responses to events that scale with what is actually occurring. If somebody bursts into tears because they get fired, I'd call that an appropriate, even proportionate response. But if they burst into tears because they spill their coffee? Well, something's up.

We've all been there. These moments of emotional overwhelm creep up on us, sometimes when we least expect them and aren't really ready to handle them. At work, with our friends, kids, or parents, in romantic relationships—we respond in ways we might later regret. We feel out of control, out of proportion, out of sync with events. If you've felt this way, it's because you are human—and some of the challenges you face are likely, at least in part, attention- and working memory–related.

It's a tricky paradox: Strong emotions can capture our attention, can invade and take over our working memory. They can cause us to dredge up off-topic, and sometimes distressing, memories and thoughts; they provide fuel for the "loop of doom." Meanwhile, we need those very same working memory resources to be able to proactively deal with the emotions that arise. There's a "driving down" effect, a kind of negative spiral: poor mood degrades working memory, and a degraded working memory causes more poor mood. So how do we pull out of that cognitive nose dive?

To start, you strengthen the capacities that will protect against distraction, dysregulation, and disconnection by engaging in mindfulness practice. Any of the core practices we've already covered will help. And by cultivating meta-awareness, as we discussed in the previous chapter, we can have higher-quality access to the contents and processes at play in our moment-to-moment experiences. We need to be aware of our *emotional state so we can intervene to regulate it, as needed.*

When I first began practicing mindfulness, I noticed that having an awareness of my emotional state helped keep my overreactions at bay. And when I overreacted (such as yelling loudly out of frustration), I apologized more quickly than I would have previously. I wasn't quite able to prevent the yelling. It bubbled out of me too fast. But I *was* able to watch the anger rise. I could track it and really feel the flushed feeling in my cheeks, the lump in my throat, the tingling in my arms, and then I could hear my (too) loud voice, yelling. Seeing this play out may not seem like an improvement, but it was. Sure, not yelling in the first place would have been better, and we'll get to that. Apologizing faster, however, meant less distress for me and the person I was yelling at. It also meant that I wouldn't have to follow my yelling with brooding or (internally) shouting at myself for fifteen minutes, regretful of my overreaction. To me, being able to apologize faster was a big win. It meant I was on my way. I could break the reactivity cycle.

You can **change the way you orient** to an experience, even if it initiated an overwhelming emotion. Here's what I mean by that: The other day, I came home very late from a long day at the lab—many back-to-back meetings, and a deadline looming the next day that still needed my attention. I felt preoccupied and exhausted. And when I walked through the door leading from our garage into the kitchen, I saw something that immediately spiked my blood pressure: the blender, still coated in that morning's smoothie at 9:00 p.m. and swarming with fruit flies.

My face got hot. I felt a swell of anger. My thoughts went immediately to Michael, my husband, who'd been home with the kids. It would have taken him a minute at the most to just rinse the blender out after using it. And I'd talked to him about the blender before—it really bothered me, and he'd promised to try to remember. My mind started leaping to conclusions: *He doesn't really listen to me! He doesn't really care!* In a matter of seconds, it was about much more than an unwashed blender.

At this point I had a couple of different options: (A) march into his office and yell at my poor husband, (B) suppress my anger and carry on as if I were just fine, (C) reappraise the situation, or (D) decenter.

All these options would have required my attention and engaging my working memory, but some more than others. Options B and C especially would. And B, suppression, doesn't work very well long-term—my anger over the blender would likely bubble up in some other situation. *Suppression* is fueled by executive attention and working memory, and it requires these resources to continue to do the suppressing. While you're actively suppressing, it leaves less cognitive bandwidth to do much else.

Which brings us to option C: *reappraisal.* Reappraisal means changing the way we think about a situation, by reevaluating or reinterpreting it in order to change its emotional impact. This is, thankfully, what I managed to do. Standing there, looking at those fruit flies dancing around my kitchen, I reframed my way of thinking about it: *Michael has been holding down the fort here at the house all day while I've been working. He's had a lot to manage! But the kids are healthy, fed, and safe. This is a small blip relative to all that is good right now.* By reappraising, we reduce the intensity of negative emotion, allowing us to take a clearer look at the situation and assess whether the impact is as negative as we initially assumed. *This isn't actually that big of a deal—nothing is ruined or broken. I can just ask him to wash the blender, or simply wash it myself.*

The strategy I use most often nowadays is option D: I *decenter*. You can go to the bird's-eye view, as we did earlier, or you can try something even faster: *stop, drop, and roll.*

- *Stop* the inner war against the actual circumstances—just accept them. It is what it is. Let me be clear: this does not mean that you are "all good" with the situation. It has nothing to do with your judgement about the actual event. It just means that you are accepting the actuality of what has occurred.

- *Drop* the story—your assessment of this situation is merely one story. Not the only one.

- *Roll* with it—keep going, keep moving, get curious about what the next moment will bring.

This approach keeps me agile, open, and receptive. It also keeps my working memory freed up, since I don't have to spin new frameworks or stories to make myself feel better, as I did with reappraising. With stop-drop-and-roll, I have confidence that I will have access to more data regarding the situation, am aware of what my story is and open to the possibility that it may be incomplete or inaccurate, and am certain that my emotional state will shift as I allow my thoughts and emotions to come and go without holding on and looping them.

By the time I approached Michael, who was at his computer busy with an emergent work demand that had no doubt maxed out all of his working memory capacity, I wasn't feeling angry anymore. I was grateful that I had these tools.

Our days, our lives, are full of "fruit flies in the blender" situations. Sometimes they're relatively minor. Other times they're bigger. And sometimes they're huge—moments of crisis or decision where a great deal hangs in the balance for you and for others. Even the minor events are impactful—since a lot of tiny instances of dysregulated emotional responses can erode our most valued relationships.

The ability to have proportionate responses affects all your interactions with others. Your ability to connect, collaborate, and communicate also hinges on your attentional stability.

When the Going Gets Tough, the Tough Stay Present

Lieutenant General Walt Piatt arrived in Kirkuk, Iraq, to broker a meeting between three leaders of local tribes that had been in conflict. As the newly arrived general from the US, he had to host these three factions and try to find a way forward. At one point they had all banded together against one common enemy, ISIS. But now that ISIS was gone from the region, they were clashing with each other, and all were furious at the US. The tension in that room was—to put it mildly—*high.*

The meeting started like a bonfire, with the tension and acrimony building rapidly. The three leaders aired their grievances about each other and about the US's involvement in their region. It might have been easiest to shift quickly into problem-solving mode, or even defensiveness. Walt decided that he was going to let them talk. He was simply going to listen. He tried to bring all of the attentional presence he had to the moment, to keep his focus on each leader as he spoke, to be completely open to what they had to say.

When each person was finished, he said, "Here's what I hear you saying." And he repeated back, with precision, what they had just expressed.

Walt didn't solve the big issues that day. He didn't come up with any grand solutions to all the thorny, difficult problems raised in that meeting. Yet, something more happened. The entire dynamic changed. The local leaders felt heard, and they felt respected.

"You could see it on their faces," Walt said. "You could see them thinking, 'This is someone we can work with.'"

The meeting ended up being a productive one. The three factions were able to talk to each other. And at the end of the meeting, one of the leaders approached Walt. He was wearing a strand of prayer beads on his wrist—beautifully decorated with a silver inscription. He un-looped it from his arm and handed it to Walt, saying, "This would not have been possible without you." A beautiful gesture of appreciation.

It's easy to think of "listening" as a passive thing. In fact, it's quite active and demanding, if you do it well. It takes your attentional con-trol, your emotional regulation, and your compassion. It takes focus, meta-awareness, and decentering. It's not passive at all. It's *heavy lift-ing*. And it's extraordinarily valuable. To listen, really listen, is often the "action" we most urgently need to perform. This story of how attention changed the course of a conflict gives me hope. It shows us what *presence*—so simple, yet so difficult—can actually achieve.

Listening Practice

Conventional wisdom tells us that if we want to be better communi-cators, we should practice communicating. But here is an important insight: to be a great communicator, you need to be able to listen, *really* listen. When you do, you will have more information regarding what to say next: what is most appropriate, kind, and strategically useful.

Here we go:

Set the stage: Choose a question to ask a close friend or family member. Pick something such as "What would you like to do this weekend?" You want something they can talk about, uninterrupted, for two minutes. (I encourage you to let them know that they are part of this exercise with you before you begin.)

Step 1: Convey the question to them.

Step 2: For the entire two minutes, make the person's response the object of your attention. Anchor to it. If you notice your mind wandering, return it back—just as you would do with any of the core practices. *This is also a practice.*

Step 3: Take one minute to write down any details about what you heard, and then convey it back to them.

Step 4: Switch places and ask them to listen to *you* for two minutes.

Debrief: When you are done, answer the following reflection questions:

How did it feel to give this person your full attention while you listened to them?
How did it feel to have this person's attention while they listened to you?

Listening is a powerful practice. It provides us with the opportunity to get comfortable being receptive. And we can even practice this simply by watching. As Yogi Berra said in his madcap way, "You can observe a lot by just watching."

Your Attention Is Your Highest Form of Love

My daughter, Sophie, had a "no homework" night from school recently, and when I asked her what she wanted to do with her evening, she said she wanted to bake something. But she was specific: she wanted to bake *with me*. She wouldn't let my husband help—she banished him from the kitchen. It was going to be a mother-daughter baking project, she insisted: just the two of us.

We found a recipe for cookies online and got going, spreading all the ingredients out on the counter, greasing the pan, preheating the oven. This wasn't a recipe we'd done before, so I had it pulled up on my phone to check and double-check the instructions. Every time I touched my phone, she was upset. "Why are you on your phone?!" she kept exclaiming whenever I so much as glanced at it. I was baffled at first—why was she overreacting? Then I realized that I'd been exceptionally busy, spending a lot of time with her brother discussing his college admissions and summer internship prospects, in addition to several late nights at the lab. It was obvious that she felt I hadn't been available to her.

I felt a pang of guilt and sadness about what she might have been feeling these past few weeks before snapping back to the present moment. I asked myself two important questions: What was needed right now, and what mattered? Baking these cookies with her, both of us together, that's what mattered. What could I do right now for what mattered most? Give her my full focus. It was all she wanted. Later that evening, after too many cookies had been consumed and Sophie was in bed, I reflected on how this evening might have unfolded differently when I was in the midst of my attention crisis— when I was far less attuned, less receptive to all that was happening around me. I would have likely missed what Sophie needed from me, and if I had figured it out, I'm not sure I could have given her what she needed. *I* didn't even have my full focus, which meant I certainly didn't have it to give.

What was different now? It felt like my mind was more present-centered, available, and pliable. I smiled, realizing: *this is what a peak mind feels like.* To me, a peak mind is not about perfection or being at some imaginary pinnacle, like you might see on a "successory" poster: woman on mountaintop, arms flung in the air relishing her peak experience. A peak mind is not about striving to get somewhere else. It's simpler, more elegant, and doable. I think of it like a triangle: the base is the present moment, and the sides are two forms of attention—one side, receptive attention so we can notice, observe, and be, and the other side, concentrative attention so we are focused and flexible.

Attention, both its receptive and concentrative forms, is not only a precious brain resource—it's a currency, one of our most valuable currencies. The people in our lives notice what, where, and who we spend it on. Attention, in a lot of ways, is our highest form of love.

In addition to attention, for us to fully connect with another person requires a unique and complex set of skills. Many of the moments of connection we want to show up for are positive and loving, but we also need to show up for those interactions that are difficult or adversarial. A whole spectrum of human relationships exists out there, and some of them are exceedingly difficult to navigate.

Connection Isn't Always Warm and Fuzzy

In 2012, Sara Flitner, a strategy and communication consultant, made a life-altering decision: she was going to run for mayor. She enjoyed her work running her own company, and she loved applying her skills, like critical thinking and empathy, to solving complex problems. Sara saw a lot of issues in her community—Jackson, Wyoming (commonly known as Jackson Hole), which is adjacent to the tourist meccas of Grand Teton and Yellowstone National Parks. Jackson had one of the highest socioeconomic divides in the nation, and with that came issues of high rates of depression and substance abuse, homelessness, high stress, and more. Sara thought she might be able to make a difference through her leadership and by influencing policy. She felt passionate about trying to move the needle from inside the system. Her goal, she says now, was to "infiltrate positions of power with compassion, civility, and basic decency and regard for fellow humans."

And how did it go?

She laughs. "I walked right into the eye of the storm."

She won the election, and once in office, Sara was confronted with the reality of how divisive politics are, even at the local level. When she ran for reelection two years later, the campaign got particularly nasty. The first time around, both Sara and her opponent had run clean, straightforward campaigns. This time, her opponent went negative. She had to decide, every day, how to respond to rhetorical attacks. She would get up every morning and do a mindfulness practice, first thing. No phone, no news, no social media. She says the practice "gave my brain rest" and allowed her time to ground herself in "what really mattered to me." She'd decided early on in her campaign that she wasn't going to "go dirty," and she held to it—even when she lost.

She jokes now that she went into her two-year term as mayor saying, "I love people!" and came out saying, "I hate people!" In all seriousness, though, she feels her time in office was valuable to her and that she *was* able to move the needle—even though it was a painful, difficult, even disillusioning time. Her mindfulness practice threw her, she says, "a lifeline," in large part because of the way it helped her connect with others and get things done—especially when those interactions were adversarial and fraught with conflict.

Thorny or difficult encounters with others can become situations where emotional reactivity gets the better of us. Or we try to escape, and find the quickest way out of the interaction. Neither strategy is great for attention or psychological health in the long term: unresolved issues, questions, and doubts become conflict states that draw your thoughts into ruminative loops. And interpersonal strife can also drain attention—disabling us from navigating a tough situation gracefully or productively.

"It's heartbreaking to see the kind of suffering we'll lay on each other when we act like there's some kind of budget for compassion or empathy," says Sara. "We have this attitude of, *I'll save my compassion for the people I like, not for you.* It's primitive brain reasoning, when we have—right here in our own heads—much more advanced technology available to us."

On-Demand Practice: "Just Like Me"

During a difficult interaction, take a moment to pause. It can be the length of one breath. Or, before a difficult interaction, take a moment and picture this person. Then, remind yourself: "This person has experienced pain, just like me. This person has experienced loss, just like me. Joy, just like me. Was born from a mother, just like me; will die someday, just like me." If these phrases don't resonate with you, feel free to substitute with other phrases that emphasize the common humanity we share with others.

Connection Is a Core Skill

When Sara Flitner finished her term as Jackson's mayor and left office, she wasn't done trying to shape her community for the better. She founded an organization, wittily named Becoming Jackson Whole, that is dedicated to training leaders across all arenas—community service, health, education, business, law enforcement, and more—in the kinds of evidence-based mindfulness skills that help build resilience and enable people to thrive personally and accomplish more professionally.

I met Sara in 2019, when her organization brought a hundred members of the community together for a research summit. I was one of the researchers invited to present my lab's mindfulness findings. In my presentation, I described the research and training that Scott Rogers and I had been doing, offering MBAT to many different groups across our various projects: teachers, business professionals, military spouses, medical professionals and trainees. After learning how adaptable MBAT was for various groups, and that it could be started in person and continued with us remotely, she invited us back to Jackson to launch it. Sara and her team assembled community leaders to participate, specifically targeting people at various levels within their respective organizations—so, alongside the CEO of the hospital system, a nurse; alongside the sheriff, a junior officer. "Just being able to focus your attention on 'the other,'" Sara recalls, "the progress was incredible. They were only there, in person with us for two days, but the kind of connections that mindfulness practice primed would never have been possible otherwise."

Sara credits her mindfulness practice for the entire existence of her organization, as well as her ability to get all these people—a lot of them busy, high-ranking professionals—in one room to begin with. Connection and compassion practices, she says, have been the bedrock of her career since the beginning. When she wanted to launch MBAT for community leaders, she needed to be able to call up the top CEOs in Jackson and say, *I need two days.* "And they said yes because *my* relationships with them are good," she reports. "When I say, 'Prioritize this, and you'll have success,' they trust me. They know their time will not be wasted."

She concludes: *Connection* is not "squishy." It's not a soft skill. It's absolutely foundational. It's not about being nice, or "getting along" with everybody. It's about using emotional literacy skills and relationship-building skills. For Sara, when it comes to navigating tough interactions, it's a question of seriousness: How much do you want to contribute? Are you going to rely on being the loudest person in the room, or "carrying the biggest club?" Or are you going to hone the connection and collaboration skills you need to operate at the highest level?

"Without them, I don't care what your other capacities are; you won't be successful," Sara says. "You could have the cure for cancer, but if nobody will listen to you, it's not worth a thing."

Our final core practice in this book is a connection practice. In the tradition of contemplative training, it's often called "loving-kindness meditation." Yet this practice is not focused exclusively on people you love—though it can often begin that way. The purpose here is to cultivate your ability to connect and offer goodwill toward others— and yourself. We start with someone you're close to, and then expand out. Shining your flashlight out into the world onto others *with well-wishes* is the next way we practice using our attention.

CORE PRACTICE: CONNECTION PRACTICE

1. Begin this practice as you have the others, sitting comfortably yet alert. Anchor on your breath and focus on breath-related sensations.

2. Now shift to bringing a sense of yourself into your mind, at this very moment in your life.

3. Silently repeat the following phrases to offer yourself well-wishes (three minutes). Remember: the point is to *offer* yourself well-wishes, not make requests or demands for them. Saying these phrases supports that:

    May I be happy
    May I be healthy
    May I be safe
    May I live with ease

    The phrases and their order are not important. Some people may say, *May I be free from suffering* instead of *May I be safe*. Others may wish to say, *May I find peace* instead of *May I live with ease*. The important thing is that you choose phrases that resonate with you *and* that convey a feeling of goodwill to the recipient.

4. Next, while allowing this sense of yourself to recede from your focus, call to mind someone who has been very good to you in this life, very kind and supportive, someone you might describe as a benefactor. Silently repeat the phrases below, offering them to this person:

    May you be happy
    May you be healthy
    May you be safe
    May you live with ease

5. Now, letting your sense of this person recede, bring to mind the image of someone with whom you have no real connection and for whom your feelings are neutral. It could be someone you see now and again but don't have strong feelings for, one way or another. Perhaps it's a neighbor you pass while walking your dog, a parking lot attendant you see daily, or a grocery store clerk. Mentally offer them the phrases.

6. As a sense of this person recedes from your focus, next bring to mind an image of someone with whom things are challenging at this

time in your life. This is often called a "difficult person." There is no need to pick the *most* challenging person in your life. Remember, you are not endorsing their view and are not necessarily even forgiving their actions in the past. You are simply offering kindness to them as a practice aimed at strengthening your ability to take another's perspective, realizing that—like you—they too wish for happiness, health, safety, and ease. With this in mind, mentally offer them the phrases.

7. Now move on to everyone in your home, community, state or province, and country, and continue to expand outward until you include all beings everywhere. Spend a few moments visualizing each place (your home, your community), and then offer the phrases to everyone there.

8. Throughout this practice, notice when your mind wanders away from the chosen focus, and gently guide your attention back.

9. When you're ready, spend a few moments anchoring on your breath to end the practice.

The instructions are straightforward, and the potential implications are profound.

A growing body of research has been examining the effects of this practice on the brain and body, such as improved positive mood and feelings of well-being, as well as the improved ability to take the perspective of someone else, which is needed for positive social emotions. Most recently several studies have reported that this connection practice provides a powerful antidote to one's implicit biases. More research needs to be done in this arena, but early results are very promising.

As you probably gathered, this practice differs quite a bit from the suite of mindfulness practices we have been doing throughout this book until now. I am offering it here for a few reasons, above and beyond the well-established benefits it has for positive mood and stress reduction. As the name indicates, this practice increases our sense of connection and reduces loneliness. Why would that be? Isn't this a solitary activity, after all?

Can You Connect with People Who Aren't Connecting Back?

The brain, remember, is a fantastic simulation machine. Subregions of the default mode network that we use to remember episodes from our lives are also used to project ourselves into the past and future. And these same regions can also be used to project ourselves into the minds of other people. Doing so allows us to simulate experiencing the world from their perspective. Perspective-taking empowers us to understand others' motivations, and therefore to extend empathy. By sending well-wishes to individuals across a full range of "closeness," as we are guided to do in this practice, we offer ourselves the experience of extending both care and concern. Granted, this is all done in the privacy of our minds, but as we have been discussing, the mind is a powerful virtual-reality simulator. Extending care can increase our feelings of connection to others in the same way receiving it can.

I experienced this firsthand when I attended a loving-kindness retreat. When it came time to select a "neutral person" as the target of this practice, I selected an administrator in my department at the University of Miami, Dr. Richard Williams. Richard was neutral in that I didn't have strong feelings for or against him. In fact, I had no real connection to him at all. I saw him every now and again when my grant budgets needed to be reviewed or when I had to make a large purchase. I'm not sure why I chose him, but I did.

A note about doing this practice daily as opposed to on a retreat: The connection practice you were asked to do on page 255 can be completed in fifteen minutes, as you cycle through silently repeating the selected phrases for about three minutes for each of the recipients. In contrast, on a week-long silent retreat, somewhere between 100 and 150 retreatants congregate daily for meditation in a large meditation hall from early morning to late at night. The practices are to be done in silence, and no ongoing guidance is given, other than the instructions the meditation teacher provides at the beginning of each day. Practices are divided into forty-five-minute sessions, with short breaks between them and longer breaks for meals. The sessions alternate between sitting meditation for forty-five minutes, followed by walking meditation, followed by sitting, and so on for the entire day. In the evening the meditation teacher presents a formal talk. On my retreat, instead of spending three minutes repeating the phrases for a neutral person as I would at home, I spent an entire day.

On day three of my loving-kindness retreat, I went to work repeating the phrases and extending the well-wishes to Richard. *May you be safe, may you be happy, may you be healthy, may you live with ease.* It felt like not much was going on. After all, I didn't know Richard well. I knew nothing about his life, his interests, his hobbies. Truth be told, the day felt really uneventful. The only thing I recall noticing was that my concentrative focus and commitment in wishing him well grew clearer and stronger over the course of the day. When I returned home from the retreat, I resumed my typical daily mindfulness practice, and on the rare occasion that I completed the connection practice, I continued to include Richard as my neutral person. But I didn't give it too much thought.

A month or so after my retreat, I was back in the psychology department building on the University of Miami's campus, where Richard had his office. I was there to hear a student's thesis defense.

After the defense was over, I decided to walk over to Richard's office. I merely wanted to say hello. He seemed surprised to see me and wondered if he had neglected to mark our meeting on his calendar. I assured him that he had not—I was just there to say hi. I'm sure he thought it was a bit odd. What was even odder was my internal experience on seeing him. I was filled with a kind of quiet joy and interest. I noticed his kind eyes, the shock of white in the hair that framed his face, that he looked a bit frail. The content of our interaction was quite ordinary. I had no sense of wanting or needing anything from the interaction. There was no lingering feeling, either.

Over the subsequent few years, I saw Richard several times for grant-related tasks. And each time, I felt that joyful connection to him. It didn't really matter to me if he didn't act any differently toward me. He was the same kind and competent administrator he had always been. If this sounds strange, I agree—it is unusual. But it gave me a glimpse into what might be happening in the minds of some exceptional people: the Dalai Lama, for one.

I remember meeting the Dalai Lama on stage when presenting our research findings at a meeting hosted by an organization that has helped catalyze the field of contemplative science, the Mind & Life Institute. He greeted each speaker, and when it was my turn, I was overcome by the feeling that I mattered to him, not because of anything I had done but just because "I matter." His attention felt intimate and interested, yet not personal or lingering. As our session was being introduced, I could see him scanning the meeting room, locking eyes, and offering a warm smile to individual audience members. And on their faces, I could sense the impact on them having received his compassionate attention for that brief moment. The experience brought to mind the many recent studies I had read reporting that in those who briefly practiced loving-kindness meditation (versus a comparison group that did not), there was a reduction in implicit racial bias.

I have no doubt that the Dalai Lama is an extraordinarily special human being, for many reasons. But perhaps his unbiased offering of care and kindness to everyone he meets is not the result of his disposition alone. Maybe it is a result of his daily compassion practice. Like Congressman Tim Ryan, the Dalai Lama too trains his mind for clarity, compassion, and connection. Maybe we all can?

To Make Change, Start with Yourself

Throughout this book, I have asked you to consider the brain and brain processes not as broken and in need of fixing, but instead as trainable and capable of being optimized. And now that you understand how to do so, consider asking yourself another important question:

WHAT WILL YOU DO WITH YOUR PEAK MIND?

Think about it. But don't use your standard analytical thinking. Try applying meta-awareness to "see what is," and try decentering to "drop the story," all while holding your attention steady and receptive.

Sadly, Richard Williams died recently. And I felt heartsick. In my grief, I questioned the value of having developed a sense of connection with him. Wouldn't I have been better off staying disconnected? Why bother getting close to anyone—aren't they just another potential heartache? I know that many people feel this way.

After some time, here's my answer: no, I would not have been "better off." Richard, even without his knowledge, gave me a great gift. He reminded me that life is not a zero-sum game. And extending care, concern, and kindness need not be transactional. It is part of what gives our lives meaning. And without it, as I said at the top of the chapter, we just die faster and less fulfilled.

Perhaps your motivation to learn about the brain science of attention and mindfulness was to uplift the lives of others you feel connected to, whether they be family members, co-workers, members of your community, or people you lead. How can you do this?

Answer: start with yourself.

"Having your own practice is the first, most important thing you do," says Sara Flitner, the former mayor from Wyoming. "As mayor, I spent time before every public meeting in some form of reflection. When things were very conflict-laden in our community, it was absolutely essential for me to be the best version of myself I could be."

When you start with yourself, you can be present "in the midst of chaos," or stress, or uncertainty—and that can make an enormous difference not just for you, but also for the people you love, the people you work with, even those you interact with once and never see again. And it means that you can be in a difficult situation, fully, and know that you have the cognitive resources to get through it. It works only if you *do the practice.*

Something we know for sure: learning about attention helps. Still, it's not enough. If you want to reap the benefits of mindfulness training, you'll need to give yourself a certain "dose" of mindfulness practice. Mindfulness practice actually *changes the structure of your brain* in ways that are beneficial to attention . . . if you do it often enough.

So what is *enough*?

10

FEEL THE BURN

Today, all around the world, people will wake up, lace up their sneakers, and take off for a morning jog. Some push *play* on a YouTube yoga class; others sweat it out on the elliptical machine. Some are lifting weights, doing sets of reps that tone and strengthen their muscles.

Whatever form of physical activity we engage in, we do it because we know it works. We understand that physical exercise makes our bodies stronger, more flexible, more capable. It's strange to think about because we take it for granted, but we didn't always know this. Sometimes, when I walk past a SoulCycle studio and glance at all the people inside, struggling up an imaginary hill, I think about how that would look to a time traveler from the past, if you plunked them down in modern-day Miami. They'd be baffled. A hundred years ago, the idea that a person would get on a bicycle that was mounted in place, then ride as hard and as fast as they possibly could to go absolutely nowhere, would have seemed absurd.

In the 1960s, an American doctor named Kenneth Cooper started researching a treatment for cardiovascular disease. Specifically, he was looking at *physical exercise.* Physical training hadn't previously been considered as a potential intervention for cardiovascular health. But

Cooper uncovered a strong correlation between aerobic exercise and heart health. He found that certain types of exercise (the kind that gets your heart pumping) strengthened respiration and strengthened the heart muscle, leading to better blood oxygenation and other benefits. This might not seem like revolutionary information, but at the time, it was. Cooper's work (which was soon adopted by the US military) found that working out the heart muscle made it stronger and healthier—and that specific ways of exercising were more effective than others at doing precisely that.

Cooper's work on aerobics would soon spread out of the lab and into homes, where many pulled on leotards, tights, and leg warmers and did their best Jane Fonda imitation on the living room rug. But it also kicked off a sea change in the way we thought about exercise. Running grew more popular as it became widely understood that the way to achieve cardiovascular health was to *physically train* for it in specific ways. We now have decades of research into *why* and *how* physical exercise makes us stronger and healthier. And public health officials use that research to issue guidelines regarding which types of activity help us to become more physically fit in specific ways.

So why aren't we getting the same kind of science-backed guidance on how to keep our *minds* fit?

Today, research on that subject is emerging at a meteoric pace. We are learning that certain forms of mental training are effective at training the brain similar to the way physical exercise works to train the body. And when it comes to better attention—to achieve better performance, better emotion regulation, better communication and connection—one form of mental training consistently shown to work is *mindfulness training*. It's no longer a mystery: mindfulness practices can train the brain to operate differently *by default*.

For Dr. Cooper, tracking heart, lung, muscle mass, and overall physical health *while* his participants were running on a treadmill gave him clues about how cardio might transform the body for improved health. Today, contemplative neuroscience labs, like mine, are bringing people into the lab to practice mindfulness exercises (their mental workout session) while lying comfortably in a brain scanner. What are we finding? As we've discussed throughout this book, during mindfulness practice the brain networks that are tied to focusing and managing attention, noticing and monitoring internal and external events, and mind-wandering are all activated. And when participants go through multiweek training programs, here's what we see: Over time there are improvements in attention and working memory. Less mind-wandering. More decentering and meta-awareness. And a greater sense of well-being, as well as better relationships.

And the really cool thing is, we see changes in brain structures and brain activity that correspond with these improvements over time: cortical thickening in key nodes within the networks tied to attention (think of this as the brain's version of better *muscle tone* for the specific muscles that a workout targets), better coordination between the attention network and the default mode network, *and* less default mode activity. These results give us insights into the *why and how of mindfulness training*, which we need before we can prescribe the *what*—meaning what specifically *you* need to do to achieve these benefits.

This was exactly what drove Walt Piatt to take on our study on mindfulness in the military when others said no: "Every day we did at least two hours of physical training," he says, "but we spent *zero* time on mental fitness."

Walt worried about sending people out on combat or diplomatic missions without any kind of mental training to really prepare them—to develop the kinds of cognitive capacities they so desperately needed to not be reactive, to see clearly, to observe and listen, and ultimately to make the right decisions in the heat of the moment.

And then, when they returned home, soldiers were having trouble integrating back into civilian life. As a leader entrusted to ensure the well-being of his soldiers and military families, Walt saw breakdowns there every day.

"We'd tell them, *Don't spend all your money, don't take out your anger on your family,*" Walt said, "but we had no tools to give them."

Our research was already showing that mindfulness training had an impact on attention—especially when you did it *a lot.* Remember our study with the seasoned meditators, whom we tracked both before and after a monthlong meditation retreat in the mountains of Colorado? As we discussed earlier, they'd shown improvements in sustained attention and alerting. They also had better working memory encoding, reduced mind-wandering, and greater meta-awareness after their retreat. So, indeed, twelve hours a day of being mindful, with many of those hours spent practicing formal mindfulness exercises, had many measurable benefits. Yet a big question lingered, namely: How much mindfulness practice did you actually need to do? We certainly couldn't go around telling people to meditate for twelve hours a day.

That study with the Marines in West Palm Beach had shown a *dose-response effect* with mindfulness practice for attention, working memory, and mood: the more that people practiced, the more they benefited. And how much did they practice to see benefits? While we asked them to practice for thirty minutes every day, we found a wide range across participants. On average, those who saw benefits practiced *twelve minutes a day over eight weeks.*

All of this—the Colorado study and the West Palm Beach study—was encouraging: promising evidence that the link between mindfulness practice and strengthened attentional capacity was real. What we needed to figure out next was what solution would have a practical application for people in the real world, in their everyday lives.

A "STRONG" Test

When my team and I flew out to the US Army's Schofield Barracks site in Hawaii to begin a study, we had a couple hiccups. The base was smack in the middle of the island of Oahu, and had no state-of-the-art brainwave lab like the one we used back on campus. What we ideally needed for a brainwave study was a Faraday cage: a room surrounded by a conductive metallic mesh that blocks out the electromagnetic fields around it. But getting a massive quantity of metal, weighing close to two thousand pounds, to encase an entire room on a military base in Hawaii wasn't really a possibility. So we did the best we could and built the brainwave recording lab in a broom closet, precariously positioning our equipment to avoid electromagnetic interference.

We cleared everything out—brooms and dustpans and boxes, cleaning supplies, industrial-size packages of toilet paper, metal shelving—and drove all over Oahu searching for materials to insulate the walls for light-and-sound dampening so that we could create a better controlled environment for our experiments. We found a Walmart and bought out all their bolts of black felt. Back on the base, we stapled layer upon layer of felt to the closet walls. We dragged in boxes of computer equipment, cables, and amplifiers that we had mailed in advance. In the room next door, we set up computer stations for the soldiers to use during testing, partitioning them as best we could with poster board from the local office supply store. It wasn't perfect, but it would have to do.

We called this the STRONG (Schofield Barracks Training and Research on Neurobehavioral Growth) project, and it was a first-of-its-kind, large-scale study of mindfulness training among active-duty US Army soldiers who were back from deployment and now preparing to deploy again—in this case, to Afghanistan. Our early studies on mindfulness training had shown a measurable impact, but while encouraging, those studies were small. The STRONG project, by contrast, would last four years and would test mindfulness across a much larger group of service members. Since then, we have gone on to do many more large-scale studies with military service members, military spouses, first responders, community leaders, and many other groups. Before we could offer a prescription for time-pressured, high-stress groups—which at some level means all of us—we would need to answer key questions about content and dosage:

- Was mindfulness training any better than getting *other* forms of mental training?

- What type of information should training contain? Was spending class time learning about stress and the benefits of mindfulness as beneficial as actually doing the practices?

- Finally, and perhaps most important, what was the *minimum* amount of time that people would have to spend in mindfulness practice in order to see attentional benefits? (For time-pressured people, answering this question was critical.)

Positivity: Worse than Nothing

We wanted to compare mindfulness training to another type of program the US Army had already begun implementing. This form of training offered exercises prompting participants to generate positive emotion by remembering positive experiences or reframing current challenges through a positive lens.

What we found: the positivity training was not only less effective than the mindfulness training, it appeared to be *actively depleting attention and working memory in these predeployment soldiers.* Since positivity *requires* reappraisal and reframing, it also requires attention. You use your attention and working memory to basically build a castle in the sky. It's fragile and requires a lot of work to keep it from falling apart—especially under demanding and stressful circumstances like these soldiers were facing. Positivity training seemed to be putting more strain on their already strained attention.

Other studies confirmed the same: mindfulness training strengthened attention better than other time-matched programs. Remember the college football players to whom we offered training in the weight room during their preseason training? We chose that setting on purpose, to align the trainings they were receiving with the idea of "exercise." One group received mindfulness training, the other relaxation exercises. Relaxation did have upsides for participants, but these upsides weren't unique to this training. Players who adhered most to either program, be it mindfulness or relaxation, reported better emotional well-being than those who adhered least, but *only* those who received mindfulness training benefited in their attention.

Finding that mindfulness training was better than other forms of training (such as positivity and relaxation) signaled a big advance. It made it clear that it was mindfulness exercises—not merely any active form of training—that were doing the work of improving attention and working memory.

Content: Just Do It!

Now to the next question: What should the training contain? Did it help participants to have what we call "didactic content," or learning *about* mindfulness and why it benefits you?

Mindfulness training in a research setting has two requirements for participants:

1. Attend the weekly course meetings, where a skilled trainer introduces them to practices and related content, and

2. Engage in the daily out-of-class mindfulness practice ("homework" exercises) that they are assigned to do.

The first study from the STRONG project (comparing mindfulness to positivity) assigned participants thirty minutes of practice, daily for eight weeks. But we'd cut the number of hours *with* the trainer from twenty-four hours down to sixteen. We were excited to discover that the mindfulness training was still beneficial, even with this reduction in hours with the trainer. This was great news for our time-pressured participants. Could we reduce it even further? Could we cut it in half?

To whittle it down that much, we needed to figure out what pieces of the training we absolutely had to keep, and what could be thrown out. Other studies across a variety of high-stress groups had shown us that *practice itself* really matters for seeing benefits. So it was this feature of the program that we keyed in on.

In the next study, we ran two simultaneous courses: both eight weeks long, both with thirty minutes of identical "homework" per day, both taught by the same trainer. The difference was that in one, the trainer spent seven out of the eight hours of class time on "didactic" mindfulness-related content—they discussed mindfulness, stress, resilience, and neuroplasticity. It was like going to the gym for a group weight training course and having the trainer tell you how great weight training is, all its benefits, and how to use the equipment and monitor your form, but not allowing very much time to actually exercise during class time. In the other course, the trainer spent far more time on mindfulness exercises—doing them and discussing them, without all the background information.

It seems fairly intuitive: if you don't do the workout, it's probably a waste of time. And that's exactly what we found. The practice-focused group outperformed the other group, which looked no different than getting no training at all. This discovery was a big win for us: we could cut the course duration *in half*, from sixteen hours down to eight, as long as we focused a lot of the class time on actual practice.

There was one more roadblock, though. We were seeing a troubling pattern across all our studies in the STRONG project, which was that participants weren't doing anywhere near as much practice as we were assigning. Their actual practice time was well below the thirty minutes. They most definitely were *not* doing their homework. What gives?

Our best guess? Practicing thirty minutes a day was just too much. It seemed like an impossible lift. It sounded too hard and too long. We wanted them to feel the burn, but they were fearful of pulling a muscle. They couldn't fit it in to their packed schedules, and so chose not to regularly practice. Sure, thirty minutes of mindfulness practice per day was going to help people if they did it, but none of this was going to help anybody if it wasn't realistic.

And I had another problem to contend with: the US Army, excited about our efforts, asked me how quickly I could scale up to offer it to many, many, more soldiers. They wanted me to get trainers out to multiple military bases—*fast*. How many trainers did I have available? My answer: *one*. Our one and only trainer on all of these studies was my colleague who had developed the program, informed by her own experience as a veteran and mindfulness practitioner.

I needed to take a different approach. The program had to be time-efficient and scalable. It had to be the lightest, most compact, most impactful version we could offer. What was the *minimum required dose* for these time-pressured people, who desperately needed this training, to see results?

Getting to the Minimum Effective Dose

If mindfulness training is beneficial, but nobody actually *does* it, who is it helping? *Nobody.*

We set out to drill down to a real "prescription" we could offer people. Now, there were a couple ways we could do this. The most obvious would be something like this: recruit a thousand participants, divide them up into groups, assign them different amounts of time (as in, Group A does thirty minutes, Group B does twenty-five, Group C does twenty, and so on), and then test them all and compare. Makes sense, right? A lot of scientific studies are run this way— for example, studies on the efficacy of drugs, when researchers want to determine a "minimum effective dose." The problem is that with mindfulness, it just doesn't work. It's not like giving a drug dosage that people can take. Participants simply don't do what you tell them to do. You can give them an assignment like "Do thirty minutes a day," but there is no guarantee that they'll do it. In fact, as we quickly learned, they probably won't.

I partnered up with Scott Rogers; he'd already written books on mindfulness for parents and lawyers, and his style was flexible, practical, and accessible. This was the kind of help we needed. Looking back at the data we'd already gathered comparing two groups—a mindfulness-training group and a group that didn't get the training—the results were not great! There was no real difference between groups afterward in the attention tests we gave them. Why? Was it because mindfulness doesn't work? Or was it because people were all over the place in their homework practice? Some did the thirty. Others did zero.

Thankfully, there was some buried treasure, data we could use that hinted at an answer and told us what might really work for people. We'd broken the training group into two smaller groups instead of lumping them all together: a high-practice group and a low-practice group. Here we hit on something. The high-practice group *did* benefit. So we zoomed in on them. The average number of minutes per day that this group practiced? *Twelve.*

We had a number. We took it and designed a new study. We asked our participants (football players this time) to do *only* twelve minutes of practice. And to help them hit the nail on the head, Scott recorded twelve-minute-long guided exercises for them to use. They didn't have to set their own timers or even push *stop*—they just had to follow along. We made it as user-friendly as possible.

We ran the monthlong study asking them to do their guided twelve-minute exercises *every day.* Once again, we broke the sample into two groups: high practice and low practice. And once again, the high-practice group showed positive results: *attentional benefits.* And on average, these guys did their twelve-minute exercises five days per week.

The pieces were falling into place. We were homing in on a recipe that time-pressured people were actually willing to do. And, when they followed it, their attention benefited. It was, to the best of our knowledge up to that point, moving us to a practical prescription, the *minimum required dosage* for training your attention: *Four weeks. Five days a week. Twelve minutes a day.*

Finally, we were able to design a program we could easily teach to other trainers so that they could deliver it more widely to demographics that needed it. And we could teach them fast. We wanted to stay with high-pressure, high-performing groups, like athletes, so we conducted a study in elite warriors, special operations forces (SOF). We were fortunate to partner with a colleague, an operational psychologist who worked with SOF, who was certified in offering mindfulness-based stress reduction. He flew to Miami and we trained him to deliver our program. We called the program Mindfulness-Based Attention Training (MBAT). As we had done before, my research team and I packed our laptops and headed to yet another military base, to see if this training actually worked outside of our campus environment and out in the field. We tried two variants of MBAT: one that would be delivered over four weeks, as we designed, and another over two weeks. The results were exciting and promising: MBAT benefited attention and working memory in these elite warriors. The benefits were *only* there when the program was delivered over four weeks. Two weeks was too short.

We were on our way. Since then, we've trained a lot of trainers: army performance coaches who then went on to train soldiers; military spouses who trained other military spouses; medical school faculty who trained med students; human resource professionals who trained employees. Most of these trainers had no prior mindfulness experience, but in just ten weeks, we were able to get them up to speed on delivering MBAT. The key to success was that even though they didn't know much about mindfulness before delivering the program, they were intimately familiar with the context and challenges of the groups they set out to train.

So what does this all mean for you? Mindfulness training does indeed have a dose-response effect, which means the more you practice, the more you benefit. But as we now know, "do as much as you can" doesn't work for most of us. Based on these many studies, what we've come to understand is that asking people to do too much, especially those with a lot of demands and very little time, de-motivates them. The key is having a goal that is not just inspiring, but *possible*. Twelve minutes worked better than thirty, and five days worked better than every single day. So this is what I want to encourage you to do: practice twelve minutes a day, five days a week. If you do this much, you are on track to really benefit. And the even better news is that if you do more, the benefits go up.

An important caveat: if you are busy and stressed but are also suffering from an ailment, disorder, or illness, this prescription may not work for you. This is not a therapy or treatment. We aren't trying to reduce symptoms or even stress. We're targeting our training to *improve attention*—that's the goal. There are other programs out there incorporating mindfulness as part of a treatment plan for psychological disorders like depression, anxiety, and PTSD, and these programs do show a lot of promise. They also require more time (forty-five minutes of daily practice, in some cases) and other interventions alongside contemplative practice. Mindfulness training at the prescription I'm offering here will help your attention. But if you are turning to mindfulness as a solution for other challenges, you may need support from a clinician or medical professional.

Now that you know what to do, how can you make sure you do it? I'd recommend putting it on your calendar or setting a phone reminder to ping you. *Twelve minutes.* It isn't a lot. But it's the minimum required dose. And if you come away from this book with anything, I want it to be a clear sense of how important this is. We're busy. We're time-pressured. We are always under the gun. But twelve more minutes of work is simply not going to catch you up as much as sitting quietly, and on purpose, with your breath. For only a little effort and a small investment of time, you can reap an enormous reward.

I get asked by many high-achieving, high-stakes professionals whether this practice can be condensed even more. Inevitably, someone will ask: "Four weeks is too long—can't we just do something in an afternoon?" Or "Twelve minutes is too hard to find in my day, so can I do less?"

My answer? Sure you can. And it might benefit you temporarily, like going for a walk can benefit you. But if you want to train for better heart health, you'd want to do more than go for the occasional leisurely walk. In the same way, if you want to protect and strengthen your attention, more is required. We have a growing body of research now. The science is clear. For this to work, *you have to work it.*

Working It . . . and Working It In

Paul Singerman is a bankruptcy attorney and co-chair at one of the most prominent business-law firms in Florida. He's one of the busiest people I know, and he operates in a world that is extremely high-stress: he spends most of his days working with and representing individuals and businesses going through Chapter 11 bankruptcy. He wakes up before dawn; spends full workdays in meetings, on calls, and in court; then caps them off with paperwork, research, and writing in the evening. Through the stay-at-home, quarantined months of the COVID-19 crisis (which is when he and I had the chance to catch up), he was still going to court—but via Zoom. It was one of the busiest times in his entire thirty-seven-year caréer—and the hardest.

"We are blessed to be busy," he said, "but it is the saddest 'busy' I have ever been. There's an immense destruction of enterprise value. People losing everything, due to no fault of their own. It's an intense time, it's a sad time, it's an exhausting time."

I inquired: Was he still able to find the time to practice mindfulness, through this crisis and all the extra demands?

"Absolutely," he said. "It's the first thing I do every morning. Taking the time to do the practice pays me back in all kinds of ways, all day long. You know what they say: if you don't have time to meditate for five minutes, then meditate for ten."

Paul wasn't always into mindfulness. He came upon it in an article in the *New York Times* Sunday Business section.

"It caught my eye because it was in the *business* section," he says. "If it had been in Sunday Styles, I probably would have flipped right past it. I thought mindfulness was bullshit."

This article was about an engineer, Chade-Meng Tan, one of the earliest engineers at Google and the 107th employee at the company, who had taken up mindfulness practice and found that it felt useful and evidence-based. Paul's interest was piqued. He gave it a shot. And he quickly found that the practice—far from being the "soft, fluffy" sort of activity he'd initially taken it for—helped him to be more effective in the courtroom, and in other areas of his law practice as well. Like a lot of lawyers in his field, he used to believe that his professional edge came from being aggressive. *Mindfulness* sounded like the sort of thing that would soften that edge. In fact, he found that it only enhanced his capacities. Made him sharper. *More* effective. And it's because of the core strengths that mindfulness develops: the ability to stay present; to stay nonreactive; to stay aware of your own mind, of others, of the immediate environment.

"I'm striving to be a more efficient, effective, and better data-gatherer in three buckets, all the time, every waking minute," he says. "Those three buckets are: myself, the other person, and the environment I'm in . . . and frequently, that's the courtroom."

For Paul, it starts with himself—with the awareness of what's going on in his own mind. And that includes not only the awareness of off-task thoughts, but also awareness of his own emotions and sensations through the high-stress, adversarial situations he regularly finds himself in. Frustration, anxiety, fatigue, anger, hunger—they can get the better of any lawyer in a courtroom situation that is both lengthy and contentious. But because of Paul's mindfulness practice, he now has the tools to bring himself quickly back to the present. In his line of work, attentional lapses really add up. He often says to his team of lawyers after meetings, courtroom encounters, and other interactions: "That would have gone so much differently ten years ago." It happens multiple times per week—the cognitive capacities built by mindfulness practice show up in impactful and practical ways and change the way things go.

"It basically gives you the ability to control the future—to meaningfully influence it," Paul says. "You avoid a reactive behavior, you avoid the mess that follows it. . . . I used to do and say things in the moment that I'd regret later, because the fallout would suck up my time—and my energy. I think of it this way: I'm now controlling the future, because I'm giving myself the ability to do more worthwhile stuff with my time."

Paul saw such an impact on himself, his work, and his capacities, that he wanted to bring others in. I met him when he invited me to the first mindfulness workshop he hosted for his entire firm. Now, my colleague Scott Rogers and I continue to provide trainings for his firm—they've seen the benefits, and they make it a priority.

For Paul and the other time-pressured, extraordinarily busy people we've met in this book—from Lieutenant General Walt Piatt, whose day is scheduled right down to the last minute, to Sara Flitner, who ran both a town and her own consulting business at the same time—their mindfulness practice is the *last* thing they would give up in a packed day where "something's gotta give." More than *taking up* time, these high-functioning, high-achieving people have found that mindfulness practice *creates* time. Paul puts it this way: "My study and practice of mindfulness has yielded the single greatest return on an investment I've ever seen."

You Can Start Now and Benefit

During the COVID-19 crisis, I heard from a lot of people who wanted to know if mindfulness training could help them cope. The pandemic was a long period of challenge. This is exactly what we mean by "period of high demand." It has all the qualifiers. We use an acronym to describe the most potent, high-demand, high-kryptonite circumstances that degrade attention: *VUCA.*

Volatility. Uncertainty. Complexity. Ambiguity.

The COVID-19 pandemic, as it unfolded throughout 2020, was an extreme example of VUCA. It was constantly changing. Information was sparse, then contradictory and incessantly updated. No easy answers or solutions were offered. It was the kind of circumstance that's excellent at engaging and draining attention. People would tell me it was the only thing they could think about—that their thoughts were racing. I heard from many people who just had this *fog.* As if their brains had gone sluggish, unable to focus on the simplest of tasks. I know that feeling. I felt it! I felt it as I re-created my lab virtually, moved my courses online, supported my family and friends as they adjusted to a new world—all with an impending sense of unease that "it's all too much. I just want to go to sleep and wake up when this thing is over."

People urgently wanted to know: Could mindfulness practice help them, right now?

My answer was: "Yes, absolutely. *Start now.*"

What I told people was this: You can pick up these practices any time. They are free. They are simple. They require no special equipment, no particular location. They are always available to you. You can use them to start protecting your attention and working memory *today.* If you're already "deployed"—in other words, in the throes of a high-demand period—you will still be able to *protect* your attention during this time.

The lesson is: Start wherever you are. Start if you're going through a time of high stress and high demand. Start even if you're *not* going through a time of high stress and high demand. Don't wait until pressures rise. Begin building your capacities now.

We are all always in "predeployment," so to speak, and we never know when the next big challenge will come along and ask us to rise to it. So start now.

How Do I Do It?

In this book, you've tried out two types of practices: the Core Practices or "formal" practices, in which you sit or stand and do the mental workout for three minutes or more, and the "On-Demand" and Optional Practices. Both are important. The first is foundational, and the second can help anchor your day in mindful moments that give you attentional boosts.

At the back of this book, you'll find a suggested weekly schedule for how to structure your first four weeks of practice. This is infinitely customizable, though. Exercising attention in the ways I've outlined can set you up for success.

We're at an exciting moment: we have an amassing evidence base of research. We are learning more and more about what works, and this is going to continue to get better over the coming years and decades. Right now, this is our best understanding of what can help you in terms of your attention and working memory.

When Should I Do It?

There's no particular time that I'd prescribe for you to do your formal daily practice. A lot of people choose to do it in the morning, to begin the day with a mental workout the same way they would start the day with a physical workout. Paul Singerman does his practice as soon as he wakes, often before the sun is up. Sara Flitner also prefers to do hers first thing in the morning—both put a premium on the time of the day before they look at their phones, read the news, see the messages that have rolled into their in-boxes overnight. The time *before* they have to engage with the demands of the day is the right time, for them, to mentally prepare.

Walt Piatt, by contrast, squeezes his in where he can. It's tough in the military, even as mindfulness is gradually becoming more accepted as a valuable "mental workout." It's still hard for him to get even five minutes to "do nothing."

"People at the Pentagon think you're crazy," Walt says. "*Five minutes to do nothing? They think, I could do ten things in those five minutes! My attitude is, Yes, but if you take five minutes to do 'nothing,' you can do a hundred more things after.*"

On his last deployment to Iraq, Walt would tie the practice to his fitness routine. After his regular morning workout, he'd end it at this particular grove of palm trees that had turned brown in the dry desert air. He would sit and gaze at them, fix his focus there, and do his breath awareness practice every day that he could manage it.

In Iraq, he had less time to practice, and it was even more critical that he do so. He wedged in micro-moments of practice wherever he could. During helicopter flights—which would always end in a new location and a new situation, whether diplomatic or otherwise—he'd take the time to do a practice. He'd turn off his headset for a few moments, silencing the chatter of the pilots. As the copter jolted and bounced along at 150 mph, he would lower his gaze and do a "drop the story" practice. He would remind himself:

This will probably not be as I expect.
There is so much more I don't know.
And what I do know is probably incomplete.

282 | PEAK MIND

"What these practices do for me is help me self-regulate," Walt reports. "You can feel when you don't have the capacity to make a good decision. When you don't have the mental energy."

In Iraq, when he started to feel that way, he would go outside and water a tiny patch of grass at night—10 p.m., 11 p.m., midnight. He would have been going since early in the morning and would still have hours of work left to do. But he knew he needed the attentional refresh.

"It was the mental exhaustion that would start to get to me," he says. "The distractions would start going up. I could feel myself not focusing, not listening."

When he first arrived on base and planted the patch of grass, nobody thought it would grow. But it did. So, late at night, when he was losing the attentional capacities he relied on, he'd go out and water it. He'd take the hose and put his thumb over the top and shower the bit of grass as gently as he could. One of the soldiers in his unit, trying to be helpful, offered to get him a sprinkler: "Sir, if you need the grass watered, we can take care of it!" He said no. The point wasn't getting the grass watered. The point was that *he* watered the grass. He used the watering time as practice time. Almost like a body scan, he filled up his mental whiteboard with the sensory experience of the activity. The cold water going smoothly past his thumb. The smell of the grass. The smell of the desert.

And then he'd end up having conversations with the people who passed by, who were perhaps startled to see the general out late at night with a hose, watering a tiny patch of struggling grass. People who worked for him would pass by, and they'd chat briefly—he'd hear things about the nitty-gritty of their days that he wouldn't have otherwise known. One of the Iraqi generals would sometimes be out strolling at the same time, and they'd end up talking. They chatted about farming. About the little town the Iraqi general came from. About how many date trees he grew on his farm at home, far away.

The practice will benefit you, too, if you make the time for it—both the formal practice and the informal practices that you can fill in throughout the day. Try this: When you wake up in the morning, don't roll over and grab your phone, or hop right up. Lie on your back. Take ten or even just five deep breaths. Focus on the breath. And maybe notice the thoughts that arise. It'll give you insight—information about yourself, your mind, your attention—that you can use today.

Try mindful teeth brushing. As you brush each tooth, direct your flashlight to those sensations. On the bus or subway, don't pull out your phone. Sit as you would in formal practice, embodying an alert, comfortable posture; close your eyes or lower your gaze, whatever works best, and take five minutes—or the length of the ride. Or perhaps offer the loving-kindness phrases to the people on the train with you. Sharon Salzberg, my friend and trusted meditation teacher to many, made a New Year's resolution one year of "no overlooked people." When standing in line, waiting for anything, or walking down the busy sidewalks of New York City, she would make a point to notice the people around her and simply offer each one a silent, simple wish for happiness: "May you be happy! May you be happy! May you be happy!" She mentally doled out well-wishes of happiness in all directions, the way Oprah used to give new cars to everyone in her TV audience. Noticing those around us and directing our attention outward in this way boomerangs back toward us, benefiting our interactions with others and our sense of happiness and well-being.

"You can do it sitting in a chair, sitting on a mat," Walt Piatt says. "I did it watering the grass."

Your Starting Point: The Mixing Board of the Mind

Amy is a freelance writer; her husband is a high school teacher. She visited our lab when she was researching an article on mindfulness and attention, and she posed an interesting question.

She'd noticed that she and her husband seemed to have wildly different attentional strengths and weaknesses. Her husband seemed to have *terrible* working memory—stuff dropped off his whiteboard right and left. At the same time, he often seemed highly skilled at staying in the moment, even when there were major pressures that might have easily pulled him into mental time travel and rumination. She'd watched him many times glance at a combative email from a parent . . . and then just close the mail app and happily move on with his day. He seemed unaffected—he was able to shield his attention from the "loop of doom."

"If I open an email like that," Amy said, "that's *it*. I'm done for. I'm sucked into thinking about it until I deal with it or solve the problem—even when I know for a fact that now is not the time, and it's not solvable. I just can't stop myself."

And yet, there were other attentional challenges when she saw herself excel—like holding a lot in working memory.

She wanted to know: Why was her husband so naturally terrible at one aspect of attention, and great at another? Where do these natural abilities and vulnerabilities come from?

My answer might not have been very satisfying: We don't really know where they come from. Your attentional profile is shaped by all kinds of forces, from the chemistry of your brain, to your upbringing and life experience, to the way you use your attention now. I call it "the mixing board of the mind." Just like the mixing board in a recording studio, we all have different levels, different settings. Each attentional profile is wildly unique. But whatever your "settings," you can benefit from mindfulness training.

Embrace the Suck

Anybody who's ever taken up a new physical exercise regimen knows how it feels at first: *worse.* If you take up running, the first few weeks are going to be rough. You'll be acutely aware of your body struggling to do what you tell it to do. The same can be true with a new mental exercise regimen, and with your brain.

One of the challenges we have is that after a week or two of participating in a mindfulness training course, some people say, "I feel worse, I feel *more* stressed."

My answer to that? *It's a good sign.* It means it's working. You temporarily feel worse because you're becoming more meta-aware. Whereas before, you might have been mostly unconscious of your own mind-wandering, now you're noticing that you're doing it all the time. You're noticing when you can't get your mind out of the loop of doom, or when your thoughts stray back to the same sore subject over and over again, and you can't stop it. It's not that these things are happening more—it's that you've *become more aware of them.*

It's hard, because the first thing that happens with mindfulness practice is that you become acutely aware of the ways your mind can rebel against what you actually want it to do. You see how it's restless and squirrelly. It doesn't want to do the twelve minutes of breath awareness. It wants to do something *else. Anything else!*

"But it's boring!" is the protest I hear most frequently from those who are just beginning mindfulness training. My response? Yes, it is! *And that's the point.*

It's hard. You get bored—*quickly.* We know how quickly the restless mind wants to move on to something else—how rapidly it reverts to its self-focused "default mode." Your mind wants to wander; your work is to notice that, and then (for some practices) to guide the mind back—over and over. *That's the workout.* When you're doing your basic breath awareness practice, each time your mind drifts, you notice the drift, you gently pull your awareness back to your breath sensations. . . *that's a push-up.*

Try reframing it this way: mindfulness can be helpful *because* it gets boring. *Boredom* is ultimately what's at the root of our 24/7 engagement—it's what drives us onto phones and news feeds in the middle of other tasks, or in any moment of downtime, denying us creative spontaneous thought and memory-consolidation time. And what we know from our lab studies is that *anything* can get boring if you do it long enough—even the most thrilling or high-stakes activity. The vigilance decrement—the waning of task performance over time—shows us that this is true even in situations where keeping your focus is a matter of life and death. Boredom drives us to pick up our phones and scroll, or even to scan our own minds for content. Boredom fuels our incessant search for other types of cognitive engagement. And what we know about continual engagement is that it saps resources.

When you feel bored, like you just want to be doing something else, that's when you need to get curious. With physical exercise, we call it feeling the burn. *That moment,* the moment of "Do I really need to do twelve minutes?" or "How much longer until the timer goes off?" or "Can't I do a different practice?"—that's your "mental burn." It's the equivalent of a muscle burn as you do a squat, though it feels like restlessness. Boredom. Discomfort. Walt Piatt says that his service members like to say, "Embrace the suck."

You have to deal with that mental chatter, resistance, and boredom, because *this is where you want to build tolerance.* The next time you're in a situation in real life, outside your formal practice, when you're dealing with that kind of mental resistance to focus and stay present, you may be able to handle it that much better.

This Is Not About "Feeling Better"

I was invited on a podcast to talk about my research on mindfulness and attention in high-stress groups. The show began with another invited guest, a self-described meditation teacher, leading a practice right on the air. The teacher began by asking us to close our eyes . . . and "imagine fields full of flowers, blue skies." This person proceeded to lead us through a mental activity focused on pleasant visualizations and relaxation.

My red flags were going up all over the place. He described this as a *mindfulness* exercise, but there was nothing emphasizing those key aspects of present-centered, nonjudgmental, and nonreactive qualities of attention. And as we've discussed throughout this book, this sort of approach does not work well under high stress; positivity and relaxation don't work under high stress. You're spending your cognitive fuel trying to build that lovely, imaginary world instead of building your core capacities: *The ability to notice where your attention is, to bring your mind back when it wanders. The ability to fill your whiteboard with the present-moment experience. The ability to resist story-making and to simply observe. The ability to become aware of when your mind needs to be redirected.* These are the skills that will serve you, especially during challenging circumstances.

After the other guest's "mindfulness" exercise was over, the host turned to me next, welcomed me warmly to the show, and began the interview. "That was lovely," she said. "Now, Dr. Jha. Why does mindfulness make us feel better?"

"Well," I said. "It doesn't."

Into the startled silence, I explained: Mindfulness practice is *not* about making you "feel better." It is not about achieving a special state of relaxation or about being blissful or joyful. Remember: the basic description of mindfulness practice is *paying attention to present-moment experience without telling a story about it.* And that's the promise: that you will become, if you engage in these exercises, more able to be your best, most skillful, most capable self through the present moment—even if that present moment is hard.

There is nothing wrong with wanting to feel better! But as we've seen in this book, those common tactics we so often use to try to feel better—avoiding upsetting thoughts, suppression, escapism—actually sabotage us, drain our attention more, and usually leave us feeling worse. We might not be able to "feel better" about the present moment. But the truth is, the present moment is the only one we are ever alive in. What we want to build is a kind of mental agility—not to push away difficulty or shield our self from it, but to *be with* the situation that arises. And with that you become better able to maneuver through difficulty.

Here's the bottom line: if you engage in mindfulness training, you *will* feel better, but not simply from the practices alone. The practices will build your attentional capacity and *that* will help you fully experience moments of joy, thrive in demanding circumstances, and successfully navigate moments of crisis with a reservoir of resilience.

I'm surrounded by people who changed their lives because of their mindfulness practice. From students who've worked in my lab, to my own family members, to some of the extraordinary people you've met throughout this book, including an Army general who meditated under thirsty brown palm trees while deployed to Iraq. I know mindfulness practice changed my life—it allowed me to continue doing all the things I wanted to do at a time when I felt like I was running out of options. To be a scientist and a mother, to run a lab and be present for my spouse every day, to have the life and career I envisioned . . . I needed mindfulness practice. Not to feel better, but to *experience my life better* . . . and then, almost as an afterthought, I started to feel better.

We Can Do Hard Things

When I went to India recently to present my research at a conference that the Dalai Lama was convening at his monastery on the topic of mindfulness and education, I was . . . well, unsettled. Buckling my seatbelt for the eighteen-hour flight, I felt preoccupied. At this late hour, I was still debating what I wanted to emphasize from all the slides I had prepared. Was my topic central to the theme of the conference? Most of the other presentations would be about research in children, but I'd done only a few studies with kids, and they were not part of my latest research. All of a sudden, I felt a twinge of worry, but was comforted by the fact that I could use the long flight to puzzle through my concerns, and finalize my presentation before landing.

The plane took off with a bit of bumpy turbulence. In the seat next to me was a girl, about eleven years old. She was looking right at me.

"Are you scared?" she asked. "If you're scared you can hold my hand."

Despite wanting to just focus on my presentation, I smiled at her. I noticed that she was hanging onto her mom's hand with a death grip. I realized that *she* was the one who was scared. She was clearly terrified of flying. A couple more air bumps and sudden dips, and she was almost hyperventilating.

So I asked, "Hey, how about I hold *your* hand?"

I started talking her through a body-scan practice. I probably picked it because I often used it with my own daughter right before gymnastics meets or dance competitions. I asked the girl to close her eyes. I asked her what was happening in her big toe. In her knees. In her stomach. I asked her to describe what she was feeling. *Afraid,* she said. I asked her what the fear felt like. She told me it felt like butterflies in her stomach, then like a tightness in her chest. She got calmer, even as she was more attuned to the fear she was feeling. The plane stabilized; eventually she drifted off to sleep, head on her mom's shoulder.

Her mother leaned over to me with soft eyes, her sleeping daughter in the seat between us. She held her hand out to show me her fingers. She had deep nail marks from where her daughter had dug into her skin.

"I'm so thankful for your help," she whispered. "It's the first time she's ever fallen asleep on a plane."

The body scan, as we talked about earlier, involves paying attention to physical sensations in the body. And while the mind may be preoccupied with worry or fear, doing a body scan occupies the mental whiteboard with something else—something more useful and productive. But it's not about distraction or suppression. I wasn't trying to distract this girl from her fear. The body scan—and so many of the other mindfulness practices we've worked on throughout this book—is about being *embodied* in the present moment. In this case, I was guiding the girl to notice the sensory experience of fear and moving her awareness toward those sensations. Locating it in her body, putting descriptors to it, and noticing these sensations would shift and change as she paid attention to them over time. It also allowed her to get a little distance from her fear, as she had to pay attention differently to report back to me what sensations were unfolding in her body as we did the practice. By the time I'd finished leading her through the practice, my own worries about the conference lessened, as well.

One way to think about mindfulness practice, and its utility in moments like these, is that it helps us build *distress tolerance*—our capacity to manage emotional distress, to be steady, effective, and resilient through the toughest times, real or perceived. It not only strengthens our attentional and working memory capacities—it also builds our understanding and confidence that we can tackle what's coming. That we can be in a hard, difficult moment and be okay. Mindfulness practice guides us to *be present* through stressful, upsetting, demanding circumstances, and know that we have the mental capacities we need to handle it.

There's this idea that a lot of us believe that resilience is something you either have or don't have. That it has to do exclusively with how you grew up, or your personality, or your coping skills. What we know from the science of attention is that cognitive resilience *is* something you can train and build.

After I did the body scan with the girl on the plane, I was able to pop my laptop open. With a clearer and less agitated mind, I could more easily identify where surgical revisions would strengthen my presentation. After making those strategic changes, I put away my computer and eased into the long journey feeling confident in the presentation I had prepared.

In my work, I research how to best train high-performing groups as they prepare for *periods of high demand.* For a lot of these groups, we know exactly when that period will be. For soldiers, it's deployment. For students, it's exams. For athletes, it's competition or playing season. However, most of us don't know when periods of high demand may occur. What we do know is, *they will occur.* Periods of high demand are really the circumstances of our lives. Mindfulness training allows you not only the peak mind you need to navigate through those periods successfully, but also the embodied confidence that you *can.* That you can be present, focused, and capable through difficult circumstances. I told the girl on the plane that the turbulence would end—and so would her fear, and all the sensations that went along with it. It would all pass, the moment would change. She just needed to realize, in each moment, that she was okay *in that moment.*

"Do you know what the pilots do when the plane runs into this kind of bumpy air?" I'd asked her. She shook her head. "Nothing!" I said. "They can't out-muscle turbulence, or swerve around it. They simply let it happen, and let the plane pass through. They hold steady until the pocket clears."

What we gain from mindfulness—from the capacity to keep our attention where we need it, in the form we need it—is this fundamental understanding that everything passes. Everything changes. This moment will pass quickly, but your presence in this moment—whether you're here or not here, reactive or nonreactive, making memories or not—will have ripple effects that expand out much more widely. So the question is: In this moment, can you be present? Can you place your flashlight on what matters to you? Let the ink fade on what doesn't? Drop your expectations and see what's right here? Avoid reactivity, judgment, and story-making and *see what is?* Can you really be here for this experience, so you can feel, learn, remember, and act in ways that make sense in your life, for your goals and aspirations, for the people around you?

You don't have to be born with expertise in these capacities—nobody is. We have to work to hone them. But now, at least, we know how.

THE PEAK MIND IN ACTION

Westminster Hall is an imposing place even if you're not there to present your life's work to members of the UK Parliament as well as top military and emergency services leaders. Huge and turreted, some parts of it almost a thousand years old, it sits in the heart of London and looms over the River Thames. The room in the House of Commons where I was presenting, along with other experts on mindfulness training, had the hushed, weighty feel of a courtroom. It was long and high-ceilinged, with deep-green walls and tall, narrow windows that looked out onto the river. Everything was antique yet pristine—the weight of history was heavy in that room. Rows of benches, a deep, polished mahogany, ran the length of it. And they were all filled with some of the most important, influential people in the country.

I already felt rattled. I'd been preparing for this presentation—at that point, one of the more high-profile ones of my career—for weeks. The original plan had been this: Walt Piatt, who was then a major general, and I would present together. He'd have ten minutes, then I'd have fifteen. I'd been told to have slides prepared and to be ready to go immediately after him. I spent hours prepping my talk, honing it down, going over the slides. I was ready.

And then, two days before the big day, Walt had to pull out. (When you're a major general and something "comes up at work," it's not negotiable.) So, we pivoted—the organizers asked me to absorb Walt's time, rework my material, and present for twenty-five minutes. I took a deep breath and dove back in, reworking my presentation. But it threw me. And arriving in London, after the long plane ride, a bit jet lagged and groggy, concerns had started to creep in. *Was my message sufficiently honed? Was my timing on track? Had I represented the broader view well, now that I was absorbing some of Walt's message?*

And there was an extra, even more personal layer to all this for me. I would be walking into the seat of government in the country that had ruled over the place of my birth for nearly ninety years. I was born in the town where Gandhi organized his nonviolent resistance against British rule. And I'd be talking about the merits of peace-promoting practices to war leaders. There was poignancy to it—and a lot of pressure. As I settled myself with the other presenters at the front of the room, I was feeling it all: the last-minute changes, the weight of history, the concerns welling up about my presentation's clarity. And then, the event organizer approached us. There was another twist.

The evening before our meeting, the room we were in had been used for a closed-door meeting about whether or not to keep Theresa May in place as the UK's prime minister. This was October 2018, in the middle of the Brexit decision—tensions were high, and everything was up in the air. The organizers had just discovered that someone had dismantled the audiovisual equipment to eliminate the possibility that the discussion regarding May could be secretly recorded. They had literally ripped it out of the wall. There was no way to get it back online. The organizers dragged in an external speaker system and scrambled around trying to find a projector, but three minutes before I was supposed to go on, they called it: *No slides. Wing it.*

As I readied myself to speak, I remember thinking, *everything in my life has brought me to this moment.* Not because if I failed, there would be dire consequences—in the grand scheme of things nothing terrible would happen if I tanked. It wasn't the same as it was with some people I worked with: I wouldn't get blown up by a grenade or engulfed by a fireball. I was not in jeopardy of losing an important case for a client or a multimillion-dollar sports contract. What I had in front of me was an opportunity. I had the chance to land my message with people who possessed the power to make decisions that radically affected other people's lives—people who *were* put in life-and-death situations every day. I had a narrow opening to make a difference. I could either take it, or let it slip away.

My thoughts seemed to settle and focus. I spread the printouts of the slides out in front of me, looked up at the crowd, and began to speak. I talked about the power of attention, how it can—and so often does—go wrong. And then I spoke about how it can go right: how mindfulness training can hone our focus *and* expand our awareness. How it lets us rise above the cacophony of a chaotic or confusing situation, take in the landscape, and in the blink of an eye make the *right* move amid so many potential wrong ones. And I talked about how the capacity to be present—to take in an experience without elaboration, judgment, or reactivity—allows us to absorb, learn, and discern so much more clearly and effectively than we would otherwise. I said that this kind of ability can change not only the moment you're in, but even the trajectory of an entire life.

When I was finished, I felt satisfied knowing I'd delivered as tight and powerful a presentation as I could have. And the last-minute changes that had threatened to undermine me had instead transformed into a kind of gift—with the longer time and the slides scrapped, I felt myself connect more fully with the audience. I had the time to expand on my ideas and results and to allow myself to relax into the rhythm of communicating my message with this esteemed audience. And instead of staring at a glowing screen as I spoke, clicking a projector remote from slide to slide, I'd looked out at my listeners, making eye contact, talking *to* them.

This was what I'd been missing all those years ago, when I lost sensation in my teeth and realized that I was numb to so much more in my life. I'd been pushing hard and moving fast, my mind always churning on something; I was overwhelmed and disconnected, never at rest and observant. I was lost in a maze, unable to see my way out. Now, I had a tool to lean on. I had learned how to find my focus and own my attention. I could zoom in to direct my mind to what mattered, and zoom out to surveil the landscape, seeing each obstacle clearly, finding a new, better way around. It was like flexing a muscle I hadn't even known was there before.

I left the grounds of Parliament practically floating. I'd accomplished exactly what I'd set out to do—I'd communicated as clearly and dynamically as I could, and maybe made a difference. I imagined the knowledge I'd shared settling in each listener like a seed, one that each parliamentarian, military leader, police chief, and first responder could carry back to their own slice of the world to take root, grow, and spread. I hoped it would help people navigate through stress and crisis, making the kinds of decisions—even under pressure—that aligned with their ethics and their goals. Maybe, like my husband, Michael, someone might achieve a better awareness of their own mind and find their focus so they could reach for their dreams. Or like the firefighter who'd sought me out thousands of miles from his home, could learn to broaden his attention to hold in mind the bigger picture, the larger goal, without getting fixated on small distractions and "engulfed" by the inevitable overwhelm of life. Or like Walt Piatt, who wrote to me while he was deployed to Iraq about his mindfulness practice, and told me how that daily mental training helps him hold to the ultimate goal—*peace*—even through stress and pressure, crisis and complexity.

People often say, "There's just too much *action* that needs to happen right now. How am I going to just sit there with my eyes closed?"

I hear this from everyone, from business leaders to social activists, from parents to police officers. And I get it—I felt the same way. People want to change the world. They want to get things done. They want to be fulfilled. To accomplish all this, it seems that we need to become a perpetual motion machine.

My response to that, as someone who once also prioritized endless motion over ever sitting still: If you want to take action for lasting change, you need to have *all your capacity to get you there.* This is about claiming, and using, *all* your resources.

As humans, we are facing unprecedented challenges with our attention systems. We live in a world that now seems built to fracture and pull at our attention. The innovative digital and technological tools that allow us to stay connected to each other, to do the work we love, to learn and progress in our lives, are the very same tools that place relentless demands on our attention, pulling us away from what we want or need to do.

When we engage in mindfulness practice, we learn to keep our attention present in the moment for the unfolding of our lives. We step away from the mode where we're simulating and planning, and we experience life directly. I said in the introduction that the present moment is the only place you can use your attention. It can't be saved up for later. It is a superpower—but it has to be used *now,* it can only be used now.

We used to think of attention as primarily *a tool for action*—a system for constraining information so we can direct our minds to do something with it. What we're seeing now through contemplative neuroscience and the *new* science of attention is that for us to lead full and successful lives, attention must not only be focused for us to take action, but it must also be receptive so we can notice and observe. We can use it to open up to what is occurring before us. We can withhold judgment and story-making and see what is. We can not only frame and reframe problems, but can *de*-frame problems and see them through new eyes. And by doing so, our thinking, decisions, and actions will all become better aligned with what is needed in the moment, and what we want out of this precious life we have.

This "new science" of attention has an empirical basis that is fast growing. What you are seeing in this book is the vanguard of this field—the push forward. We are breaking new and exciting ground on the incredible value of mindfulness and other contemplative practices. This is a direction we vitally need to go, and because I've seen the impact this work has had on people across a broad range of professions, people from many walks of life, I'm thrilled to be a part of it.

That day in historic London, presenting to Parliament, I had only one regret: that I would not be able to share anything about it with my father. During each of the highs of my life—getting my PhD, my wedding, opening my lab, the births of my children—there has always been one missing piece, a shadow in the shape of him.

Earlier, when I talked about trauma and triggers, I mentioned how many of us have experienced them. In my life, it was a car accident that had a big impact on me. It changed my life, because it took my father's. Driving back from a family road trip to Yosemite National Park, a drunk driver slammed into our car, veering us off a cliff and onto a field below. My sister and I, aged thirteen and five, in the backseat, were spared the worst of it; my mother on the passenger's side, less so. My father, in the driver's seat, was not.

My memories from the accident are vivid but choppy. I remember the way the car moved just as I woke up into an unfolding nightmare. Then: the car on its side, the hissing of the engine, the slow realization that this was *not* merely a dream. I remember how quiet it was all around us. I could see a man on the cliff looking down and it struck me that he wasn't running to help. We later surmised that he was likely the driver. It had been a hit-and-run—at some point after I spotted him, he must have just left, because nobody called for help. In the distance, I could see a small house. I knew we needed to get to it, call an ambulance. I picked up my sister and carried her toward it, through the field.

I was only a kid then, and I didn't know the first thing about how the brain worked, or how mindfulness could transform it. This fatal accident that took my father's life, and severely injured my mother, was an experience that shaped a great deal of my life, including my work as a neuroscientist. When I first started on this journey, embarking on my research into the science of attention, I didn't know exactly what I would discover. And yet a part of me knew what I was searching for: that it's not simply about being able to focus on an assignment or project or task. It's not only about being more productive, or performing better at work, or being a more-present parent or partner. It *is* about those things, but it's about something more, something bigger. Having a peak mind means living fully in the face of everything we have to deal with as human beings. Through stress and grief, through joy and tragedy.

I said at the beginning of this book that the battle for your attention is the battle for the resources to live your life. In my decades of research into the science of attention and mindfulness, everything I've uncovered along the way has only served to prove how true that really is. It *is* a battle—but it's one you can win, over and over.

CORE TRAINING FOR THE BRAIN

As we've discussed throughout this book, you need attention for almost everything you want to do, and to do it well. The brain's attention system serves as our *mental* core. Like the body's physical core:

- it's engaged during most of our activities,

- its core strength determines how stable and agile we feel as we maneuver through the world, and

- there are effective exercises we can do to strengthen it.

While a plank, bridge, or sit-up each targets slightly different muscles, they all improve coordination between muscle groups and bolster core strength. Mindfulness exercises are intended to strengthen and improve coordination between brain networks that carry out a variety of attentional functions: our ability to direct and maintain focus, notice and monitor ongoing conscious experience, and manage goals and behavior. With more repetition comes improved coordination between these brain networks—and greater core strength. What this feels like in our lives is greater mental stability and agility, which ultimately empower our effectiveness and fulfillment, and deepen our sense of well-being and purpose.

This book has introduced you to three types of practices that work to strengthen attention. The first category of practices was about strengthening concentrative focus—the intention was to narrow and steady the beam of your attentional flashlight. These practices build your attentional control. Your goal was to direct your attention first to a specific target object—your breath (*Find Your Flashlight*)—and then to specific bodily sensations (*Body Scan*), and maintain it there for some period of time. When your attention wandered away from that object, you brought it back. Together, each of these steps comprises the "attentional reps" of the practice. Focus, maintain, notice, redirect. Repeat. The more reps you do, the more you strengthen these aspects of your attention.

The second category of practices is about *keeping watch*, as you monitor and notice the ongoing processes and content in your moment-to-moment experiences. Unlike the concentrative practices, here your attention should be receptive and broad. These were the *open monitoring practices* you tried. The challenge with these was different: There was no particular target for your attention; instead, you maintained a stable watch—noticing, monitoring, receptive, open. You took an observational stance. You allowed thoughts, emotions, and sensations to arise and then pass away.

We find that when people train using open monitoring techniques, which are some of the more challenging exercises, they strengthen that open, receptive form of attention. Practice this regularly, and you will be more capable of recognizing, faster, that your thoughts are not facts. You'll be able to decenter and drop the story with more ease. Just as your body grows stronger by doing regular physical training, this mental training will build *meta-awareness*, a heightened awareness of the rising and passing away of the contents and processes of consciousness, such as thinking, feeling, and perceiving.

Doing these practices consistently over time will change the functioning and structures of your brain. In fact, even the *very first twelve minutes* you spend will immediately change how your brain operates—*but only for those twelve minutes.* After, it will "default" back to its typical mode of processing. But over time, as you establish a consistent practice of five or more days per week, week after week, these new ways of paying attention increasingly become the default. While this adds up to better brain functionality, how do concentrative and receptive practices support us in the real world? How do they help support a *peak mind*?

William James, the philosopher and psychologist who long ago pointed out that training a wandering mind would be the best kind of education we could offer, also observed: "Like a bird's life, [the stream of consciousness] seems to be made [up] of an alternation of flights and perchings." A peak mind balances and values the flights and perchings, the doing and being, the directing and receiving.

You learned a third type of practice as well, which emphasized connection and built on your strengthening of concentrative and receptive attention. But unlike the prior practices that emphasize observing the unfolding of whatever is occurring in the here and now, the connection practice is prescriptive: We are directing attention in a concentrative manner to the concept of well-wishes toward ourselves and others. During this practice, attention is utilized for reappraising and perspective-taking. This type of practice is designed to help us move out of a limited but accustomed way of paying attention and to experiment with using a different angle: we look at ourselves as worthy of receiving well-wishes for our happiness, safety, health, and ease. For example, you may be used to thinking of yourself as "too busy" for this kind of activity; you may even find it uncomfortable to accept these wishes. This practice is experimenting with allowing ourselves to receive them. We also do this for others as we progress through the practice. This is another key aspect of a peak mind—the capacity to be connected and caring toward ourselves and others.

Here, I've laid out a recommended weekly schedule, based on our most current data from the lab and the field, for training your attention. The instructions are informed by current science on behavior change: Start with extremely small goals, achieve them, don't miss out on the feel-good sense of success (this is key!), and repeat. Slowly increase the size of the goal and keep achieving it, and you'll continue the rewarding feeling of accomplishing it. This is how to best support yourself in creating a habit—go small, feel the success of completion.

Success here does not mean that your mind never wandered, or that you didn't move at all, or that you experienced bliss, peace, or relaxation. Rather, success means you put in the time and did the practice. Success is completion. To ensure that you complete the practice, tie it to some other activity that you successfully complete each day. It could be brushing your teeth, exercising, making yourself a cup of coffee. Researchers on the science of behavior change and habit creation recommend choosing an "anchor activity" for any new thing you want to add to your day. When you do the "anchor," you perform the new habit you want to build. So, for example, your anchor could be *coffee:* "When I turn on the coffee maker to brew, I sit down and do my practice."

Throughout this book, I asked you to do three minutes per practice when I introduced you to each of the practices. As you embark on habit formation of daily practice, I encourage you to keep the time demands to 50 percent of what you feel is comfortable. Then once you are consistent, slowly expand the time. In the formal program, I recommend twelve minutes of daily practice. Remember: it's not a race. Do what's manageable. Straining doesn't make for faster progress.

The schedule runs for four weeks. My hope is that, once you hit the end of week four, you'll begin to experience practice-driven shifts in your daily life and that those results will keep you inspired to keep going. But here is the key: for mindfulness training to work for you, you've got to work it. This means a commitment to practice. Practice equals progress.

PART ONE

WEEK ONE

We begin with the fundamental exercise that is the building block for every other practice: *Find Your Flashlight*. This simple but powerful breath awareness exercise is your foundational skill.

CORE PRACTICE			
DAY 1	Find Your Flashlight	12 minutes	page 117
DAY 2	Find Your Flashlight	12 minutes	
DAY 3	Find Your Flashlight	12 minutes	
DAY 4	Find Your Flashlight	12 minutes	
DAY 5	Find Your Flashlight	12 minutes	Goal
DAY 6	Find Your Flashlight	12 minutes	Stretch
DAY 7	Find Your Flashlight	12 minutes	Big Reach

What to Focus On This Week

A reminder: in this exercise, we are *focusing* our attention on the breath, but not constraining or controlling it. This is not about deep breathing—a valuable activity for relaxation, but not what we're do-ing here. Instead of controlling the breath, you are watching it as it occurs in real time, with an awareness of doing so. You may find your breath slows down a bit during the practice, or you have moments where you drift into deeper breathing. This is fine, since as we said this practice is about noticing your breath, not controlling it. The fact that you notice natural variations in your breathing patterns is a good sign. You're on-task!

Going beyond the formal practice, integrate this into your life as much as possible. Add a mindful orientation to an activity you al-ready have to do. Example: mindful teeth brushing. If you're already thinking about your to-do list as you're scrubbing, bring your flash-light back. Steady it on the sensations: the cool, refreshing tingle of the toothpaste, the feel of the bristles, the muscles of your hand and arm moving. It takes zero extra minutes to layer a mindful orienta-tion into some of your existing daily routines.

What Week One Might Feel Like

A lot of people report that their mind is "too busy." I hear it all the time: "It's not working; my mind won't sit still." But understand this: Your brain is *not* too busy—you just have a human brain! As we discussed, it works like a "thought pump." That's exactly what it does. Your job is not to stop it—your job is to exist with it, and to do the work of placing your attention back where you want it. *That* is the workout.

Frequently Experienced Challenges

Many new practitioners go into this carrying a lot of "mindfulness myths" along with them. These can be destructive and demoralizing. Here are a couple of reminders, to debunk any damaging expectations that may be lingering from what you've heard about mindfulness in the popular discourse:

- *You are not "clearing your mind."* This is not possible, and not what mindfulness practice asks you to do.

- *Your goal is not to feel peaceful or relaxed.* Images of mindfulness practitioners often exude this expectation—remember, this is not what's happening. This is an *active* mental workout.

- *There is no special state to achieve.* There's no "blissed-out" state you are aiming to experience; you don't need to feel transported. In fact, the whole point is to be *more* present in your current moment. You're not traveling elsewhere. You're going to feel your hip bones against the chair. You're going to notice every itch, every desire to move, every shift away from the present moment. You'll notice every small sensation and outrageous or distressing thought. *That's success.*

What Success Looks Like in Week One

That you did it! If you did your five days, for twelve minutes each day, you get a gold star. It doesn't matter how squirrely your mind felt, or if you opened your eyes to check the time every minute. You got yourself in the chair with the intention to practice, and you did it—that's a win.

You might have caught yourself mind-wandering a lot this week. Guess what? That's great. No matter how long you were mind-wandering, the moment you *notice* it is your success point. So, if you caught yourself mind-wandering a hundred times in a session, that's a lot of success. This is a big reframe, but an important one: what we think is a failure is actually a win.

How Week One Skills Will Show Up in Your Life

If you're really able to *find your flashlight*—that is, know where your attention is, moment by moment—you can then realize whenever you're mind-wandering during a conversation or not mentally present in a meeting, or notice any moment in your life when you're displaced in time and space. You'll notice this happening more and more, and you'll be able to guide your flashlight back, just as you do in practice. You'll also develop more confidence in redirecting it, in a supportive yet firm manner.

WEEK TWO

Last week you found your flashlight.

Now, we're going to move it.

CORE PRACTICE			
DAY 1	Find Your Flashlight	12 minutes	page 117
DAY 2	Body Scan	12 minutes	page 178
DAY 3	Find Your Flashlight	12 minutes	
DAY 4	Body Scan	12 minutes	
DAY 5	Find Your Flashlight	12 minutes	Goal
DAY 6	Body Scan	12 minutes	Stretch
DAY 7	Find Your Flashlight	12 minutes	Big Reach

What to Focus On This Week

The target of your attention in this week's practice is body sensations. The workout is not only keeping the flashlight steady, but also moving it—your focus becomes something you smoothly sweep through the body. Notice that this week's schedule is still asking you to continue with your basic *Find Your Flashlight* practice, every other day. What we've found through our work with various cohorts is that interleaving the practices in this way is the most effective way to build that core attentional strength.

Find Your Flashlight is going to be a lifelong practice—you don't "progress" past it. You keep expanding this practice—noticing more-nuanced changes in your moment-to-moment experience; the arising of an emotion, sensation, or thought; the urge to shift away; the feeling of returning back. The granularity will also increase the more you practice. It will strengthen your capacity to perform and benefit from the other practices as well; meanwhile, the other practices will inform this one. You may feel more moments of insight—*aha!* moments when you suddenly feel a sense of knowing, understanding, or perceiving something that had previously eluded you. This could be about a mental habit you have, or a challenge in a relationship, or a more fundamental understanding of the nature of things (for example, impermanence and interdependence).

What Week Two Might Feel Like

Be aware that when you introduce the *Body Scan*, you may notice more pain and discomfort in the body. This can seem like a downside at first, and in fact we wondered exactly this with soldiers: Why do we want to make them more aware of discomfort and pain when they have to go out and experience it? But more knowledge of the body translates into greater capacity to act to intervene with anything you notice going on. (Foot pain, when attended to, could signal a soldier to notice that she needs more padding in her boot. This can be the difference between completing a fifty-mile hike successfully versus spraining her foot.) You will also notice that your story about the pain may keep the pain around for longer or with more intensity. You'll be able to parse the monolithic experience of pain, separating it into undulating shifts of sensations—tightening, piercing, warmth, and so on. The pain will begin to be seen as more of a constellation, and the stories about physical sensations may quiet, as you notice the mind-wandering and return back to the raw data of the physical sensations.

Frequently Experienced Challenges

Some people find it challenging to perform the *Body Scan* on their own. If you find it difficult or distracting to guide yourself through it, seek out guidance, such as a recording to follow.

And, watch out for a feeling of "chasing the high." You might have had a couple really good, successful-feeling sessions last week. Don't let yourself fall into this striving or chasing mode. Mindfulness practice as attention training won't look (or feel) like exponential upward improvement. Often, "success" doesn't *look* like success. A session that feels like a failure was probably a great workout for your brain.

How Week Two Skills Will Show Up in Your Life

Whenever anything happens—at work, at home, wherever you are—there's a whole constellation of sensations that show up in the body. Stress, anxiety, elation, fear, sadness, excitement—they each have associated physical sensations. You'll be noticing this more and more. This means that you can take action as you tap into these sensations, notice them quickly, and understand what they mean. For example: I know that I've gotten a lot better at realizing the sensations that begin to build when worry sets in. I feel it first in my chest, but then I check in with my jaw, which I usually find I've been clenching. With this awareness, I can intentionally relax my jaw and pay attention to the issue causing the worry, or at least acknowledge that I've gotten lost in a simulation, and then be able to engage with the next moment in the best way. These are micro-interventions that can help us course-correct as we become more attuned to our minds and bodies.

Integrate the *Body Scan* into your day. Remember: it takes *zero minutes* to add this into a task you might otherwise perform mindlessly. Do the *Body Scan* in the shower as you wash from head to toe, or as you just step in and feel the water washing over you. Don't miss it.

WEEK THREE

This week, your focus becomes attention itself.

CORE PRACTICE			
DAY 1	Find Your Flashlight	12 minutes	page 117
DAY 2	River of Thought	12 minutes	page 230
DAY 3	Find Your Flashlight	12 minutes	
DAY 4	River of Thought	12 minutes	
DAY 5	Find Your Flashlight	12 minutes	Goal
DAY 6			Stretch
DAY 7			Big Reach

What to Focus On This Week

This week, *Find Your Flashlight* is still your touchstone practice. But as we shift into *River of Thought*, the focus of your attention is now your own mind. Remember: with *River of Thought*, you visualize your own mind as a moving river. All kinds of stuff is going to float by in that moving water—your job is to observe it and let it go. Don't reach down to grab any of those thoughts or worries or memories—simply notice them and let them float on by. Draw on the decentering and *Watch Your Whiteboard* mini-practices offered to exercise your capacity to step back and observe the mind. If you do find yourself wrapped up in something, go back to your breath—think of it as a boulder in that river that you can rest your attention on and regain your stability. Then begin observing the moving water again.

What Week Three Might Feel Like

Not engaging and not elaborating are active attentional skills that require core strength to perform. You will build this capacity over time, but doing this for the first time in a twelve-minute formal practice can feel as hard as trying to hold a plank when you can't yet do a push-up. You'll get better at this. If you find yourself engaged with thoughts, worries, or memories that have floated up, remember: that realization is a win. *That's* meta-awareness—you just did it. Reclaim your flashlight, redirect it to the breath to anchor yourself for a bit, and then move back into observing the River of Thought again.

Frequently Experienced Challenges

You'll start to become more aware of how much your mind is wandering. This can feel uncomfortable, or make you wonder if you're getting worse instead of better. You're not! You're simply growing more aware. Remember: your mind has always been wandering, but you're just catching yourself more. Again: success point.

You may start noticing what's arising in your mind more and more (both during formal practice and throughout the day), and it might not always be nice. You may find yourself realizing, *Man, I get angry a lot.* Or: *I'm obsessing over food (or sex or video games) and can't stop.* These are not fun things to realize. Reframe it: this is information you can use. It's like getting to know a new friend. You are supportive yet firm, befriending yourself, quirks and all.

How Week Three Skills Will Show Up in Your Life

You grow the capacity to reflexively ask yourself, *What's happening right now? What's my mind doing? What am I really upset about? Why am I consumed by this?*

You'll notice that you start defaulting to taking a more observational stance toward your own thought processes; you get in the habit of checking with yourself to see if you have a story, and how it might be affecting your interpretation of events or feelings. This is an important part of what having a peak mind means, and you're starting to get there: you are able take a broad, receptive, observational stance.

You can "monitor" your mind in this way, outside of formal practice. Try this: While driving, walking, or riding the subway, don't listen to music or a podcast; don't take a phone call. Just sit and let your mind roam. Notice where it goes and what comes up.

WEEK FOUR

The flashlight of your attention moves outward, toward others.

CORE PRACTICE			
DAY 1	Find Your Flashlight	12 minutes	page 117
DAY 2	Connection Practice	12 minutes	page 255
DAY 3	Find Your Flashlight	12 minutes	
DAY 4	Connection Practice	12 minutes	
DAY 5	Find Your Flashlight	12 minutes	Goal
DAY 6	Connection Practice	12 minutes	Stretch
DAY 7	Find Your Flashlight	12 minutes	Big Reach

What to Focus On This Week

This week's new practice is not only about directing your flashlight toward other people, but also about having well-wishes for yourself, even and perhaps especially when you mind-wander or end up in the loop of doom. Big parts of this practice involve remembering that the human brain works this way by default, and then having kindness for yourself as you begin again.

Notice that *Find Your Flashlight* is still interleaved: this foundational practice is now reinforcing *all three* of the other practices. You draw on this key skill as you focus on body sensations, notice what arises in your mind, and practice directing well-wishes to yourself and others. *Find Your Flashlight* is the lifelong work of attention training: it reinforces all the other practices.

What Week Four Might Feel Like

You might notice that spending twelve minutes each day making well-wishes makes you more likely to be supportive instead of punitive, curious instead of righteous, hoping for the best instead of expecting the worst. You may find yourself more easily able to "see it from someone else's eyes" during a disagreement. This is what reappraisal and perspective-taking look like in our lived experience.

Frequently Experienced Challenges

You may find that sometimes the phrases feel empty, as if you're merely reciting a word salad, or the words lose their meaning. If this happens, remind yourself that this is a concentrative practice. You want to use each phrase as the *complete* focus of your attention. Slow it down. Understand each word. Fully comprehend its meaning. And if the phrases feel too prone to elaboration and mind-wandering, try to just use your inner speech to say the words, one by one. The key is to comprehend and extend the well-wishes, without checking out or diving into the story of each.

If you experience discomfort with directing phrases with well-wishes toward yourself, remember that this is part of the workout: we are intentionally practicing this new perspective. Notice this discomfort, but continue.

You may also feel nothing at all—this is normal! And it's still doing the work—so keep going. The effects of the workout can show up much later. Here's an example: You're saying these things for a week or two, and you feel as if there's nothing really going on. Then all of a sudden you're about to raise your voice or snap at your spouse or child and you catch yourself, realizing that your intention *is* for them to be happy, and there might be a better way to say this. You can shift from reacting to responding. You end up communicating the same message, but without the reactive tone.

How Week Four Skills Will Show Up in Your Life

And finally—as always—integrate this into your day. You don't have to be sitting with your eyes closed to extend well-wishes toward others, or even toward yourself. Again, layer this into your routine. Try it as you're walking: With the cadence of your steps, say silently to yourself, *May I be happy, may I be healthy. . . .* Wish it for yourself or someone you know, or extend it toward any living thing that you see. Have you ever been in a store or other public setting and become annoyed with a person you don't know? *May you be happy!* No reason to waste time occupying your thoughts with anger. You may notice that you are more easily able to "get on the same page" with people as you tune in to their mental models, or that interpersonal conflicts are more easily resolved, or that people you previously looked past come alive to you.

WEEKS FIVE
THROUGH FOREVER

Keep going!

DAY 1		
DAY 2		
DAY 3		
DAY 4		
DAY 5		Goal
DAY 6		Stretch
DAY 7		Big Reach

From here on out, the schedule is up to you! You know by now that you'll need to practice for a minimum of twelve minutes, aiming for five times per week, in order to see benefits in your attention system. But the combination of practices is completely customizable. Most people report that they have a practice they particularly like.

Remember: They are all mutually reinforcing, and they each incorporate components of the others. They are all part of the core workout. So choose what works for you.

You can select a different practice each day. You can combine the practices to equal twelve minutes. I like to do *Find Your Flashlight* or *River of Thought* for the first twelve minutes, then finish with a shorter *Connection Practice*.

As you practice these skills for twelve minutes, in a chair in your living room (or wherever you do this attentional workout), they're going to start showing up for you: in your work, in your relationships, in the arc of your life as you meet challenges and try to hold to your goals and dreams. If those twelve minutes feel too hard, remind yourself: You're not doing this to be an Olympic-level breath follower! You're doing it to strengthen your mental core, to power up your attentional stability and agility.

With mindfulness training, you can use your attention to disrupt old, ineffective ways of navigating the world. When you have a peak mind, you have the power to flip the script.

The Peak Mind Pivot

There's the standard way of thinking, and then there's the Peak Mind Pivot. It's not that the standard way of thinking isn't valuable—it's that the Peak Mind Pivot greatly *expands your options*.

- Standard view: *To think better,* practice thinking.
  Peak Mind Pivot: Practice being aware that you are thinking.

- Standard view: *To focus better,* practice directing your attention.
  Peak Mind Pivot: Practice noticing and monitoring when you are not focused.

- Standard view: *To communicate better,* get clear on what you want to say.

  Peak Mind Pivot: Get better at listening.

- Standard view: *To understand yourself,* identify qualities of who you are.

  Peak Mind Pivot: Disidentify and unyoke your perspective from me/I so you can see yourself and the situation more clearly.

- Standard view: *To feel less pain,* distract yourself from it.

  Peak Mind Pivot: Practice focusing on it non-elaboratively. Don't make up a story about it—simply observe it, and notice how it changes over time.

- Standard view: *To know your mind and emotional disturbances,* analyze them.

  Peak Mind Pivot: Focus on the body when you are experiencing strong emotion to gain more data and greater insight into what is arising.

- Standard view: *If something is intolerable,* reject and suppress it.

  Peak Mind Pivot: Accept and allow it.

- Standard view: *To show your power,* be aggressive.

  Peak Mind Pivot: Extend kindness and show compassion.

- Standard view: *To help others regulate,* control them.

  Peak Mind Pivot: Regulate yourself (first). *Be calm to get calm.*

- Standard view: *To be less distracted,* remove all distractions.

  Peak Mind Pivot: Accept that distractions will arise. Notice them, and practice coming back.

ACKNOWLEDGMENTS

When I finish reading a good book, I'm often left with a longing for more words to savor. And in that afterglow, I turn to the acknowledgments page. Doing so always helps. In seeing the whole of the iceberg, my respect for the deliberateness taken in what captured me at the surface (of the page) is deepened. My experience writing this book gives me a different perspective. Those who allowed me to convey the words on the page are not just the rest of the iceberg, they are the entire ocean. Their mentoring, encouragement, collaboration, and friendship throughout the journey of writing this book kept me afloat. And now, I'm eager to thank all the *peak minds* that guided, inspired, challenged, and comforted me along the way.

First, I wish to thank the incredible team at Idea Architects: Doug Abrams, Rachel Neumann, Lara Love, Ty Love, Boo Prince, and Alyssa Knickerbocker. I arrived with a fuzzy blueprint and a "big idea" of what I wanted to convey in a book. But they saw the edifice that could be created from the "building blocks" I had to offer, and they encouraged me to build it. Their guidance provided much-needed scaffolding, ensuring that the structure of this book was sturdy and strong. And in working with Alyssa Knickerbocker for writing support, I struck gold. She helped me sharpen my thinking to better communicate complex concepts—serving as my oxygen supply to breathe a lifetime of ideas, research findings, and compelling stories from compelling people into words on the page.

Next, I'd like to thank Gideon Weil, Judith Curr, Laina Adler, Aly Mostel, Dan Rovzar, Lucile Culver, Lisa Zuniga, Terri Leonard, Adrian Morgan, and Sam Tatum at HarperOne. Gideon first wrote to me a stunning eleven years ago, and seeded the idea that I might consider writing a book. He gently yet persistently tended to my germinating ideas and research over these years. And although it took nearly a decade, I'm so grateful that we found our way to working together formally in 2019. His grit coupled with his direct, insightful editorial guidance, transparent style, and patience have meant the world to me.

I am deeply greatly to four trusted readers who provided their compelling and helpful feedback on the full first draft of this book. Thank you Liz Buzone, Jonathan Banks, Mirabai Bush, and Mike McConville.

Thank you to my family. My husband, Michael, read every word of multiple drafts, serving as my in-house editor, late-night sounding board, motivational coach, mindfulness practice partner, and chef-chauffeur-and-concierge for the whole family on my many weekends and late evenings working away. Michael, this book would not have been possible without you. Leo and Sophie, you cheered me on throughout this process with humor, patience, and self-sufficiency. Your relentless curiosity, drive to learn, and the deliberateness of your choices—from what you eat, wear, and do to promote awareness about the climate crisis—make me want to pay attention, *better*. One member of our household I know will never read this book but who helped me every day is our sweet dog, Tashi. You are such a good boy.

My father, Parag, died many decades before this book was conceptualized, let alone written. But his clarity and kindness have served as a guiding light throughout my life and throughout this book-writing journey. I am very fortunate for the loving support of my inspiring and spirited mother, Vandana. Thank you for reminding me to pay attention to myself! My sister, Toral Livingston-Jha; my brother-in-law, Simon; my nephew, Rohan; my cousin, Birju Pandya; and my parents in-law, Jeanne and Tony, have been much appreciated sounding boards as well as sources of love and support. Thank you to each of you.

In addition to my dear family, I wish to thank Liz Buzone, who gently encouraged me to leave my writing cave for much-needed walks and talks. Their ripples are expressed in this book. I'm lucky to have such an attentive friend in you. I also want to thank a dear group of friends I've loved for nearly three decades now, known collectively as The Borg. Turns out, we were right all along, even from an attentional perspective—resistance is futile!

I'm very fortunate that one of my close friends is someone with whom I have had the honor of collaborating on dozens of our large-scale research studies. Scott Rogers, your humor, creativity, kindness, openness, and deep knowledge and practice of mindfulness have made our work together not only fun but fulfilling and successful. Thank you.

I wish to thank Walt and Cynthia Piatt for their years of collaboration and support of our research efforts. When I first met him, I was struck by Walt's description of various leaders he'd met during his deployments as his friends. But I've since learned that he seeks to understand others, learn from them, and when he calls you his friend, he means it. I thank you both for seeking to understand attention and mindfulness, and for allowing me to understand what military service requires of leaders and their families. It has been a privilege to learn from you. I am fortunate to have each of you as my friend.

My interest in the science of attention began in the laboratory of Patti Reuter-Lorenz at the University of Michigan. Thank you,

Patti

Patti, for guiding me during those early days, and for continuing to be a trusted mentor throughout my career. Beyond what you taught me, it was seeing you actualize the life of a strong, successful academic leader and mom that helped me dream that it might be possible for me. I count my lucky stars that you accepted me into your lab all those years ago! And my good fortune continued in having Ron Mangun as my graduate school advisor at UC Davis. Ron, if it weren't for the strong foundation you provided on the brain science of attention, I would have never had the confidence and courage to expand and pivot my program of research into unchartered waters over these years. I am deeply grateful to you both.

I also want to thank Richie Davidson. I was asked recently by a reporter if I would have considered studying mindfulness if Richie hadn't said the word *meditation* at the end of a seminar at Penn nearly two decades ago. My answer: "No way!" Thank you for your leadership in our nascent field of contemplative neuroscience, and for being an activist-scientist. For their support of this field, I'd also like to acknowledge the Mind & Life Institute. Thank you to Adam Engle and Susan Bauer-Wu for your leadership of this important organization, to which I am very grateful.

For her scientific mentoring and wise counsel over the past decade as we've pursued studies in a variety of high-demand cohorts, I wish to thank Amy Adler, who patiently guided me over the years to take a rigorous yet flexible approach to research in complex real-world environments. You helped me see that we should aim to not only advance our knowledge of attention and the utility of mindfulness, but also to best position our research to provide actionable and much-needed solutions. Thank you for taking the time and interest in our research efforts, and providing invaluable advice. The many studies in applied settings that I reference in this book benefited from your guidance.

Throughout this book, I use the term "we" in describing the research studies conducted in my lab. This was deliberate, so that every reader is aware that science is a team sport. I am very fortunate to have teammates who are some of the smartest, most collaborative, strategic, wise, and kind people I've encountered. I am unable to mention every trainee here, but I have valued each. Ekaterina Denkova, I want to especially thank you for advising, guiding, and supporting all of our lab activities during those short bursts of time during the book-writing process when I've had to "disappear." And beyond that, I thank you for your brilliant scientific insights, integrity, and care for the scientific process, as well as the success of our efforts. I thank Tony Zanesco for temporarily joining the team during the STRONG project, and returning back to our lab as a post-doctoral researcher. Thank you for leading many of the statistical and methodological innovations we've been able to pursue. I also want to thank past and current members of my lab, including Alex Morrison, Kartik Sreenivasan, Joshua Rooks, Marissa Krimsky, Joanna Witkin, Marieke Van Vugt, Cody Boland, Malena Price, Jordan Barry, Costanza Alessio, Bao Tran Duang, Cindy Ripoll-Martinez, Lindsey Slavin, Emily Brudner, Keith Chichester, Nicolas Ramos, Justin Dainer-Best, Suzanne Parker, Nina Rostrup, Anastasia Kiyonaga, Jason Krompinger, Melissa Ranucci, Ling Wong, Merissa Goolsarran, Matt Gosselin, and many other wonderful research assistants and trainees.

When I decided to give meditation a try, I "randomly" happened upon Jack Kornfield's book *Meditation for Beginners*. He was my first meditation teacher, and for that I am grateful. I'm also very grateful to have Sharon Salzberg and Jon Kabat-Zinn as two mentors and teachers in my life. Sharon, thank you for your love and friendship. Thank you also for all of your support through the book writing process, including reading the practice guide at the end of this book, as well as the practices provided throughout. I appreciate you taking the time to do so and for providing such helpful guidance. To Jon Kabat-Zinn, I want to say thank you for creating MBSR, and for serving as an advisor on our military MBAT studies. When I first told you I wanted to offer mindfulness training to military service members, and that I may need to do so in as few as eight hours, you were skeptical. And that respectful skepticism provided a very fruitful ground to have active, honest dialogue with you over all of these years. For that, as well as your ongoing loving interest and support of our efforts, I am very grateful.

This book describes many of the research studies we have conducted in high demand professionals and others. I thank the funders, the participants in all of these studies, as well as the leadership of various organizations that partnered with us. A special thanks to: Gus Castellanos, John Gaddy, Stephen Gonzales, Margaret Cullen, Elana Rosenbaum, Jannell MacAulay, Michael Baime, Liz Stanley, Jane Carpenter Cohn, and Tom Nassif. In addition, I am grateful for the advisory role played by the following individuals in our work as well as in specific book passages: Michael Brumage, Michael Hosie, Dennis Smith, and Phillip Thomas.

To Goldie Hawn, Marshall Ames, Maria Tussi Kluge, Bill Macnulty, Maurice Sipos, and Ed Cardon, I am deeply appreciative for not only your collaboration, but also for your invaluable support, wisdom, and friendship over the many years leading up to the writing of this book.

I was very fortunate to be able to include in-depth interviews and narratives from Jeff Davis, Jason Spitaletta, Walt Piatt, Paul Singerman, Chris McAliley, Sara Flitner, Richard Gonzales, and Eric Schoomaker. Thank you for allowing me to share your insights and journey within these pages. You inspire me in so many ways, and I know that learning about each of you will inspire many others as well.

Over the course of this daunting, confounding, but ultimately satisfying journey, I learned that I needed to apply everything I was aiming to convey in this book in the writing of it. Writing this book was my own high-demand interval. Thankfully, I had practiced getting very quiet, slowing down, watching my mind, focusing, and broadening as needed. And I had other trusted tools to keep me going, day or night, on-demand, whenever I needed an extra boost—tools that took many forms, from practice to poetry, prose, and music. I am very grateful for silence, Miami rainstorms, Rumi, Pema Chodron, and Polo & Pan.

Lastly, I thank everyone who chose to read this book. May it be of benefit to you.

NOTES

Introduction—"May I Have Your Attention, Please?"

1 *missing 50 percent of your life*: Numerous studies have reported mind-wandering by sampling participants during everyday life (Killingsworth and Gilbert, 2010; Kane et al., 2007) as well as during experimental task performance (Broadway et al., 2015; Unsworth et al., 2012). Across these studies, the rates of mind-wandering range from 30 to 50 percent, with a high degree of variability across participants. Rates of mind-wandering are known to vary as a function of age (Maillet et al., 2018), time of day (Smith et al., 2018), and how participants are asked about it (Seli et al., 2018).

Killingsworth, M. A., and Gilbert, D. T. A Wandering Mind Is an Unhappy Mind. *Science* **330**, no. 6006, 932 (2010). https://doi.org/10.1126/science .1192439.

Kane, M. J. et al. For Whom the Mind Wanders, and When: An Experience-Sampling Study of Working Memory and Executive Control in Daily Life. *Psychological Science* **18**, no. 7, 614–21 (2007). https://doi.org/10.1111/j .1467–9280.2007.01948.x.

Broadway, J. M. et al. Early Event-Related Brain Potentials and Hemispheric Asymmetries Reveal Mind-Wandering While Reading and Predict Comprehension. *Biological Psychology* **107**, 31–43 (2015). http://dx.doi.org /10.1016/j.biopsycho.2015.02.009.

Unsworth, N. et al. Everyday Attention Failures: An Individual Differences Investigation. *Journal of Experimental Psychology: Learning, Memory, and Cognition* **38**, 1765–72 (2012). https://doi.org/10.1037/a0028075.

Maillet, D. et al. Age-Related Differences in Mind-Wandering in Daily Life. *Psychology and Aging* **33**, no. 4, 643–53 (2018). https://doi.org/10.1037 /pag0000260.

Smith, G. K. et al. Mind-Wandering Rates Fluctuate Across the Day: Evidence from an Experience-Sampling Study. *Cognitive Research Principles and Implications* **3**, no. 1 (2018). https://doi.org/10.1186/s41235-018-0141-4.

Seli, P. et al. How Pervasive Is Mind Wandering, Really? *Conscious Cognitive* **66**, 74–78 (2018). https://doi.org/10.1016/j.concog.2018.10.002.

2 *our attention waxes and wanes*: Views on why attention is prone to distractibility include evolutionary survival pressures (opportunity costs: Kurzban et al., 2013; information foraging: Pirolli, 2007; attentional cycling: Schooler et al., 2011) and

benefits for learning and memory formation (dishabituation: Schooler et al., 2011; episodic memory: Mildner and Tamir, 2019).

Kurzban, R. et al. An Opportunity Cost Model of Subjective Effort and Task Performance. *Behavioral and Brain Sciences* **36**, no. 6, 661 (2013). https://doi.org/10.1017/S0140525X12003196.

Pirolli, P. *Information Foraging Theory: Adaptive Interaction with Information* (New York: Oxford University Press, 2007).

Schooler, J. W. et al. Meta-Awareness, Perceptual Decoupling and the Wandering Mind. *Trends in Cognitive Sciences* **15**, no. 7, 319–26 (2011). https://doi.org/10.1016/j.tics.2011.05.006.

Mildner, J. N., and Tamir, D. I. Spontaneous Thought as an Unconstrained Memory Process. *Trends in Neuroscience* **42**, no. 11, 763–77 (2019). https://doi.org/10.1016/j.tins.2019.09.001.

4 *commercial value of attention has taken center stage*: There is growing awareness, as described recently by Myllylahti (2020) and Davenport and Beck (2001), about the economics of attention as news and social media companies use our attention as their product for sale.

Myllylahti, M. Paying Attention to Attention: A Conceptual Framework for Studying News Reader Revenue Models Related to Platforms. *Digital Journalism* **8**, no. 5, 567–75 (2020). https://doi.org/10.1080/21670811.2019.1691926.

Davenport, T. H., and Beck, J. C. *The Attention Economy: Understanding the New Currency of Business*. (Cambridge, MA: Harvard Business Review Press, 2001).

6 *Whatever we pay attention to is* amplified: Task-relevant information that is attended is enhanced neurally (Posner and Driver, 1992) and phenomenologically in our perceptual awareness (Carrasco et al., 2004).

Posner, M. I., and Driver, J. The Neurobiology of Selective Attention. *Current Opinion in Neurobiology* **2**, no. 2, 165–69 (1992). https://doi.org/10.1016/0959-4388(92)90006-7.

Carrasco, M. et al. Attention Alters Appearance. *Nature Neuroscience* **7**, no. 3, 308–13 (2004). https://doi.org/10.1038/nn1194.

6 *When we experience stress, threat, or poor mood . . . this valuable resource is drained*: Attention is thought to have evolved to prioritize information that advantages an organism's survival. Yet, this can lead to attention being derailed from the task-at-hand. Both acute and chronic stress are known to degrade attentional performance and perturb prefrontal cortical functioning (Arnsten, 2015). Threat increases mind-wandering (Mrazek et al., 2011) as well as captures attention (Koster et al., 2004). Negative mood and repetitive negative thinking decrease performance on tasks of attention and working memory (Smallwood et al., 2009). The costs of stress, threat, and poor mood in psychological disorders have been attributed to the hijacking of attentional resources to process such content, which drains the availability of these resources for other forms of information processing (Eysenck et al., 2007).

Arnsten, A. Stress Weakens Prefrontal Networks: Molecular Insults to Higher Cognition. *Nature Neuroscience* **18**, no. 10, 1376–85 (2015). https://doi.org/10.1038/nn.4087.

Mrazek, M. D. et al. Threatened to Distraction: Mind-Wandering as a Consequence of Stereotype Threat. *Journal of Experimental Social Psychology* **47**, no. 6, 1243–48 (2011). https://doi.org/10.1016/j.jesp.2011.05.011.

Koster, E. W. et al. Does Imminent Threat Capture and Hold Attention? *Emotion* **4**, no. 3, 312–17 (2004). https://doi.org/10.1037/1528-3542.4.3.312.

Smallwood, J. et al. Shifting Moods, Wandering Minds: Negative Moods Lead the Mind to Wander. *Emotion* **9**, no. 2, 271–76 (2009). https://doi.org/10.1037/a0014855.

Eysenck, M. W. et al. Anxiety and Cognitive Performance: Attentional Control Theory. *Emotion* 7, no. 2, 336–53 (2007). https://doi.org/10.1037/1528-3542.7.2.336.

8 *To win one hundred victories in one hundred battles is not the acme of skill*: Sun Tzu. *The Art of War* (Bridgewater, MA: World Publications, 2007), 13.

9 *We have records of medieval monks in the year 420*: Kreiner, J. How to Reduce Digital Distractions: Advice from Medieval Monks. *Aeon*, April 21, 2019. https://aeon.co/ideas/how-to-reduce-digital-distractions-advice-from-medieval-monks.

9 *The faculty of voluntarily bringing back a wandering attention, over and over again, is the very root of judgment, character, and will*: James, W. (1890). *The Principles of Psychology*, vols. 1–2 (New York: Holt, 1890), 424.

10 *The mind's nature is to forage for information and engage with it*: Todd, P. M., and Hills, T. Foraging in Mind. *Current Directions in Psychological Science* 29, no. 3, 309–15 (2020). https://doi.org/10.1177/0963721420915861.

11 *Research participants couldn't continuously pay attention when they were instructed to*: They couldn't do it when the stakes were high or when they were motivated to. They couldn't do it even when they were paid to. Attention lapses and performance failures occur even when the stakes (Mrazek et al., 2012) and motivation (Seli et al., 2019) are high, as well as when rewards are offered for not lapsing (Esterman et al., 2014).

Mrazek, M. D. et al. The Role of Mind-Wandering in Measurements of General Aptitude. *Journal of Experimental Psychology General* 141, no. 4, 788–98 (2012). https://doi.org/10.1037/a0027968.

Seli, P. et al. Increasing Participant Motivation Reduces Rates of Intentional and Unintentional Mind Wandering. *Psychological Research* 83, no. 5, 1057–69 (2019). https://doi.org/10.1007/s00426-017-0914-2.

Esterman, M. et al. Reward Reveals Dissociable Aspects of Sustained Attention. *Journal of Experimental Psychology General* 143, no. 6, 2287–95 (2014). https://doi.org/10.1037/xge0000019.

14 *escapism along with other mental coping tactics, like positive thinking and suppression . . . don't help us under high-stress circumstances*: Escapism, formally referred to as avoidance, as well as suppression have been found to increase symptoms of psychological disorders such as depression (Aldao et al., 2010). While positive mood can be beneficial (Le Nguyen and Fredrickson, 2018), under high acute stress (Hirshberg et al., 2018) or longer high-stress intervals (Jha et al., 2020), aiming to increase positive emotion can lead to greater mood and performance disturbances.

Aldao, A. et al. Emotion-Regulation Strategies Across Psychopathology: A Meta-Analytic Review. *Clinical Psychology Review* 30, no. 2, 217–37 (2010). https://doi.org/10.1016/j.cpr.2009.11.004.

Le Nguyen, K. D., and Fredrickson, B. L. *Positive Psychology: Established and Emerging Issues* (New York: Routledge/Taylor & Francis Group, 2018), 29–45.

Hirshberg, M. J. et al. Divergent Effects of Brief Contemplative Practices in Response to an Acute Stressor: A Randomized Controlled Trial of Brief Breath Awareness, Loving-Kindness, Gratitude or an Attention Control Practice. *PLoS One* 13, no. 12, e0207765 (2018). https://doi.org/10.1371/journal.pone.0207765.

Jha, A. P. et al. Comparing Mindfulness and Positivity Trainings in High-Demand Cohorts. *Cognitive Therapy and Research* 44, no. 2, 311–26 (2020). https://doi.org/10.1007/s10608-020-10076-6.

16 *how much and what kind of mindfulness practice is most beneficial is a rapidly developing field*: There are many studies actively underway examining mindfulness practice. For example, see Birtwell, K. et al. An Exploration of Formal and

Informal Mindfulness Practice and Associations with Wellbeing. *Mindfulness* **10**, no. 1, 89–99 (2019). https://doi.org/10.1007/s12671-018-0951-y.

16 *for as little as twelve minutes per day, you can protect against that stress- and overwhelm-related decline in attention*:

Jha, A. P. et al. Examining the Protective Effects of Mindfulness Training on Working Memory Capacity and Affective Experience. *Emotion* **10**, no. 1, 54–64 (2010). https://doi.org/10.1037/a0018438.

Rooks, J. D. et al. "We Are Talking About Practice": The Influence of Mindfulness vs. Relaxation Training on Athletes' Attention and Well-Being over High-Demand Intervals. *Journal of Cognitive Enhancement* **1**, no. 2, 141–53 (2017). https://doi.org/10.1007/s41465-017-0016-5.

Chapter 1—Attention Is Your Superpower

24 *brain imaging research shows that this mental rehearsal activates the motor cortex similar to the way actual physical movement does*: Slimani, M. et al. Effects of Mental Imagery on Muscular Strength in Healthy and Patient Participants: A Systematic Review. *Journal of Sports Science & Medicine* **15**, no. 3, 434–50 (2016). https://pubmed.ncbi.nlm.nih.gov/27803622.

26 *There's a famous study on attention that goes like this*: There have been many studies done on inattentional blindness, akin to the famous "dancing gorilla" study. Simons, D. J., and Chabris, C. F. Gorillas in Our Midst: Sustained Inattentional Blindness for Dynamic Events. *Perception* **28**, no. 9, 1059–74 (1999). https://doi.org/10.1068/p281059.

28 *How much of your brain do you think is devoted to vision?*: Hagen, S. The Mind's Eye. *Rochester Review* **74**, no. 4, 32–37 (2012).

31 *certain neurodegenerative diseases that impair cognition, movement, vision, and more—neurons lose their clear marching orders and stop coordinating the way they're supposed to*: There is growing evidence of not only impaired structural connectivity found postmortem but also impaired resting state functional activity and connectivity indexed with fMRI in diseases such as Parkinson's (van Eimeren et al., 2009), Alzheimer's (Greicius et al., 2004), and Huntington's (Werner et al., 2014).

van Eimeren, T. et al. Dysfunction of the Default Mode Network in Parkinson Disease: A Functional Magnetic Resonance Imaging Study. *JAMA Neurology* **66**, no. 7, 877–83 (2009). https://doi.org/10.1001/archneurol.2009.97.

Greicius, M. D. et al. Default-Mode Network Activity Distinguishes Alzheimer's Disease from Healthy Aging: Evidence from Functional MRI. *Proceedings of the National Academy of Sciences of the United States of America* **101**, no. 13, 4637–42 (2004). https://doi.org/10.1073/pnas.0308627101.

Werner, C. J. et al. Altered Resting-State Connectivity in Huntington's Disease. *Human Brain Mapping* **35**, no. 6, 2582–93 (2014). https://doi.org/10.1002/hbm.22351.

32 *if I showed you two faces at the same time, the N170 would suddenly drop to being smaller in amplitude*: I am referring to the well-established phenomenon of competitive interactions among visual stimuli for neural representation, especially when these stimuli recruit a common population of neurons (Desimone and Duncan, 1995). This phenomenon is observed with EEG recordings, such as the N170 component in humans (Jacques and Rossion, 2004) as well as in single-unit studies in nonhuman primates (Rolls and Tovee, 1995).

Desimone, R., and Duncan, J. Neural Mechanisms of Selective Visual Attention. *Annual Review of Neuroscience* **18**, 193–222 (1995). https://doi.org/10.1146/annurev.ne.18.030195.001205.

Jacques, C., and Rossion, B. Concurrent Processing Reveals Competition Between Visual Representations of Faces. *Neuroreport* 15, no. 15, 2417–21 (2004). https://doi.org/10.1097/00001756–200410250–00023.

Rolls, E. T., and Tovee, M. J. The Responses of Single Neurons in the Temporal Visual Cortical Areas of the Macaque When More Than One Stimulus Is Present in the Receptive Field. *Experimental Brain Research* 103, 409–20 (1995). https://doi.org/10.1007/BF00241500.

33 *There are actually three subsystems that work together to allow us to fluidly and successfully function in our complex world*: Petersen, S. E., and M. I. Posner. The Attention System of the Human Brain: 20 Years After. *Annual Review of Neuroscience* 35, 73–89 (2012). https://doi.org/10.1146/annurev-neuro-062111–150525.

38 *Attention and working memory work together*: Unsworth, N. et al. Are Individual Differences in Attention Control Related to Working Memory Capacity? A Latent Variable Mega-Analysis. *Journal of Experimental Psychology General* 38, no. 6, 1765–72 (2020). https://doi.org/10.1037/xge0001000.

39 *Attention and working memory form not only the current contents of our conscious experience, but also our ability to* use *that information as we maneuver through life*: LeDoux, J. E., and Brown, R. A Higher-Order Theory of Emotional Consciousness. *Proceedings of the National Academy of Sciences of the United States of America* 114, no. 10, E2016–E2025 (2017). https://doi.org/10.1073/pnas.1619316114.

Baddeley, A. The Episodic Buffer: A New Component of Working Memory? *Trends in Cognitive Sciences* 4, no. 11, 417–23 (2000). https://doi.org/https://doi.org/10.1016/S1364–6613(00)01538–2.

39 *heart pumps* two thousand *gallons of blood per day*: "Facts About Your Heart," MetLife AIG (accessed September 10, 2020). https://tcs-ksa.com/en/metlife/facts-about-your-heart.php.

40 *In a variant of the experiment, we showed the same face/scene images. But every now and then, we'd flicker a different image on the screen: a negative image, something violent or upsetting*: In Paczynski et al. (2015), we examined the consequences of negative versus neutral distraction on attention, and found that the presentation of irrelevant negative images reduced the N170 attention effect. It is important to note that there is a well-established "negativity bias" wherein negative information has stronger effects (relative to equally extreme and arousing positive information) on a broad range of functions, such as attention, perception, and memory; motivation; and decision making (see Norris, 2019 for a recent review). In addition to negative external stimuli capturing attention, as proposed to have occurred in Paczynski et al. (2015), there is growing evidence that negative, more so than positive or neutral, content that is internally generated (i.e., negatively valanced memories and thoughts, negative mind-wandering) captures attention to a greater degree. And there is mounting evidence that negatively valanced mind-wandering impairs performance on tasks of attention and working memory (Banks et al., 2016).

Paczynski, M. et al. Brief Exposure to Aversive Stimuli Impairs Visual Selective Attention. *Journal of Cognitive Neuroscience* 27, no. 6, 1172–9 (2015). https://doi.org/10.1162/jocn_a_00768.

Norris, C. J. The Negativity Bias, Revisited: Evidence from Neuroscience Measures and an Individual Differences Approach. *Social Neuroscience* 16 (2019). https://doi.org/10.1080/17470919.2019.1696225.

Banks, J. B. et al. Examining the Role of Emotional Valence of Mind Wandering: All Mind Wandering Is Not Equal. *Consciousness and Cognition* 43, 167–76 (2016). https://doi.org/10.1016/j.concog.2016.06.003.

Chapter 2— . . . But There's Kryptonite

45 *The neuroscience literature points to three main factors that determine when our attention is deployed*: Theeuwes, J. Goal-Driven, Stimulus-Driven, and History-Driven Selection. *Current Opinion in Psychology* 29, 97–101 (2019). https://doi.org/10.1016/j.copsyc.2018.12.024.

47 *Take a look at the graph*: In addition to the inverted U pattern of correspondence between performance and stress described initially by Yerkes and Dodson (1908; also see Teigen, 1994) and many other studies since, there is recent evidence as reviewed by Qin et al. (2009) that the precise levels of certain stress-related neurotransmitters, such as norepinephrine (NE), that drive activity in brain regions such as the locus coeruleus (LC) show an inverted U pattern related to performance. Optimal performance is associated with NE levels that result in an intermediate level of LC activity. But when NE levels lead to LC hypoactivity and hyperactivity, performance is impaired. The point here is that it is not that stress is bad or good, but that the consequences are tied to the amount of stress. Distress, as opposed to eustress, is often shorthanded as stress. Tasks that demonstrate this stress-related inverted U pattern are those that require effortful engagement of attention and working memory for successful task performance.

Yerkes, R. M., and Dodson, J. D. The Relation of Strength of Stimulus to Rapidity of Habitat-Formation. *Journal of Comparative Neurology and Psychology* 18, 459–82 (1908). https://doi.org/10.1002/cne.920180503.

Teigen, K. H. Yerkes-Dodson: A Law for All Seasons. *Theory Psychology* 4, 525 (1994). https://doi.org/10.1177/0959354394044004.

Qin, S. et al. Acute Psychological Stress Reduces Working Memory-Related Activity in the Dorsolateral Prefrontal Cortex. *Biological Psychiatry* 66, no. 1, 25–32 (2009). https://doi.org/10.1016/j.biopsych.2009.03.006.

49 *Performance is always worse—lower accuracy, slower and more variable responses—after the negative mood induction*: This is describing performance on a task of sustained attention (Smallwood et al., 2009). Note that the relationship between attention, working memory, and mood has been examined using a variety of tasks and a variety of methods for probing mood and affective distraction. Negative distractors presented during the experiment (e.g., Witkin et al., 2020; Garrison and Schmeichel, 2018) as well as dispositional and disordered negative mood are associated with impaired performance on tasks of attention and working memory (Eysenck et al., 2007; Gotlib and Joormann, 2010). See also Schmeichel and Tang (2015) and Mitchell and Phillips (2007).

Smallwood, J. et al. Shifting Moods, Wandering Minds: Negative Moods Lead the Mind to Wander. *Emotion* 9, no. 2, 271–76 (2009). https://doi.org/10.1037/a0014855.

Witkin, J. et al. Dynamic Adjustments in Working Memory in the Face of Affective Interference. *Memory & Cognition* 48, 16–31 (2020). https://doi.org/10.3758/s13421-019-00958-w.

Garrison, K. E., and Schmeichel, B. J. Effects of Emotional Content on Working Memory Capacity. *Cognition and Emotion* 33, no. 2, 370–77 (2018). https://doi.org/10.1080/02699931.2018.1438989.

Eysenck, M. W. et al. Anxiety and Cognitive Performance: Attentional Control Theory. *Emotion* 7, no. 2, 336–53 (2007). https://doi.org/10.1037/1528-3542.7.2.336.

Gotlib, I. H., and Joormann, J. Cognition and Depression: Current Status and Future Directions. *Annual Review of Clinical Psychology* 6, 285–312 (2010). https://doi.org/10.1146/annurev.clinpsy.121208.131305.

Schmeichel, B. J., and Tang, D. Individual Differences in Executive Functioning and Their Relationship to Emotional Processes and Responses. *Current Directions in Psychological Science* 24, no. 2, 93–98 (2015). https://doi.org/10.1177/0963721414555178.

Mitchell, R. L., and Phillips, L. H. The Psychological, Neurochemical and Functional Neuroanatomical Mediators of the Effects of Positive and Negative Mood on Executive Functions. *Neuropsychologia* 45, no. 4, 617–29 (2007). https://doi.org/10.1016/j.neuropsychologia.2006.06.030.

50 *If you feel threatened all the time, you aren't going to be able to engage deeply in any other task or experience*: There is growing evidence that threat-related information can capture and hold attention (Koster et al., 2004) and can perturb working memory (Schmader and Johns, 2003), which may impair ongoing task performance (Shih et al., 1999).

Koster, E. H. W. et al. Does Imminent Threat Capture and Hold Attention? *Emotion* 4, no. 3, 312–17 (2004). https://doi.org/10.1037/1528–3542.4.3.312.

Schmader, T., and Johns, M. Converging Evidence that Stereotype Threat Reduces Working Memory Capacity. *Journal of Personality and Social Psychology* 85, no. 3, 440–52 (2003). https://doi.org/10.1037/0022–3514.85.3.440.

Shih, M. et al. Stereotype Susceptibility: Identity Salience and Shifts in Quantitative Performance. *Psychological Science* 10, no. 1, 80–83 (1999). https://doi.org/10.1111/1467–9280.00111.

50 *they haven't changed in thirty-five thousand years*: Neubauer, S. The Evolution of Modern Human Brain Shape. *Science Advances* 4, no. 1 (2018). https://doi.org/10.1126/sciadv.aao5961.

51 *A study on Asian undergraduate women played two common stereotypes against each other*: Gibson, C. E. et al. A Replication Attempt of Stereotype Susceptibility: Identity Salience and Shifts in Quantitative Performance. *Social Psychology* 45, no. 3, 194–98 (2014). http://dx.doi.org/10.1027/1864–9335/a000184.

54 *Many things leaders deal with—high-cognitive demands, evaluative pressure, tense social interactions, uncertainty—are known to degrade attention, as well*: Beyond stress, threat, and poor mood, many factors impair performance on tasks of attention and working memory. Blasiman, R. N., and Was, C. A. Why Is Working Memory Performance Unstable? A Review of 21 Factors. *Europe's Journal of Psychology* 14, no. 1, 188–231 (2018). https://doi.org/10.5964/ejop.v14i1.1472.

54 *In a recent study, participants were told that they might have to give a speech after completing an attentionally demanding task that would take several minutes*: Alquist, J. L. et al. What You Don't Know Can Hurt You: Uncertainty Impairs Executive Function. *Frontiers in Psychology* 11, 576001 (2020). https://doi.org/10.3389/fpsyg.2020.576001.

57 *drains can take the shape of anything from an uncomfortably low temperature to mortality salience (thinking about your own death)*: For more on mortality salience and performance decline, see Gailliot, M. T. et al. Self-Regulatory Processes Defend Against the Threat of Death: Effects of Self-Control Depletion and Trait Self-Control on Thoughts and Fears of Dying. *Journal of Personality and Social Psychology* 91, no. 1, 49–62 (2006). https://doi.org/10.1037/0022–3514.91.1.49.

58 *Your job is to say the color of the ink for each cluster of letters, as quickly as you can*: Stroop, J. R. Studies of Interference in Serial Verbal Reactions. *Journal of Experimental Psychology* 18, no. 6, 643–62 (1935). https://doi.org/10.1037/h0054651.

59 *Responses are faster and more accurate for high-conflict trials that follow other high-conflict trials versus those that follow low-conflict trials—which sounds like a good thing*: The pattern of better performance after a high- vs. low-conflict trial is referred to as the conflict adaptation effect. It is proposed to result from the dynamic upregulation of cognitive control resources elicited by high-conflict as

well as other high-cognitive demands, such as working memory load and distractor interference.

Ullsperger, M. et al. The Conflict Adaptation Effect: It's Not Just Priming. *Cognitive, Affective, & Behavioral Neuroscience* 5, 467–72 (2005). https://doi.org /10.3758/CABN.5.4.467.

Witkin, J. E. et al. Dynamic Adjustments in Working Memory in the Face of Affective Interference. *Memory & Cognition* 48, 16–31 (2020). https://doi.org /10.3758/s13421-019-00958-w.

Jha, A. P., and Kiyonaga, A. Working-Memory-Triggered Dynamic Adjustments in Cognitive Control. *Journal of Experimental Psychology, Learning, Memory, and Cognition* 36, no. 4, 1036–42 (2010). https://doi.org/10.1037/a0019337.

59 *challenging situations are often "conflict states"*: These different mind states are aligned with Buddhist descriptions of the Five Hindrances. Wallace, B. A. *The Attention Revolution: Unlocking the Power of the Focused Mind* (Boston: Wisdom Publications, 2006).

61 *don't think about a polar bear*: "Try to pose for yourself this task: not to think of a polar bear, and you will see that the cursed thing will come to mind every minute" ("Winter Notes on Summer Impressions," Fyodor Dostoevsky, 1863). This quote motivated a classic study that found that there was a paradoxical increase in the frequency of a thought that was to be suppressed (Wegner et al., 1987; see also Winerman, 2011; and Rassin et al., 2000). There is growing evidence that thought suppression and expressive suppression, which refers to the effortful control of automatic emotional responses, impair working memory (Franchow and Suchy, 2015) and result in poor psychological health outcomes (Gross and John, 2003).

Wegner, D. M. et al. Paradoxical Effects of Thought Suppression. *Journal of Personality and Social Psychology* 53, no. 1, 5–13 (1987). https://doi.org/10 .1037//0022–3514.53.1.5.

Winerman, L. Suppressing the "White Bears." *American Psychological Association* 42, no. 9, 44 (2011). https://www.apa.org/monitor/2011/10/unwanted -thoughts.

Rassin, E. et al. Paradoxical and Less Paradoxical Effects of Thought Suppression: A Critical Review. *Clinical Psychology Review* 20, no. 8, 973–95 (2000). https:// doi.org/10.1016/S0272–7358(99)00019–7.

Franchow, E., and Suchy, Y. Naturally-Occurring Expressive Suppression in Daily Life Depletes Executive Functioning. *Emotion* 15, no. 1, 78–89 (2015). https:// doi.org/10.1037/emo0000013.

Gross, J. J., and John, O. P. Individual Differences in Two Emotion Regulation Processes: Implications for Affect, Relationships, and Well-Being. *Journal of Personality and Social Psychology* 85, no. 2, 348–62 (2003). https://doi.org/10 .1037/0022–3514.85.2.348.

Chapter 3—Push-ups for the Mind

65 *researchers ran a study comparing the brains of bus drivers with those of cab drivers*: Maguire, E. A. et al. London Taxi Drivers and Bus Drivers: A Structural MRI and Neuropsychological Analysis. *Hippocampus* 16, no. 12, 1091–1101 (2006). https:// doi.org/10.1002/hipo.20233.

67 *fMRI illuminates the ongoing levels of oxygenated blood in different parts of the brain over time*: Fundamentally, brain functions occur via electrochemical processes, specifically those that occur during the firing of neurons. fMRI is not indexing electrical activity in the brain but rather the increase in blood flow that accompanies this activity. As such, fMRI is an indirect measure of neural activity.

de Haan, M., and Thomas, K. M. Applications of ERP and fMRI Techniques to Developmental Science. *Developmental Science* 5, no. 3, 335–43 (2002). https://doi.org/10.1111/1467–7687.00373.

69 *no solid scientific consensus that playing most of these kinds of games leads to any benefits beyond simply getting better at that particular game*:
Parong, J., and Mayer, R. E. Cognitive Consequences of Playing Brain-Training Games in Immersive Virtual Reality. *Applied Cognitive Psychology* 34, no. 1, 29–38 (2020). https://doi.org/10.1002/acp.3582.

A Consensus on the Brain Training Industry from the Scientific Community. Max Planck Institute for Human Development and Stanford Center on Longevity. News release (October 20, 2014). https://longevity.stanford.edu/a-consensus-on-the-brain-training-industry-from-the-scientific-community-2/.

Kable, J. W. et al. No Effect of Commercial Cognitive Training on Brain Activity, Choice Behavior, or Cognitive Performance. *Journal of Neuroscience* 37, no. 31, 7390–7402 (2017). https://doi.org/10.1523/JNEUROSCI.2832–16.2017.

Slagter, H. A. et al. Mental Training as a Tool in the Neuroscientific Study of Brain and Cognitive Plasticity. *Frontiers in Human Neuroscience* 5, no. 17 (2011). https://doi.org/10.3389/fnhum.2011.00017.

75 *after the retreat, the meditators only mistakenly pressed the space bar* 30 *percent of the time*: Witkin, J. et al. Mindfulness Training Influences Sustained Attention: Attentional Benefits as a Function of Training Intensity. Poster presented at the International Symposium for Contemplative Research, Phoenix, Arizona (2018).

75 *A version of the SART was conducted with live-fire simulation*: Biggs, A. T. et al. Cognitive Training Can Reduce Civilian Casualties in a Simulated Shooting Environment. *Psychological Science* 26, no. 8, 1064–76 (2015). https://doi.org/10.1177/0956797615579274.

75 *we also conducted studies that let us dig into the subsystems of attention with mindfulness training*: Jha, A. P. et al. Mindfulness Training Modifies Subsystems of Attention. *Cognitive, Affective & Behavioral Neuroscience* 7, no. 2, 109–19 (2007). https://doi.org/10.3758/CABN.7.2.109.

77 *intercepted the University of Miami football team*: Rooks, J. D. et al. "We Are Talking About Practice": The Influence of Mindfulness vs. Relaxation Training on Athletes' Attention and Well-Being over High-Demand Intervals. *Journal of Cognitive Enhancement* 1, no. 2, 141–53 (2017). https://doi.org/10.1007/s41465-017-0016-5.

78 *something we'd discovered about attention and high-demand periods: everybody degrades*: We have found a pattern of performance decline over high-stress intervals in a wide range of groups, from undergraduates over the academic semester (Morrison et al., 2014) and predeployment Marines over eight weeks of training (Jha et al., 2010) to incarcerated youth (Leonard et al., 2013) and football players over preseason training (Rooks et al., 2017).

Morrison, A. B. et al. Taming a Wandering Attention: Short-Form Mindfulness Training in Student Cohorts. *Frontiers in Human Neuroscience* 7, 897 (2014). https://doi.org/10.3389/fnhum.2013.00897.

Jha, A. P. et al. Examining the Protective Effects of Mindfulness Training on Working Memory Capacity and Affective Experience. *Emotion* 10, no. 1, 54–64 (2010). https://doi.org/10.1037/a0018438.

Leonard, N. R. et al. Mindfulness Training Improves Attentional Task Performance in Incarcerated Youth: A Group Randomized Controlled Intervention Trial. *Frontiers in Psychology* 4, no. 792, 2–10 (2013). https://doi.org/10.3389/fpsyg.2013.00792.

Rooks, J. D. et al. "We Are Talking About Practice": The Influence of Mindfulness vs. Relaxation Training on Athletes' Attention and Well-Being over High-

Demand Intervals. *Journal of Cognitive Enhancement* **1**, no. 2, 141–53 (2017). https://doi.org/10.1007/s41465-017-0016-5.

79 *Many studies on mindfulness practice suggest that if you* accept and allow *instead of* resist: Lyndsay, E. K., and Creswell, J. D. Mindfulness, Acceptance, and Emotion Regulation: Perspectives from Monitor and Acceptance Theory (MAT). *Current Opinion in Psychology* **28**, 120–5 (2019). https://doi.org/10.1007/s41465-017-0016-5.

Chapter 4—Find Your Focus

93 *A recent survey of social media use in the workplace reported that while it can help provide a "mental break," fifty-six percent of employees said it distracts them from the work they need to do*: Lampe, C., and Ellison, N. Social Media and the Workplace. Pew Research Center, June 22, 2016. https://www.pewresearch.org/internet/2016/06/22/social-media-and-the-workplace/.

93 *We conducted a study with undergraduate students at the University of Miami*: Cameron, L. et al. Mind Wandering Impairs Textbook Reading Comprehension and Retention. Poster presented at the Cognitive Neuroscience Society Annual Meeting, Boston, Massachusetts (April 2014).

94 *Other experiments have found the same thing with easier parameters*: See, for example, Zanesco, A. P. et al. Meditation Training Influences Mind Wandering and Mindless Reading. *Psychology of Consciousness: Theory, Research, and Practice* **3**, no. 1, 12–33 (2016). https://doi.org/10.1037/cns0000082.

94 *people fail to immediately notice that the words are meaningless thirty percent of the time . . . before they realize the text they're reading is actually gibberish*: Smallwood, J. et al. The Lights Are On but No One's Home: Meta-Awareness and the Decoupling of Attention When the Mind Wanders. *Psychonomic Bulletin & Review* **14**, no. 3, 527–33 (2007). https://doi.org/10.3758/BF03194102.

95 *People cannot hold their focus, no matter what. Not if they are paid. Not if their task is solely to enjoy an activity. Not even if the consequences for losing focus are disastrous*: Esterman, M. et al. In the Zone or Zoning Out? Tracking Behavioral and Neural Fluctuations During Sustained Attention. *Cerebral Cortex* **23**, no. 11, 2712–23 (2013). https://doi.org/10.1093/cercor/bhs261.

Mrazek, M. D. et al. The Role of Mind-Wandering in Measurements of General Aptitude. *Journal of Experimental Psychology General* **141**, no. 4, 788–98 (2012). https://doi.org/10.1037/a0027968.

Wilson, T. D. et al. Just Think: The Challenges of the Disengaged Mind. *Science* **345**, no. 6192, 75–7 (2014). https://doi.org/10.1126/science.1250830.

97 *referred to as a need for* cognitive closure: Webster, D. M., and Kruglanski, A. W. Individual Differences in Need for Cognitive Closure. *Journal of Personality and Social Psychology* **67**, no. 6, 1049–62 (1994). https://doi.org/10.1037//0022-3514.67.6.1049.

98 load theory: Lavie, N. et al. Load Theory of Selective Attention and Cognitive Control. *Journal of Experimental Psychology* **133**, no. 3, 339–54 (2004). https://doi.org/10.1037/0096-3445.133.3.339.

98 *and the* vigilance decrement: The vigilance decrement, also referred to as time-on-task effects, is the behavioral pattern of reduced performance with longer periods of engagement in a task. There is debate regarding the causes of this phenomenon, from resource depletion to attentional cycling, and consideration of opportunity costs. See Rubinstein (2020) for discussion as well as Davies and Parasuraman (1982).

Rubinstein, J. S. Divergent Response-Time Patterns in Vigilance Decrement Tasks. *Journal of Experimental Psychology: Human Perception and Performance* **46**, no. 10, 1058–76 (2020). https://doi.org/10.1037/xhp0000813.

Davies, D. R., and Parasuraman, R. *The Psychology of Vigilance* (London: Academic Press, 1982).

99 *Participants sit at a computer screen that shows them a different face every half second*: Denkova, E. et al. Attenuated Face Processing During Mind Wandering. *Journal of Cognitive Neuroscience* 30, no. 11, 1691–1703 (2018). https://doi.org/10.1162 /jocn_a_01312.

102 *You experience "perceptual decoupling"*: Schooler, J. W. et al. Meta-Awareness, Perceptual Decoupling and the Wandering Mind. *Trends in Cognitive Sciences* 15, no. 7, 319–26 (2011). https://doi.org/10.1016/j.tics.2011.05.006.

103 *Mind-wandering, it turns out, potentially happens at the same rate when someone's sitting on the couch reading a magazine as when they're performing brain surgery*: While mind-wandering can occur in many real-world contexts, real-world rates of mind-wandering and performance- and laboratory-based rates may not always be aligned across individuals (Kane et al., 2017) and factors such as self-imposed effort to concentrate, task demands, and other individual differences may result in a misalignment in mind-wandering and working memory in real-life vs. laboratory contexts. Kane, M. J. et al. For Whom the Mind Wanders, and When, Varies Across Laboratory and Daily-Life Settings. *Psychological Science* 28, no. 9 1271–1289 (2017). https://doi.org/10.11 https:// doi.org/10.1177/0956797617706086.

103 *You amp up your stress*: Crosswell, A. D. et al. Mind Wandering and Stress: When You Don't Like the Present Moment. *Emotion* 20, no. 3, 403–12 (2020). https:// doi.org/10.1037/emo0000548.

103 *the moment afterward is going to be riddled with a little bit of negativity*: Killingsworth, M. A., and Gilbert, D. T. A Wandering Mind Is an Unhappy Mind. *Science* 330, no. 6006, 932 (2010). https://doi.org/10.1126/science.1192439.

107 *We call this phenomenon the* inhibition of return: Posner, M. I. et al. Inhibition of Return: Neural Basis and Function. *Cognitive Neuropsychology* 2, no. 3, 211–28 (1985). https://doi.org/10.1080/02643298508252866.

108 *Mind-wandering may have ultimately been selected over the course of human evolution to maximize* opportunity costs: Ward, A. F., and Wegner, D. M. Mind-Blanking: When the Mind Goes Away. *Frontiers in Psychology* 4, 650 (2013). https://doi.org /10.3389/fpsyg.2013.00650.

109 attentional cycling: Some studies have suggested that slow temporal fluctuations in performance and brain activity patterns may reflect the cycling of attention to various goals one after another. Smallwood, J. et al. Segmenting the Stream of Consciousness: The Psychological Correlates of Temporal Structures in the Time Series Data of a Continuous Performance Task. *Brain and Cognition* 66, no. 1, 50–6 (2008). https://doi.org/10.1016/j.bandc.2007.05.004.

110 *They* did *improve*: Rosen, Z. B. et al. Mindfulness Training Improves Working Memory Performance in Adults with ADHD. Poster presented at the Annual Meeting of the Society for Neuroscience, Washington, DC (2008).

120 *Multitasking—or, more specifically,* task switching: Rubinstein, J. S. et al. Executive Control of Cognitive Processes in Task Switching. *Journal of Experimental Psychology: Human Perception and Performance* 27, no, 4, 763–97 (2001). https:// doi.org/10.1037/0096-1523.27.4.763.

122 *But also:* monotask as much as possible: Levy, D. M. et al. The Effects of Mindfulness Meditation Training on Multitasking in a High-Stress Information Environment. *Proceedings of Graphics Interface*, 45–52 (2012). https://dl.acm.org /doi/10.5555/2305276.2305285.

123 *You'll miss less, make fewer errors, and (science suggests!) stay happier*: Etkin, J., and Mogilner, C. Does Variety Among Activities Increase Happiness? *Journal of Consumer Research* 43, no. 2, 210–29 (2016). https://doi.org/10.1093/jcr/ucw021.

Chapter 5—Stay In *Play*

128 *topic of* working memory: Working memory is a cognitive system that allows for the short-term maintenance of information in a highly accessible state and the manipulation of this information in the service of goals. There are several prominent models of working memory. For example, whereas Baddeley's model (Baddeley 2010) emphasizes the component structure of working memory, Engle's model (Engle and Kane, 2004) emphasizes an individual differences approach and the role of executive control (akin to the central executive system of attention) in accounting for individual differences in working memory capacity.

Baddeley, A. Working Memory. *Current Biology* 20, no. 4, R136–R140 (2010). https://doi.org/10.1016/j.cub.2009.12.014.

Engle, R. W., and Kane, M. J. Executive Attention, Working Memory Capacity, and a Two-Factor Theory of Cognitive Control. In B. Ross (ed.), *The Psychology of Learning and Motivation* 44, 145–99 (2004).

128 *Directing the flashlight of your attention to the contents of your working memory essentially "refreshes" that content*: Raye, C. L. et al. Refreshing: A Minimal Executive Function. *Cortex* 43, no. 1, 134–45 (2007). https://doi.org/10.1016/s0010–9452(08)70451–9.

132 *certain prefrontal brain regions were much more active when participants were doing the 3-back task*: Braver, T. S. et al. A Parametric Study of Prefrontal Cortex Involvement in Human Working Memory. *NeuroImage* 5, no. 1, 49–62 (1997). https://doi.org/10.1006/nimg.1996.0247.

133 *They showed participants a series of adjectives while they were in the scanner*: Many studies have been done with event-related fMRI comparing activation during adjective judgments for self and for close "others" versus famous or unfamiliar persons. Activation is greater in key nodes of the default mode network such as the medial prefrontal cortex, posterior cingulate cortex, and the precuneus during judgments regarding self and close "others" versus famous or unfamiliar persons.

van der Meer, L. et al. Self-Reflection and the Brain: A Theoretical Review and Meta-Analysis of Neuroimaging Studies with Implications for Schizophrenia. *Neuroscience & Biobehavioral Reviews* 34, no. 6, 935–46 (2010). https://doi.org/10.1016/j.neubiorev.2009.12.004.

Zhu, Y. et al. Neural Basis of Cultural Influence on Self-Representation. *NeuroImage* 34, no. 3, 1310–6 (2007). https://doi.org/10.1016/j.neuroimage.2006.08.047.

Heatherton, T. F. et al. Medial Prefrontal Activity Differentiates Self from Close Others. *Social Cognitive & Affective Neuroscience* 1, no. 1, 18–25 (2006). https://doi.org/10.1093/scan/nsl001.

133 *"default mode network"*: Raichle, M. E. The Brain's Default Mode Network. *Annual Review of Neuroscience* 38, 433–47 (2015). https://doi.org/10.1146/annurev-neuro-071013–014030.

134 *the attention network was "online"*: Weissman, D. H. et al. The Neural Bases of Momentary Lapses in Attention. *Nature Neuroscience* 9, no. 7, 971–8 (2006). https://doi.org/10.1038/nn1727.

134 *emotionally charged thoughts can capture attention just as powerfully as someone shouting your name*: Andrews-Hanna, J. R. et al. Dynamic Regulation of Internal Experience: Mechanisms of Therapeutic Change. In Lane, R. D., and Nadel, L., *Neuroscience of Enduring Change: Implications for Psychotherapy* (New York: Oxford University Press, 2020), 89–131. https://doi.org/10.1093/oso/9780190881511.003.0005.

134 *Working memory is critical for social connection and communication*: Barrett, L. F. et al. Individual Differences in Working Memory Capacity and Dual-Process Theories

of the Mind. *Psychological Bulletin* **130**, no. 4, 553–73 (2004). https://doi.org/10 .1037/0033–2909.130.4.553.

135 *And it's where you experience emotion*:
Mikels, J. A., and Reuter-Lorenz, P. A. Affective Working Memory: An Integrative Psychological Construct. *Perspectives on Psychological Science* **14**, no. 4, 543–59 (2019). https://doi.org/https://doi.org/10.1177/1745691619837597.
LeDoux, J. E., and Brown, R. A Higher-Order Theory of Emotional Consciousness. *Proceedings of the National Academy of Sciences of the United States of America* **114**, no. 10, E2016–E2025 (2017). https://doi.org/10.1073/pnas .1619316114.

135 *One study had participants come in and watch a disturbing movie*: Schmeichel, B. J. et al. Working Memory Capacity and the Self-Regulation of Emotional Expression and Experience. *Journal of Personality and Social Psychology* **95**, no. 6, 1526–40 (2008). https://doi.org/10.1037/a0013345.

137 *frontal lobes were springing forward*: Klingberg, T. Development of a Superior Frontal-Intraparietal Network for Visuo-Spatial Working Memory. *Neuropsychologia* **44**, no. 11, 2171–7 (2006). https://doi.org/10.1016/j .neuropsychologia.2005.11.019.

138 *And you can "open" three or four of those channels at once and still keep them separate from each other*: Noguchi, Y., and Kakigi, R. Temporal Codes of Visual Working Memory in the Human Cerebral Cortex: Brain Rhythms Associated with High Memory Capacity. *NeuroImage* **222**, no. 15, 117294 (2020). https://doi.org/10 .1016/j.neuroimage.2020.117294.

139 *"The Magical Number Seven, Plus or Minus Two"*: Miller, G. A. The Magical Number Seven, Plus or Minus Two: Some Limits on Our Capacity for Processing Information. *Psychological Review* **101**, no. 2, 343–52 (1956). https://doi.org/10 .1037/0033–295x.101.2.343.

139 *the time it takes to say seven numbers in English is roughly the "time buffer" of our auditory working memory*: Lüer, G. et al. Memory Span in German and Chinese: Evidence for the Phonological Loop. *European Psychologist* **3**, no. 2, 102–12 (2006). https://doi.org/10.1027/1016–9040.3.2.102.

139 *"Cognitive offloading"*: Morrison, A. B., and Richmond, L. L. Offloading Items from Memory: Individual Differences in Cognitive Offloading in a Short-Term Memory Task. *Cognitive Research: Principles and Implications* **5**, no. 1 (2020). https://doi.org/10.1186/s41235-019-0201–4.

139 *the opposite:* blanking: Kawagoe, T. et al. The Neural Correlates of "Mind Blanking": When the Mind Goes Away. *Human Brain Mapping* **40**, no. 17, 4934–40 (2019). https://doi.org/10.1002/hbm.24748.

140 *Another hypothesis is that there is a "sudden death" of neural activity*: Zhang, W., and Luck, S. J. Sudden Death and Gradual Decay in Visual Working Memory. *Psychological Science* **20**, no. 4, 423–8 (2009). https://doi.org/10.1111/j.1467–9280 .2009.02322.x.

141 *This temporarily cuts off access to working memory and impairs any functions that rely on it (like long-term memory, social connection, and emotion regulation)*: Datta, D., and Arnsten, A. F. T. Loss of Prefrontal Cortical Higher Cognition with Uncontrollable Stress: Molecular Mechanisms, Changes with Age, and Relevance to Treatment. *Brain Sciences* **9**, no. 5 (2019). https://doi.org/10.3390/brainsci 9050113.

142 *In 2013, our lab collaborated on a large-scale study*: Roeser, R. W. et al. Mindfulness Training and Reductions in Teacher Stress and Burnout: Results from Two Randomized, Waitlist-Control Field Trials. *Journal of Educational Psychology* **105**, no. 3, 787–804 (2013). https://doi.org/10.1037/a0032093.

143 *Colleagues at the University of California, Santa Barbara, had the same hunch and*

tested it out in a clever experiment: Mrazek, M. D. et al. The Role of Mind-Wandering in Measurements of General Aptitude. *Journal of Experimental Psychology General* **141**, no. 4, 788–98 (2012). https://doi.org/10.1037/a0027968.

145 *Rumination is one of the most potent forms of mental time travel*: Beaty, R. E. et al. Thinking About the Past and Future in Daily Life: An Experience Sampling Study of Individual Differences in Mental Time Travel. *Psychological Research* **83**, no. 4, 805–916 (2019). https://doi.org/10.1007/s00426-018-1075-7.

147 *But this time, we put the brain cap on our participants while they did the experiment, and we only gave them one face to remember*: Sreenivasan, K. K. et al. Temporal Characteristics of Top-Down Modulations During Working Memory Maintenance: An Event-Related Potential Study of the N170 Component. *Journal of Cognitive Neuroscience* **19**, no. 11, 1836–44 (2017). https://doi.org/10.1162/jocn.2007.19.11.1836.

154 *They are able to allow the ink to fade when it's appropriate for it to do so, selectively*: Visual working memory capacity is tied to the efficiency with which distractors can be filtered.

Vogel, E. K. et al. The Time Course of Consolidation in Visual Working Memory. *Journal of Experimental Psychology: Human Perception and Performance* **32**, no. 6, 1436–51 (2006). https://doi.org/10.1037/0096-1523.32.6.1436.

Luria, R. et al. The Contralateral Delay Activity as a Neural Measure of Visual Working Memory. *Neuroscience & Biobehavioral Reviews* **62**, 100–8 (2016). https://doi.org//10.1016/j.neubiorev.2016.01.003.

Chapter 6—Press *Record*

163 *memory for experiences, involves* selective encoding of only those aspects of experience that were most attended to and held in working memory: Recent studies suggest that working memory capacity is moderately to strongly related with measures of long-term memory (Mogle et al., 2008; Unsworth et al, 2009). Working memory may serve as a scratch space for long-term memory where information can be manipulated (that is, reordered, organized, integrated; see Blumenfeld and Ranganath, 2006) for more efficient storage. Yet, there is still active debate regarding the dissociable neural systems that may or may not uniquely have a role in working memory and long-term memory (Ranganath and Blumenfeld, 2005).

Mogle, J. A. et al. What's So Special About Working Memory? An Examination of the Relationships Among Working Memory, Secondary Memory, and Fluid Intelligence. *Psychological Science* **19**, 1071–7 (2008). https://doi.org/10.1111/j.1467-9280.2008.02202.x.

Unsworth, N. et al. There's More to the Working Memory–fluid Intelligence Relationship Than Just Secondary Memory. *Psychonomic Bulletin & Review* **16**, 931–7 (2009). https://doi.org/10.3758/pbr.16.5.931.

Blumenfeld, R. S., and Ranganath, C. Dorsolateral Prefrontal Cortex Promotes Long-Term Memory Formation Through Its Role in Working Memory Organization. *Journal of Neuroscience* **26**, no. 3, 916–25 (2006). https://doi.org/10.1523/jneurosci.2353-05.2006.

Ranganath, C., and Blumenfeld, R. S. Doubts About Double Dissociations Between Short- and Long-Term Memory. *Trends in Cognitive Sciences* **9**, no. 8, 374–80 (2005). https://doi.org/10.1016/j.tics.2005.06.009.

164 *Yes, we remember negative information better than positive information*: Spaniol, J. et al. Aging and Emotional Memory: Cognitive Mechanisms Underlying the Positivity Effect. *Psychology and Aging* **23**, no. 4, 859–72 (2008). https://doi.org/10.1037/a0014218.

164 *the things that are outliers are more privileged—they become more salient in our*

memory: Schroots, J. J. F. et al. Autobiographical Memory from a Life Span Perspective. *International Journal of Aging and Human Development* 58, no. 1, 69–85 (2004). https://doi.org/10.2190/7A1A-8HCE-0FD9–7CTX.

166 Forgetting is a good thing: Forgetting is often studied using directed forgetting paradigms. Williams, M. et al. The Benefit of Forgetting. *Psychonomic Bulletin & Review* 20, 348–55 (2013). https://doi.org/10.3758/s13423-012-0354-3.

166 *A 2018 social media study set out to investigate an important question*: Tamir, D. I. et al. Media Usage Diminishes Memory for Experiences. *Journal of Experimental Social Psychology* 76, 161–8 (2018). https://doi.org/10.1016/j.jesp.2018.01.006.

167 *studies have found that media use in the classroom*: Allen A. et al. Is the Pencil Mightier Than the Keyboard? A Meta-Analysis Comparing the Method of Notetaking Outcomes. *Southern Communication Journal* 85, no. 3, 143–54 (2020). https://doi.org/10.1080/1041794X.2020.1764613.

169 *H. M. received an experimental brain surgery to treat his epilepsy*: Squire, L. R. The Legacy of Patient H. M. for Neuroscience. *Neuron* 61, no. 1, 6–9 (2009). https://doi.org/10.1016/j.neuron.2008.12.023.

175 *Those attention-grabbing thoughts have as their raw materials long-term memory traces*: Andrews-Hanna, J. R. et al. Dynamic Regulation of Internal Experience: Mechanisms of Therapeutic Change. In Lane, R. D., and Nadel, L., *Neuroscience of Enduring Change: Implications for Psychotherapy* (New York: Oxford University Press, 2020), 89–131. https://doi.org/10.1093/oso/9780190881511.003.0005.

175 *It pumps out content like memory traces and other mental chatter generated by raw memory input*: Mildner, J. N., and Tamir, D. I. Spontaneous Thought as an Unconstrained Memory Process. *Trends in Neuroscience* 42, no. 11, 763–77 (2019). https://doi.org/10.1016/j.tins.2019.09.001.

177 *called* autonoetic consciousness: Wheeler, M. A. et al. Toward a Theory of Episodic Memory: The Frontal Lobes and Autonoetic Consciousness. *Psychological Bulletin* 121, no. 3, 331–54 (1997). https://doi.org/10.1037/0033–2909.121.3.331.

180 *Another study involving participants taking photographs of artwork in a museum*: Henkel, L. A. Point-and-Shoot Memories: The Influence of Taking Photos on Memory for a Museum Tour. *Psychological Science* 25, no. 2, 396–402 (2014). https://doi.org/10.1177/0956797613504438.

183 *to be* mentally present in the moment, *and then to have* space to let the mind roam free, unconstrained by any task or demand:
Christoff, K. et al. Mind-Wandering as Spontaneous Thought: A Dynamic Framework. *Nature Reviews Neuroscience* 17, no. 11, 718–31 (2016). https://doi.org/10.1038/nrn.2016.113.
Fox, K. C. R., and Christoff, K. (eds.), *The Oxford Handbook of Spontaneous Thought: Mind-wandering, Creativity, and Dreaming* (New York: Oxford University Press, 2018). http://dx.doi.org/10.1093/oxfordhb/9780190464745.001.0001.

184 *Traumatic memories can feel indelibly written*: There is controversy regarding whether traumatic memories are different than other memories and the mechanisms by which that may be so.
Geraerts, E. et al. Traumatic Memories of War Veterans: Not So Special After All. *Consciousness and Cognition* 16, no. 1, 170–7 (2007). https://doi.org/10.1016/j.concog.2006.02.005.
Martinho, R. et al. Epinephrine May Contribute to the Persistence of Traumatic Memories in a Post-Traumatic Stress Disorder Animal Model. *Frontiers in Molecular Neuroscience* 13, no. 588802 (2020). https://doi.org/10.3389/fnmol.2020.588802.

184 *There is growing evidence that clinical treatments involving mindfulness can help PTSD patients*: Boyd, J. E. et al. Mindfulness-Based Treatments for Posttraumatic

Stress Disorder: A Review of the Treatment Literature and Neurobiological Evidence. *Journal of Psychiatry & Neuroscience* **43**, no. 1, 7–25 (2018). https://doi.org/10.1503/jpn.170021.

Chapter 7—Drop the Story

188 *Confirmation bias is common—it happens when people essentially "see what they expect to see," discounting any information that doesn't line up with their expectation*: Kappes, A. et al. Confirmation Bias in the Utilization of Others' Opinion Strength. *Nature Neuroscience* **23**, no. 1, 130–7 (2020). https://doi.org/10.1038/s41593-019-0549-2.

189 *We are incessantly concocting narratives*: Schacter, D. L., and Addis, D. R. On the Nature of Medial Temporal Lobe Contributions to the Constructive Simulation of Future Events. *Philosophical Transactions of the Royal Society* **364**, no. 1521, 1245–53 (2009). https://doi.org/10.1098/rstb.2008.0308.

190 mental models *that guide our thinking, decision making, and actions*: Jones, Natalie A. et al. Mental Models: An Interdisciplinary Synthesis of Theory and Methods. *Ecology and Society* **16**, no. 1 (2011). http://www.jstor.org/stable/26268859.

Johnson-Laird, P. N. Mental Models and Human Reasoning. Proceedings of the National Academy of Sciences of the United States of America 107, no. 43, 18243–50 (2010). https://doi.org/10.1073/pnas.1012933107.

192 *Emotion is how the brain determines the value of something (say, an event or a choice)*: Verweij, M. et al. Emotion, Rationality, and Decision-Making: How to Link Affective and Social Neuroscience with Social Theory. *Frontiers in Neuroscience* **9**, 332 (2015). https://doi.org/10.3389/fnins.2015.00332.

194 *Studies on the impact of advertising have shown that* vividness *is what grabs people's attention and convinces them to buy*: Blondé, J., and Girandola, F. Revealing the Elusive Effects of Vividness: A Meta-Analysis of Empirical Evidences Assessing the Effect of Vividness on Persuasion. *Social Influence* **11**, no. 2, 111–29 (2016). https://doi.org/10.1080/15534510.2016.1157096.

194 *"Our eyes are not only viewers"*: Maharishi International University. Full Speech: Jim Carrey's Commencement Address at the 2014 MUM Graduation [video]. YouTube, May 30, 2014. https://www.youtube.com/watch?v=V80-gPkpH6M.acce.

195 *referred to as* maladaptive repetitive thought: Andrews-Hanna, J. R. et al. Dynamic Regulation of Internal Experience: Mechanisms of Therapeutic Change. In Lane, R. D., and Nadel, L., *Neuroscience of Enduring Change: Implications for Psychotherapy* (New York: Oxford University Press, 2020) 89–131. https://doi.org/10.1093/oso/9780190881511.003.0005.

198 *brain science suggests that we have little to no conscious awareness of it*: Ellamil, M. et al. Dynamics of Neural Recruitment Surrounding the Spontaneous Arising of Thoughts in Experienced Mindfulness Practitioners. *NeuroImage* **136**, 186–96 (2016). https://doi.org/10.1016/j.neuroimage.2016.04.034.

202 *stepping* out *of your simulations and mental models "decentering"*: Bernstein, A. et al. Metacognitive Processes Model of Decentering: Emerging Methods and Insights. *Current Opinion in Psychology* **28**, 245–51 (2019). https://doi.org/10.1016/j.copsyc.2019.01.019.

203 *in the early months of the COVID-19 crisis, we ran a study offering mindfulness training to older adults*: Barry, J. et al. The Power of Distancing During a Pandemic: Greater Decentering Protects Against the Deleterious Effects of COVID-19-Related Intrusive Thoughts on Psychological Health in Older Adults. Poster presented at the Mind & Life 2020 Contemplative Research Conference, online (November 2020).

204 *But many other studies that have offered participants specific instructions on how to decenter found the same beneficial effects and more*: Kross, E., and Ayduk, O. Self-Distancing: Theory, Research, and Current Directions. In J. M. Olson (ed.), *Advances in Experimental Social Psychology* 55, 81–136 (2017). https://doi.org/10.1016/bs.aesp.2016.10.002.

204 *In one study, researchers prompted people to call up negative memories from their past*: Kross, E. et al. Coping with Emotions Past: The Neural Bases of Regulating Affect Associated with Negative Autobiographical Memories. *Biological Psychiatry* 65, no. 5, 361–6 (2009). https://doi.org/10.1016/j.biopsych.2008.10.019.

206 *decentering leads to reduced stress and even reduced symptoms of disorders like anxiety and depression*:

Hayes-Skelton, S. A. et al. Decentering as a Potential Common Mechanism Across Two Therapies for Generalized Anxiety Disorder. *Journal of Consulting and Clinical Psychology* 83, no. 2, 83–404 (2015). https://doi.org/10.1037/a0038305.

Seah, S. et al. Spontaneous Self-Distancing Mediates the Association Between Working Memory Capacity and Emotion Regulation Success. *Clinical Psychological Science* 9, no. 1, 79–96 (2020). https://doi.org/10.1177/2167702620953636.

King, A. P., and Fresco, D. M. A Neurobehavioral Account for Decentering as the Salve for the Distressed Mind. *Current Opinion in Psychology* 28, 285–93 (2019). https://doi.org/10.1016/j.copsyc.2019.02.009.

Perestelo-Perez, L. et al. Mindfulness-Based Interventions for the Treatment of Depressive Rumination: Systematic Review and Meta-Analysis. *International Journal of Clinical and Health Psychology* 17, no. 3, 282–95 (2017). https://doi.org/10.1016/j.ijchp.2017.07.004.

Bieling, P. J. et al. Treatment-Specific Changes in Decentering Following Mindfulness-Based Cognitive Therapy Versus Antidepressant Medication or Placebo for Prevention of Depressive Relapse. *Journal of Consulting and Clinical Psychology* 80, no. 3, 365–72 (2012). https://doi.org/10.1037/a0027483.

208 *my team's research findings on offering a program called Mindfulness-Based Attention Training (MBAT)*:

Jha, A. P. et al. Bolstering Cognitive Resilience via Train-the-Trainer Delivery of Mindfulness Training in Applied High-Demand Settings. *Mindfulness* 11, 683–97 (2020). https://doi.org/10.1007/s12671-019-01284-7.

Zanesco, A. P. et al. Mindfulness Training as Cognitive Training in High-Demand Cohorts: An Initial Study in Elite Military Servicemembers. In *Progress in Brain Research* 244, 323–54 (2019). https://doi.org/10.1016/bs.pbr.2018.10.001.

210 *Studies are finding that mindfulness training can indeed help people* act *in less-biased ways*: Lueke, A., and Gibson, B. Brief Mindfulness Meditation Reduces Discrimination. *Psychology of Consciousness: Theory, Research, and Practice* 3, no. 1. 34–44 (2016). https://doi.org/10.1037/cns0000081

Chapter 8—Go Big

215 *Simulations create mental models that lead to decisions*: Endsley, M. R. The Divergence of Objective and Subjective Situation Awareness: A Meta-Analysis. *Journal of Cognitive Engineering and Decision Making* 14, no. 1, 34–53 (2020). https://doi.org/10/ggqfzd.

216 *we call this* goal neglect: Recent studies suggest a correspondence between neglecting one's goals, working memory capacity, and mind-wandering. McVay, J. C., and Kane, M. J. Conducting the Train of Thought: Working Memory Capacity, Goal Neglect, and Mind Wandering in an Executive-Control Task.

Journal of Experimental Psychology: Learning, Memory, and Cognition **35**, no. 1, 196–204 (2009). 218

218 *Meta-awareness is the ability to take explicit note of and monitor the current contents or processes of your conscious experience*: Schooler, J. W. et al. Meta-Awareness, Perceptual Decoupling and the Wandering Mind. *Trends in Cognitive Sciences* **15**, no. 7, 319–26 (2011). https://doi.org/10.1016/j.tics.2011.05.006.

221 *We brought 143 undergraduate students into the lab to test their* awareness *of their own mind-wandering*: Krimsky, M. et al. The Influence of Time on Task on Mind Wandering and Visual Working Memory. *Cognition* **169**, 84–90 (2017). https://doi.org/10.1016/j.cognition.2017.08.006.

222 *The human brain may simply be designed to cyclically pull away from the task-at-hand*: Some studies have suggested that slow temporal fluctuations in performance and brain activity patterns may reflect the cycling of attention to various goals one after another. Smallwood, J. et al. Segmenting the Stream of Consciousness: The Psychological Correlates of Temporal Structures in the Time Series Data of a Continuous Performance Task. *Brain and Cognition* **66**, no. 1, 50–6 (2008). https://doi.org/10.1016/j.bandc.2007.05.004.

222 *as mind-wandering was going up, meta-awareness was going down. We are mind-wandering more and more over time, and growing less and less able to catch ourselves doing it*: Krimsky, M. et al. The Influence of Time on Task on Mind Wandering and Visual Working Memory. *Cognition* **69**, 84–90 (2017). https://doi.org/10.1016/j.cognition.2017.08.006.

223 *But if the task demands suddenly rise, and performance starts slipping, attentional resources will be diverted back to the task-at-hand. Your own mind cues you*: During challenging activities requiring concentration and effort, higher-working memory capacity (WMC) subjects maintained on-task thoughts better, and mind-wandered less, than did lower-WMC subjects. Kane, M. J. et al. For Whom the Mind Wanders, and When: An Experience-Sampling Study of Working Memory and Executive Control in Daily Life. *Psychological Science* **18**, no. 7, 614–21 (2007). https://doi.org/10.1111/j.1467–9280.2007.01948.x.

223 *ADHD patients tend to have high mind-wandering—so high that it can lead to detrimental real-life outcomes. A recent study found that . . . the "costs" of mind-wandering were abated in patients who were more* meta-aware: Franklin, M. S. et al. Tracking Distraction: The Relationship Between Mind-Wandering, Meta-Awareness, and ADHD Symptomatology. *Journal of Attention Disorders* **21**, no. 6, 475–86 (2017). https://doi.org/10.1177/1087054714543494.

226 *Study after study shows that the more* aware *people are of where their attention is, the better their performance is*:
Smallwood, J. et al. Segmenting the Stream of Consciousness: The Psychological Correlates of Temporal Structures in the Time Series Data of a Continuous Performance Task. *Brain and Cognition* **66**, no. 1, 50–56 (2008). https://doi.org/10.1016/j.bandc.2007.05.004.
Polychroni, N. et al. Response Time Fluctuations in the Sustained Attention to Response Task Predict Performance Accuracy and Meta-Awareness of Attentional States. *Psychology of Consciousness: Theory, Research, and Practice* (2020). https://doi.org/10.1037/cns0000248.

226 *we know that some things cause meta-awareness to tank—like cigarette cravings and drinking alcohol*: Sayette, M. A. et al. Lost in the Sauce: The Effects of Alcohol on Mind Wandering. *Psychological Science* **20**, no. 6, 747–52 (2009). https://doi.org/10.1111/j.1467–9280.2009.02351.x.

226 reduced default mode activity:
Brewer, J. A. et al. Meditation Experience Is Associated with Differences in Default Mode Network Activity and Connectivity. *Proceedings of the National Academy of*

Sciences of the United States of America **108**, no. 50, 20254–9 (2011). https://doi
.org/10.1073/pnas.1112029108.

Kral, T. R. A. et al. Mindfulness-Based Stress Reduction-Related Changes in
Posterior Cingulate Resting Brain Connectivity. *Social Cognitive and
Affective Neuroscience* **14**, no. 7, 777–87 (2019). https://doi.org/10.1093
/scan/nsz050.

Lutz, A. et al. Investigating the Phenomenological Matrix of Mindfulness-Related
Practices from a Neurocognitive Perspective. *American Psychologist* **70**, no. 7,
632–58 (2015). https://doi.org/10.1037/a0039585.

228 *The force applied is minute but the results enormous*: Sun Tzu. *The Art of War*
(Bridgewater, MA: World Publications, 2007), 95.

234 *There is a concept in Buddhism called the "Second Arrow." It comes from a famous
parable*: Bhikkhu, T. (trans.). Sallatha Sutta: The Arrow. Access to Insight (BCBS
edition), November 30, 2013, https://www.accesstoinsight.org/tipitaka/sn/sn36
/sn36.006.than.html.

235 *One important node in the brain network for meta-awareness is located at the very
front of the prefrontal cortex—it also happens to be part of a brain network for social
connection*: McCaig, R. G. et al. Improved Modulation of Rostrolateral Prefrontal
Cortex Using Real-Time fMRI Training and Meta-Cognitive Awareness.
NeuroImage **55**, no. 3, 1298–305 (2011). https://doi.org/10.1016/j.neuroimage
.2010.12.016.

Chapter 9—Get Connected

240 *Loneliness and social isolation are risk factors for poor health as well as accelerated
mortality*: Perissinotto, C. M. et al. Loneliness in Older Persons: A Predictor of
Functional Decline and Death. *Archives of Internal Medicine* **172**, no. 14,
1078–984 (2012). https://doi.org/10.1001/archinternmed.2012.1993.

240 *Conversations rely on* shared mental models:

Alfred, K. L. et al. Mental Models Use Common Neural Spatial Structure for
Spatial and Abstract Content. *Communications Biology* **3**, no. 17 (2020). https://
doi.org/10.1038/s42003-019-0740–8.

Jonker, C. M. et al. Shared Mental Models: A Conceptual Analysis. *Lecture Notes
in Computer Science* **6541**, 132–51 (2011). https://doi.org/10.1007/978-3-642
-21268-0_8.

242 *Sadly, a recent study examining parental behavior and working memory capacity found
that parents with lower (vs. higher) working memory capacity were more likely to
engage in verbally or emotionally abusive behavior toward their children*: Deater-
Deckard, K. et al. Maternal Working Memory and Reactive Negativity in
Parenting. *Psychological Sciences* **21**, no. 1, 75–9 (2010). https://doi.org/10.1177
/0956797609354073

245 *While you're actively suppressing, it leaves less cognitive bandwidth to do much else*:
Franchow, E. I., and Suchy, Y. Naturally-Occurring Expressive Suppression in
Daily Life Depletes Executive Functioning. *Emotion* **15**, no. 1, 78–89 (2015).
https://doi.org/10.1037/emo0000013.

Brewin, C. R., and Beaton, A. Thought Suppression, Intelligence, and Working
Memory Capacity. *Behaviour Research and Therapy* **40**, no. 8, 923–30 (2002).
https://doi.org/10.1016/S0005-7967(01)00127-9.

257 *A growing body of research has been examining the effects of this practice on the brain
and body*: These papers provide comprehensive reviews of findings across numerous
studies.

Dahl, C. J. et al. The Plasticity of Well-Being: A Training-Based Framework for the
Cultivation of Human Flourishing. *Proceedings of the National Academy of*

Sciences of the United States of America **117**, no. 51, 32197–206 (2020). https://doi.org/10.1073/pnas.2014859117.

Brandmeyer, T., and Delorme, A. Meditation and the Wandering Mind: A Theoretical Framework of Underlying Neurocognitive Mechanisms. *Perspectives on Psychological Science* **16**, no. 1, 39–66 (2021). https://doi.org/10.1177/1745691620917340.

261 *in those who briefly practiced loving-kindness meditation (versus a comparison group that did not), there was a reduction in implicit racial bias*: Kang, Y. et al. The Nondiscriminating Heart: Lovingkindness Meditation Training Decreases Implicit Intergroup Bias. *Journal of Experimental Psychology: General* **143**, no. 3, 1306–13 (2021). https://doi.org/10.1007/s11031-015-9514-x.

Chapter 10—Feel the Burn

264 *Cooper uncovered a strong correlation between aerobic exercise and heart health*: Cooper, K. H. The History of Aerobics (50 Years and Still Counting). *Research Quarterly for Exercise and Sport* **89**, no. 2, 129–34 (2018). https://doi.org/10.1080/02701367.2018.1452469.

264 *And when it comes to better attention*: Prakash, R. S. et al. Mindfulness and Attention: Current State-of-Affairs and Future Considerations. *Journal of Cognitive Enhancement* **4**, 340–67 (2020). https://doi.org/10.1007/s41465-019-00144-5.

265 *the brain networks that are tied to focusing and managing attention, noticing and monitoring internal and external events, and mind-wandering are all activated*: Hasenkamp, W. et al. Mind Wandering and Attention During Focused Meditation: A Fine-Grained Temporal Analysis of Fluctuating Cognitive States. *NeuroImage* **59**, no. 1, 750–60 (2012). https://doi.org/10.1016/j.neuroimage.2011.07.008

265 *we see changes in brain structures and brain activity that correspond with these improvements over time*:
Brandmeyer, T., and Delorme, A. Meditation and the Wandering Mind: A Theoretical Framework of Underlying Neurocognitive Mechanisms. *Perspectives on Psychological Science* **16**, no. 1, 39–66 (2021). https://doi.org/10.1177/1745691620917340.

Fox, K. C. R. et al A. Functional Neuroanatomy of Meditation: A Review and Meta-Analysis of 78 Functional Neuroimaging Investigations. *Neuroscience & Biobehavioral Reviews* **65**, 208–28 (2016). https://doi.org/10.1016/j.neubiorev.2016.03.021.

266 *they'd shown improvements in sustained attention and alerting. They also had better working memory encoding, reduced mind-wandering, and greater meta-awareness*: There are several studies from other research groups (e.g., Lutz et al., 2008, for review; Zanesco et al., 2013; Zanesco et al., 2016) reporting benefits on attention as a function of participation in longer-term retreats. The specific benefits on SART performance (Witkin et al., 2018) include improvements in sustained attention performance, reductions in self-reported mind-wandering, increases in meta-awareness, improvements in alerting (Jha et al., 2007), and improvements in working memory encoding (van Vugt and Jha, 2011). These were all studies conducted at the Shambhala Mountain Center. The study by Witkin et al. (2018) was conducted in collaboration with Naropa University with my colleague Jane Carpenter Cohn. In addition to studies examining cognitive effects of mindfulness retreats, many studies have been conducted examining other benefits (McClintock et al., 2019).

Lutz, A. et al. Attention Regulation and Monitoring in Meditation. *Trends in Cognitive Sciences* **12**, no. 4, 163–9 (2008). https://doi.org/10.1016/j.tics.2008.01.005.

Zanesco, A. et al. Executive Control and Felt Concentrative Engagement Following Intensive Meditation Training. *Frontiers in Human Neuroscience* 7, 566 (2013). https://doi.org/10.3389/fnhum.2013.00566.

Zanesco, A. P. et al. Meditation Training Influences Mind Wandering and Mindless Reading. *Psychology of Consciousness: Theory, Research, and Practice* 3, no. 1, 12–33 (2016). https://doi.org/10.1037/cns0000082.

Witkin, J. et al. *Mindfulness Training Influences Sustained Attention: Attentional Benefits as a Function of Training Intensity.* Poster presented at the International Symposium for Contemplative Research, Phoenix, Arizona (2018).

Jha, A. P. et al. Mindfulness Training Modifies Subsystems of Attention. *Cognitive, Affective & Behavioral Neuroscience* 7, no. 2, 109–19 (2007). https://doi.org/10.3758/CABN.7.2.109.

van Vugt, M., and Jha, A. P. Investigating the Impact of Mindfulness Meditation Training on Working Memory: A Mathematical Modeling Approach. *Cognitive, Affective & Behavioral Neuroscience* 11, 344–53 (2011). https://doi.org/10.3758/s13415-011-0048-8.

McClintock, A. S. et al. The Effects of Mindfulness Retreats on the Psychological Health of Non-Clinical Adults: A Meta-Analysis. *Mindfulness* 10, 1443–54 (2019). https://doi.org/10.1007/s12671-019-01123-9.

266 *That study with the Marines in West Palm Beach had shown a* dose-response effect *with mindfulness practice for attention, working memory, and mood*:

Jha, A. P. et al. Minds "At Attention": Mindfulness Training Curbs Attentional Lapses in Military Cohorts. *PLoS One* 10, no. 2, 1–19 (2015). https://doi.org/10.1371/journal.pone.0116889.

Jha, A. P. et al. Examining the Protective Effects of Mindfulness Training on Working Memory Capacity and Affective Experience. *Emotion* 10, no. 1, 54–64 (2010). https://doi.org/10.1037/a0018438.

268 *many more large-scale studies with military service members, military spouses, first responders, community leaders, and many other groups*:

Service Members:

Jha, A. P. et al. Bolstering Cognitive Resilience via Train-the-Trainer Delivery of Mindfulness Training in Applied High-Demand Settings. *Mindfulness* 11, 683–97 (2020). https://doi.org/10.1007/s12671-019-01284-7.

Zanesco, A. P. et al. Mindfulness Training as Cognitive Training in High-Demand Cohorts: An Initial Study in Elite Military Servicemembers. In *Progress in Brain Research* 244, 323–54 (2019). https://doi.org/10.1016/bs.pbr.2018.10.001.

Military Spouses:

Brudner, E. G. et al. The Influence of Training Program Duration on Cognitive Psychological Benefits of Mindfulness and Compassion Training in Military Spouses. Poster presented at the International Symposium for Contemplative Studies. San Diego, California (November 2016).

Firefighters:

Denkova, E. et al. Is Resilience Trainable? An Initial Study Comparing Mindfulness and Relaxation Training in Firefighters. *Psychiatry Research* 285, 112794 (2020). https://doi.org/10.1016/j.psychres.2020.112794.

Community and Workplace Leaders:

Alessio, C. et al. Leading Mindfully: Examining the Effects of Short-Form Mindfulness Training on Leaders' Attention, Well-Being, and Workplace Satisfaction. Poster presented at The Mind & Life 2020 Contemplative Research Conference, online (November 2020).

Accountants:

Denkova, E. et al. Strengthening Attention with Mindfulness Training in Workplace Settings. In Siegel, D. J. and Solomon, M., *Mind, Consciousness, and Well-Being* (New York: W. W. Norton & Company, 2020), 1–22.

269 *than the mindfulness training, it appeared to be* actively depleting attention and
working memory in these predeployment soldiers:
Jha, A. P. et al. Comparing Mindfulness and Positivity Trainings in High-Demand
Cohorts. *Cognitive Therapy and Research* 44, no. 2, 311–26 (2020). https://doi
.org/10.1007/s10608-020-10076-6. We note that positivity training is known
to have beneficial effects when offered in other contexts, typified by normative
levels of distress and challenge, particularly those suffering from dysphoria.
Becker, E. S. et al. Always Approach the Bright Side of Life: A General Positivity
Training Reduces Stress Reactions in Vulnerable Individuals. *Cognitive Therapy
and Research* 40, 57–71 (2016). https://doi.org/10.1007/s10608-015-9716-2.
270 *In the next study, we ran two simultaneous courses: both eight weeks long, both with
thirty minutes of "homework" per day, both taught by the same trainer.* Jha, A. P.
Short-Form Mindfulness Training Protects Against Working Memory Degradation
Over High-Demand Intervals. *Journal of Cognitive Enhancement* 1, 154–71 (2017).
https://doi.org/10.1007/s41465-017-0035-2.
275 *this is what I want to encourage you to do: practice twelve minutes a day, five days a
week*: To determine if there is a "minimum effective dose" of mindfulness training,
we first needed to examine if dose matters. To do so, we examined if there are
dose-response effects, which refer to patterns in which the magnitude of a response
varies as a function of the dose of exposure to something. In our studies, the "dose"
was the actual amount of time that healthy participants engaged in mindfulness
training exercises outside of the formal time they spent in a training course with a
qualified trainer. The "response" was their performance on our evaluation metrics
of attention and working memory after (versus before) the formal training interval.
We have observed dose-response effects on cognitive task performance in many of
our studies in high-stress cohorts. Many other research teams have reported
dose-response effects in noncognitive domains as well (Lloyd et al., 2018; Parsons
et al., 2017). The benefits of mindfulness training are greater in those with more
(versus less) practice engagement.

A key point about "dose" in studies of mindfulness training is that assigning
participants a specific amount of practice time each day does not mean that they
will adhere to these requirements. In fact, in our studies in high-stress cohorts, we
have found that there is considerable variability in adherence to assigned practice.
Learning this suggested that determining what a "minimum effective dose" is by
experimentally prescribing dose (assigning subgroups of participants in the
mindfulness training or comparison training conditions to different amounts of
daily practice) was unlikely to be fruitful, since we would likely find variability in
actual self-reported practice engagement in all the practice subgroups. Instead, we
opted for a data emergent approach using the participants' self-reports of how
much they actually practiced. Specifically, participants were median split into
high-practice and low-practice subgroups based on their self-reported practice. We
then statistically tested to see which of these two groups significantly differed from
each other as well as from their respective active-training comparison or no-
training control groups, which were also part of these studies.

In our initial studies (Jha et al., 2010; Jha et al., 2015), we assigned thirty
minutes of practice every day for the entire eight-week training interval. Very few
participants reported engaging in this dose. No significant differences were found
when we compared the entire training group (which comprised those with low and
high practice) to the no-training control group. But after parsing the training
group into high- and low-practice subgroups, we found that the high-practice
group's performance was significantly better than the low-practice and no-training
control groups. The high-practice group in this study practiced an average of
twelve minutes daily. We used this number to guide our next step. In our next

large-scale study (Rooks et al., 2017), we preset practice at twelve minutes a day for the duration of a four-week training interval (the guided practice recordings each lasted twelve minutes and participants were encouraged to complete the entire recording). Once again, there was variability, with some participants practicing only a few days per week, and some practicing more. And again, we did not find that the mindfulness training group as a whole significantly differed from the comparison group, which received relaxation training. We parsed each training group into high- and low-practice subgroups. We found that for those who received mindfulness training, performance was significantly better in the high-practice vs low-practice subgroup. The mindfulness high-practice group also performed significantly better than the relaxation high-practice group. The mindfulness high-practice group engaged in twelve minutes of practice, on average five days per week. In two follow-up studies (Zanesco et al., 2019; Jha et al., 2020), we constrained the practice requirements to five days a week instead of requiring them to practice every day throughout the entire training interval as our previous studies had required. In addition, we slightly increased the daily dose to fifteen minutes by providing fifteen-minute recordings (instead of twelve) because we were now relying on the trainers we had quickly trained instead of expert trainers. In both of these studies, participants largely adhered to the assigned practice, and the mindfulness training group as a whole performed significantly better than the no-training control group at the end of the training interval. These studies suggested that practicing for four to five days a week benefited cognitive performance.

Thus, collectively these studies suggest that a minimum effective dose for benefits to attention and working memory over high-demand intervals in healthy participants is twelve to fifteen minutes a day, five days a week. We acknowledge that many more studies are required to further explore this prescription and that these results may differ for other metrics and other types of groups. Nonetheless, through these series of studies, we seem to have landed upon a recipe that many participants are willing to adhere to. In addition, it opens up many fascinating new lines of research regarding factors (such as personality, prior life experiences, current life demands, and so on) that may determine how much time people are willing to practice. For example, in our initial studies with Marines we found that those with openness as a personality trait and those who had been previously deployed were more willing to practice than others. And finally, it is critical to keep in mind that any research-informed prescription is based on statistics that rely on aggregate data such as averages, trends, and correlations. As such, it is entirely plausible that any one individual may experience beneficial effects of mindfulness training without conforming to this or other research-derived prescriptions.

Lloyd, A. et al. The Utility of Home-Practice in Mindfulness-Based Group Interventions: A Systematic Review. *Mindfulness* 9, 673–692 (2018). https://doi.org/10.1007/s12671-017-0813-z.

Parsons, C. E. et al. Home Practice in Mindfulness-Based Cognitive Therapy and Mindfulness-Based Stress Reduction: A Systematic Review and Meta-Analysis of Participants' Mindfulness Practice and Its Association with Outcomes. *Behaviour Research and Therapy* 95, 29–41 (2017). https://doi.org/10.1016/j.brat.2017.05.004.

Jha, A. P. et al. Examining the Protective Effects of Mindfulness Training on Working Memory Capacity and Affective Experience. *Emotion* 10, no. 1, 54–64 (2010). https://doi.org/10.1037/a0018438.

Jha, A. P. et al. Minds "At Attention": Mindfulness Training Curbs Attentional Lapses in Military Cohorts. *PLoS One* 10, no. 2, 1–19 (2015). https://doi.org/10.1371/journal.pone.0116889.

Rooks, J. D. et al. "We Are Talking About Practice": The Influence of Mindfulness vs. Relaxation Training on Athletes' Attention and Well-Being over High-Demand Intervals. *Journal of Cognitive Enhancement* 1, no. 2, 141–53 (2017). https://doi.org/10.1007/s41465-017-0016-5.

Zanesco, A. P. et al. Mindfulness Training as Cognitive Training in High-Demand Cohorts: An Initial Study in Elite Military Servicemembers. In *Progress in Brain Research* 244, 323–54 (2019). https://doi.org/10.1016/bs.pbr.2018.10.001.

Jha, A. P. et al. Bolstering Cognitive Resilience via Train-the-Trainer Delivery of Mindfulness Training in Applied High-Demand Settings. *Mindfulness* 11, 683–97 (2020). https://doi.org/10.1007/s12671-019-01284-7.

275 *There are other programs out there incorporating mindfulness as part of a treatment plan for psychological disorders like depression, anxiety, and PTSD*: There are many resources on mindfulness-based stress reduction (Kabat-Zinn, 1990) and mindfulness-based cognitive therapy for stress and symptom reduction (Segal et al., 2002), as well as meta-analyses on the stress and health benefits of these programs (Goyal et al., 2014).

Kabat-Zinn, J. *Full Catastrophe Living: How to Cope with Stress, Pain and Illness Using Mindfulness Meditation* (New York: Bantam Dell, 1990).

Segal, Z. V. et al. *Mindfulness-Based Cognitive Therapy for Depression: A New Approach to Preventing Relapse* (New York: Guilford, 2002).

Goyal, M. et al. Meditation Programs for Psychological Stress and Well-Being: A Systematic Review and Meta-Analysis. *JAMA Internal Medicine* 174, no. 3, 357–68 (2014). https://doi.org/10.1007/s41465-017-0016-5.

290 *One way to think about mindfulness practice, and its utility in moments like these*: Nila, K. et a. Mindfulness-Based Stress Reduction (MBSR) Enhances Distress Tolerance and Resilience Through Changes in Mindfulness. *Mental Health & Prevention* 4, no. 1, 36–41 (2016). https://doi.org/10.1016/j.mhp.2016.01.001.

The Peak Mind Practice Guide

303 *Like a bird's life, [the stream of consciousness] seems to be made [up]*: James, W. *Principles of Psychology* (vols. 1–2). (New York: Holt, 1890). 243.

304 *The instructions are informed by current science on behavior change: Start with extremely small goals, achieve them*: Fogg, B. J. *Tiny Habits: The Small Changes That Change Everything* (New York: Houghton Mifflin Harcourt, 2020). http://tinyhabits.com.

322 *Be calm to get calm*: Personal communication from Walt Piatt (October 4, 2018), conveying quote from Cynthia Piatt, referring to the need and value of emotionally regulating oneself, prior to requesting or requiring it of others.